The Romantic Period

Longman Literature in English Series

General Editors:
David Carroll, formerly University of Lancaster
Chris Walsh, University College Chester
Michael Wheeler, Director of the Gladstone Project

The Romantic Period: The Intellectual and Cultural Context of English Literature, 1789–1830

Robin Jarvis

PEARSON

Longman

Harlow, England • London • New York • Boston • San Francisco • Toronto • Sydney • Singapore • Hong Kong
Tokyo • Seoul • Taipei • New Delhi • Cape Town • Madrid • Mexico City • Amsterdam • Munich • Paris • Milan

PEARSON EDUCATION LIMITED

Edinburgh Gate
Harlow CM20 2JE
Tel: +44 (0)1279 623623
Fax: +44 (0)1279 431059
Website: www.pearsoned.co.uk

First edition published in Great Britain in 2004

© Pearson Education Limited 2004

The right of Robin Jarvis to be identified as author
of this work has been asserted by him in accordance
with the Copyright, Designs and Patents Act 1988.

ISBN 0 582 38239 4

British Library Cataloguing in Publication Data
A CIP catalogue record for this book can be obtained from the British Library

Library of Congress Cataloging in Publication Data
A CIP catalog record for this book can be obtained from the Library of Congress

10 9 8 7 6 5 4 3 2 1

Set in 10/12pt Sabon by 35
Printed in Malaysia

The Publisher's policy is to use paper manufactured from sustainable forests.

Contents

In memory of
KATE FULLBROOK
1950–2003

Editors' Preface

The multi-volume Longman Literature in English Series provides students of literature with a critical introduction to the major genres in their historical and cultural context. Each volume gives a coherent account of a clearly defined area, and the series, when complete, will offer a practical and comprehensive guide to literature written in English from Anglo-Saxon times to the present. The aim of the series as a whole is to show that the most valuable and stimulating approach to the study of literature is that based upon awareness of the relations between literary forms and their historical contexts. Thus the areas covered by most of the separate volumes are defined by period and genre. Each volume offers new and informed ways of reading literary works, and provides guidance for further reading in an extensive reference section.

In recent years, the nature of English studies has been questioned in a number of increasingly radical ways. The very terms employed to define a series of this kind – period, genre, history, context, canon – have become the focus of extensive critical debate, which has necessarily influenced in varying degrees the successive volumes published since 1985. But however fierce the debate, it rages around the traditional terms and concepts.

As well as studies on all periods of English and American literature, the series includes books on criticism and literary theory and on the intellectual and cultural context. A comprehensive series of this kind must of course include other literatures written in English, and therefore a group of volumes deals with Irish and Scottish literature, and the literatures of India, Africa, the Caribbean, Australia and Canada. The forty-seven volumes of the series cover the following areas: Pre-Renaissance English Literature, English Poetry, English Drama, English Fiction, English Prose, Criticism and Literary Theory, Intellectual and Cultural Context, American Literature, Other Literatures in English.

David Carroll
Chris Walsh
Michael Wheeler

Author's Preface

The chronological boundaries of this contextual survey have been dictated by its positioning within the Longman Literature in English Series. The forty-odd years from 1789 to 1830 now seem an unsatisfactorily tight compartment to many scholars, with the result that Romantic literature is frequently allowed to sprawl over a much more generous stretch of time (the *Oxford Companion to the Romantic Age*, for instance, defines that age as 1776–1832), or alternatively is subsumed by a 'long eighteenth century' or something similar. On the other hand, those forty years probably still encompass most of the writers or texts that students typically encounter in places where Romantic literature is still taught, certainly at undergraduate level. Suffice to say that, in this book, wherever I refer (as I often do) to 'the period', I mean the period 1789–1830, without making the foolish assumption that those dates are when Romanticism began or ended. In some places, indeed, I have been obliged to 'disapply' the chronological limits: it would be ridiculous, for example, to talk about cultural primitivism without mentioning Rousseau (1712–78), or to treat Romantic aesthetics without reference to Burke's treatise on the sublime and beautiful (1757).

My main aim is to contextualise the modern Romantic canon, a canon no longer monopolised by a small number of male poets but including novels and non-fictional prose (Romantic drama is still uncommon on university syllabuses) as well as poetry, by both male and female authors. This welcome diversification of the canon has introduced a need for different kinds of contextual insight: the material in Chapter 4 on education and the family should, for example, be of great help to students tackling any of the novels of manners and sentiment produced in great numbers by women authors in the late eighteenth and early nineteenth centuries. I have tried to attend, as far as possible, to the international dimensions of British Romanticism. The importance of travel literature, and of colonial and imperial perspectives, to constructions of personal and national identity in the period is increasingly being recognised, and I have endeavoured to take these issues on board, most obviously in Chapter 2; equally, I have sought to restore some sense of the European intellectual culture in which the British Romantics flourished, as opposed to the rather narrow focus upon domestic politics that has prevailed since the bicentenary of the French Revolution in 1789 authorised a 'return to history' in Romantic studies. That new historicism is itself contextualised in Chapter 7, which explores the complexities of the Romantic period's own developing historical consciousness. Meanwhile, neglected areas of interest like religion (Chapter 6) and aesthetics (Chapter 8) are overdue a recovery, and I have tried to give students the wherewithal to take an interest in such matters. Throughout the book, it has been my intention to provide as much material as possible that I think will be helpful to students of Romantic literature in the twenty-first century, without pointing up links between context and specific literary texts directly: that task – and the intellectual fun – falls to the students themselves as they make their individual journeys through the literature. One final point: this book is primarily a study of the background of English Romantic literature, and I am aware that Scottish literature and Irish literature of the period are served by other volumes in the series. However, given the importance of developments in Scotland, Ireland, and Wales to political and cultural life at this time, I have tried to keep the broader national context in mind, and where I choose between terms like 'English' or 'British' I hope I do so advisedly.

The very selective bibliographies at the back of this book are designed to supplement, rather than simply summarise, the suggestions for further reading contained in the notes to individual chapters. There is a deliberate – though not exclusive – emphasis on books accessible and helpful to students, as opposed to research-intensive studies that offer little purchase to the inexperienced. It is in the general bibliographies that some attempt is made to bridge the gap between literature and context that I abstain from crossing in the main body of the book.

The Research Committee of the Faculty of Humanities at the University of the West of England has granted me two periods of research leave to further my work on this book, and I very much appreciate its support. The second period was augmented by an award under the Arts and Humanities Research Board's Research Leave Scheme, and I acknowledge this too with gratitude. I owe sincere thanks to Pete Broks and Madge Dresser for their invaluable feedback on Chapters 5 and 6, respectively. Chris Walsh has been a most amenable and helpful general editor. My greatest scholarly debt, involving constant support and encouragement as well as the services of a discriminating reader, is to the friend and colleague whose tragically early death is commemorated in my dedication. This dreadful event, which has afflicted so many people with a sense of loss and waste, has made me all the more conscious of my good fortune in the constant presence of my loved ones: my wife, Carol, and son, William.

Robin Jarvis
Bristol, September 2003

Chapter One

The Political and Economic Scene

Revolution

An event described by one of the leading English Romantic poets as 'the master-theme of the epoch in which we live' has obvious claims to be put first in any contextual study of the period. It is inconvenient that the event Shelley refers to – the French Revolution – is one which has been the source of profound and lasting disagreement among historians, and the subject of a frightening estimated two thousand publications a year; inevitably, the version of the Revolution that literature students are served up is vastly simplified and possibly very partisan. To make matters worse, the other revolution that traditionally features in introductions to the period, the industrial revolution (discussed in a later section), is a historical battlefield of similar proportions. The student is therefore required to come to terms with a 'dual revolution'[1] the causes, nature, consequences – even the very existence – of which are hotly contested; nevertheless, the obligation to offer some kind of route map of this disputed territory is clear.

Although frequently described as a 'world-historical event' of immense significance, the word 'event' is awkwardly applied to the French Revolution, which appears rather as a concatenation of events stretching over a number of years – a complex process, riddled with contingency, with no inevitable beginning and no predetermined outcome. Popular identification of the Revolution with a single day of action, the storming of the Bastille on 14 July 1789, finds little support among historians, who tend rather to distinguish a 'pre-Revolution' from the Revolution itself, and to dissolve the unity of the latter into multiple overlapping phenomena: a 'bourgeois revolution' and a 'popular revolution'; the revolution in Paris, the municipal revolution in provincial towns, the revolution in the countryside. What seems reasonably clear is that the events of 1789, which amounted to the collapse of an entire social and political system, were the product of accumulating tensions and discontents at all levels of society, exaggerated by accidents of nature and given expression in a new political vocabulary disseminated by Enlightenment thinkers. The aristocracy resisted attempts to make it bear the crippling cost of the country's involvement in the American War of Independence; the bourgeoisie increasingly resented barriers to free trade, their exclusion from public office, and their lack of representation in government; the peasantry reacted angrily to measures taken by 'improving' landowners to raise productivity and the imposition of new feudal obligations; and they, in common with urban wage-earners and craftsmen, were hit hard by disastrous harvests in 1787–9 which pushed food prices up to starvation levels. There was, therefore, as George Rudé describes it, a 'merging' of quite separate movements that, by the middle of 1789, had produced a 'common bond of interest' between the urban and rural labouring classes and the more politically motivated bourgeoisie.[2] What began as an 'aristocratic revolt' against the royal government thus turned in 1789 into a revolt of the 'Third Estate' (basically everyone except the nobility and the clergy) against the privileged orders, a conflict that became a challenge to the very legitimacy of the state. The course of the Revolution was thenceforth determined at key points by just such unstable alliances between the propertied classes and the common people as occurred in Paris on 14 July, or again on 5 October when the men and women of Paris marched to Versailles and, through overwhelming force, secured the king's acceptance of the Declaration of the Rights of Man.

The development of the Revolution was rapid and bewildering, as illustrated by the fact that France went through three constitutions in five years, none of which lasted long enough to be fully implemented. It was variously exhilarating, empowering, disorientating, or terrifying, depending on one's point of view and the fortunes of the moment. In the first phase of the Revolution, the self-declared National Assembly replaced absolute with constitutional monarchy and devised a Constitution (1791) which, building on the principles enshrined in the 1789 Declaration (liberty, equality, fraternity), established a limited form of representative government, refashioned the administrative and judicial systems from scratch, and drastically curtailed the wealth and status of the Church. The violent overthrow of the king in August 1792 and his execution early the following year took the Revolution in what would now be called a 'far Left' direction, masterminded by the more populist Jacobin faction within the new National Convention and its enigmatic leader, Maximilien Robespierre. The Jacobin constitution of 1793, which provided for full male suffrage, a right to work or welfare for all, freedom of worship and universal primary education, was the most radical the world had ever seen; it was quietly shelved under pressure of war and civil disorder, to be replaced by an authoritarian revolutionary government dispensing summary justice (the 'Reign of Terror') through the infamously titled Committee of Public Safety. When Robespierre fell victim to a renewed power struggle in July 1794, the Revolution fell into the hands of much more moderate and business-minded republicans, who produced their own Constitution (1795) that enshrined government by men of property and good education. However, the new regime proved unstable, with the Directory (as it was called) seesawing between Jacobin survivors on the left and a royalist revival on the right, and eventually republican diehards persuaded the rising military hero, Napoleon Bonaparte, to take control in a *coup d'état* in November 1799.

This event conventionally marks the end of the Revolutionary decade: with Napoleon's rapid rise from First Consul (within a triumvirate) in 1800 to Consul for life in 1802 to hereditary Emperor in 1804, military dictatorship extinguished the beleaguered experiment in democratic republicanism. It is, of course, as a military genius and imperial colossus that Napoleon is best known:

having moved from defending the infant republic, to exporting revolution to sympathetic neighbour states, to unfettered imperial expansionism, by 1812 the territory under his command or influence stretched from Copenhagen in the north to Naples in the south, and from Cadiz in the west to Warsaw in the east. Nevertheless, social and political reform was consolidated or extended during Napoleon's reign. The Civil Code, or Napoleonic Code, promulgated in 1804 was applied to all territories under direct French control and was an innovation of lasting international significance. It coupled the consolidation of the egalitarian principles of 1789, encompassing the destruction of feudalism, abolition of primogeniture, and religious toleration, with a reactionary authoritarianism on matters concerning the family and gender relations. Throughout the Empire, Napoleon promoted to varying degrees equality before the law, civil marriage, secular education, and individual property rights, though he also discarded unwelcome principles like popular sovereignty and representative government and reinstated slavery in French colonies. It is not hard to see why he is seen as having 'fulfilled and distorted the legacy of the French Revolution'.[3]

That legacy was substantial and durable, despite the restitution of monarchical regimes in France and across Europe after the final defeat of Napoleon in 1815 and the establishment of a new conservative balance of power on the Continent. The monarchy, the aristocracy, and the Church all suffered permanent loss of status, privileges, and authority, and the resulting society was more open and fluid and reflected more clearly the interests of the middle classes. The orthodox 'Marxist' interpretation of the Revolution is therefore that it began the inevitable historical process of modernising society and paved the way for the development of industrial capitalism. More recently this interpretation has been criticised for its alleged overidentification with the perceptions of certain favoured participants within the revolutionary drama itself. Firmly rejecting a tradition of what he calls 'commemorative' historiography, François Furet has challenged both the assumption that the Revolution constituted a radical break with the past and the notion of its historical inevitability: the 'occupational disease' of historians, he observes, is 'to reduce the potential outcomes of a situation to a single one, since it alone occurred'. For Furet, nothing can mitigate the sheer singularity of the revolutionary phenomenon, 'a new type of historical action and consciousness' that took shape within the power vacuum that developed in France in the late 1780s. Irreducible to socioeconomic causes, what emerged from a fortuitous convergence of events was something definitively political: a new belief in the capacity of human beings to determine their lives through collective action – democratic politics not as a set of institutions but as a 'national ideology'. According to Furet, the 'secret of the success of 1789, its message and its lasting influence lie in that invention, which was unprecedented and whose legacy was to be so widespread'.[4]

It is therefore only a particular kind of 'radical break' – one that assumes that *ancien régime* France was socially and economically moribund – that Furet and others would disallow. For innovation was indeed everywhere in the 1790s: the revolutionary vanguard set out to change everything, from the administrative map of France to the very organisation of time and space (the revolutionary calendar used between 1793 and 1805 created a week of ten days, while the metre and the gram applied the decimal principle to weights and measures). In a general retrospect written in the bicentenary year, Robert Darnton, disturbed though he is by the 'mystery' of revolutionary violence, remains overawed by the complementary 'utopian energy', the sense of 'possibilism against the givenness of things' that provides the most conspicuous face of the Revolution:

> How can we grasp those moments of madness, of suspended disbelief, when anything looked possible and the world appeared as a tabula rasa, wiped clean by a surge of popular emotion and ready to be redesigned?[5]

Such euphoric 'possibilism' was, for a time, shared in Britain, where early responses to the Revolution were broadly favourable. The legal reformer, Samuel Romilly, declared that the Revolution should be especially welcome to Englishmen, who 'have long known the value of liberty, and many of whom are descended from ancestors who had the honor of shedding their blood in its defence'. He also highlighted the advantages for Britain of what had happened on the Continent, naively asserting that hostilities with France, its oldest enemy, would now be a thing of the past, since France would require the consent of its people to go to war: 'no force formidable to the liberties of this country can ever exist, while France is free.'[6] This combination of self-regarding applause (seeing the French Revolution as a belated successor to England's own 'Glorious Revolution' of 1688, by which constitutional monarchy was established) and political pragmatism was typical of the early liberal or Whig reaction. Radicals, on the other hand, who were less enamoured of the virtues of the British constitution, were more likely to see the Revolution as an inspiration for social change both domestically and further afield. The radical peer, Charles Stanhope, compared new French legislation on religious toleration favourably with the English Test and Corporation Acts that barred Catholics and Protestant Dissenters from public office, and declared that the Revolution would 'disseminate throughout Europe, liberality of sentiment, and a just regard for Political, Civil, and Religious Liberty'.[7] It should also be noted that conservatives were by no means antagonistic to the Revolution at first: even William Pitt, the Prime Minister, thought that 'The present convulsions of France must, sooner or later, terminate in general harmony and regular order'.[8]

This fragile, positive consensus across the political spectrum lasted at best until the middle of 1792. The dramatic raising of the revolutionary temperature, epitomised by the so-called 'September Massacres' of suspected traitors and plotters, and the execution of Louis XVI, rapidly polarised opinion in Britain. In Parliament, the unity of the Whig opposition, already strained after its muddled response to the Regency crisis of 1788–9, worsened into a formal party split: its leader, Charles James Fox, was left at the head of around fifty diehard radicals and reformers, while the remaining conservative Whigs entered an alliance with Pitt to form a powerful coalition in defence of property and the existing order. The authorities became increasingly preoccupied with the perceived threat of insurrection from 'English Jacobins', a catch-all term to denote anyone who persisted in the cause of reform or who sought the importation of 'French principles'. The most notorious official outcomes of this backlash were the 'Treason Trials' of three leading radicals in 1794, by which the government hoped to deliver a crushing blow to dissidence, and the 'Two Acts' of 1795, which extended the law of treason to the spoken and written word and clamped down on public meetings. The trials resulted (sensationally) in acquittal, and the new legislation was in fact rarely deployed, but the combination of these legal measures with more covert machinery of repression (such as an elaborate spy network) and a systematic government-backed propaganda campaign succeeded in uniting the propertied classes behind King and Constitution, and the radical movement was effectively driven underground or relegated to clandestine plotting by the mid-1790s.

The Revolution and its aftermath had other, far-reaching consequences for the 'state of the nation'. Great Britain had been created in 1707 by the Act of Union, joining the kingdoms of England and Scotland. The motive for Union had been to prevent the Scots choosing James Edward Stuart (the 'Old Pretender') as their next monarch, which would have raised the spectre of a Catholic dynasty on England's doorstep. Support from Scottish Highlanders for the Jacobite rebellions in 1715 and 1745 meant that mutual suspicion and aggression between the English and the Scots remained strong for much of the century, but the concept of a British identity had begun slowly to take hold. This process was helped significantly by the large numbers of Scots who enlisted in the war against Revolutionary France, either in the regular army or in volunteer regiments, and who thus promoted the ideal of a *British* nation in arms. Wales was differently circumstanced: its connection to England was much older, yet in some respects (such as a separate language spoken by the majority of the population) it was still a foreign country. Mobilisation of Welshmen during the war helped to fray this internal border and further the process of integrating the 'Celtic fringe' within the nation as a whole.

However, it was on Britain's relation to its troublesome colony, Ireland, that the Revolution had its greatest impact. In the eighteenth century Ireland consisted essentially of a Catholic peasantry exploited by absentee Protestant landlords and governed by a corrupt, pseudo-autonomous Parliament that chiefly minded British interests. Under the direct inspiration of the French Revolution, the United Irish Society was formed in 1791 as a moderate, cross-denominational reform movement, its early development hindered by tensions between Protestants (its leader, Wolfe Tone, was a Protestant) and Catholics. Suppressed in 1794, it re-emerged as a revolutionary society and looked to France to provide military assistance to the 'friends of liberty'. A French invasion in December 1796 was in fact only derailed by a string of accidents. A brutal campaign of repression in 1797–8 then caused plans for a full-blown United Irish rebellion to be brought forward before the French – preoccupied in Egypt – were ready, and the result was a bloodbath in which twenty thousand people lost their lives. One consequence of the rebellion was a widening of the religious divide, or, in Marianne Elliott's careful summary, 'a deeply polarised populace and the running sores of militantly sectarian republicanism and loyalism'.[9] Another outcome was that the British government decided that a parliament of wealthy Protestants in Dublin was incapable of maintaining social order, and bribery was used freely to secure the passage of the Act of Union (1800) that merged Ireland with Britain.

One unexpected side-product of the British response to the Revolution was a new role for the monarch of this less than united kingdom. George III had already begun to cultivate a public image of father of the nation, quite at odds with the remote splendour of his predecessors, but after the Revolution he increasingly and deliberately became the focus for sentiments of national unity. He toured the country and became visible to his subjects to an unprecedented extent, and his jubilee celebrations in 1809, the first event of their kind, were conducted on a huge scale. According to Linda Colley's biting analysis, George III practised a new kind of 'royal magic', appearing as both a special being and a husband and father like anyone else, and thereby launched a myth which still has residual appeal in some quarters; just as importantly, he managed to use his long reign to cast himself as 'a symbol of his nation's relative stability', reinforcing the argument for leaving things as they were constitutionally.[10]

War

Britain had been involved in a number of essentially commercial wars in the eighteenth century. Defeat in the most recent of these, the American War of Independence (1775–83), was a humiliating blow, which has been likened in terms of its demoralising and disorientating effects to the USA's defeat in Vietnam. Economically, however, Britain recovered well from the loss of its colony, with international trade, especially with the East, receiving a significant stimulus. The political fallout from a conflict that had left Britain virtually isolated in Europe (France and Spain, notably, had joined the Americans) was more difficult to redress, but the Triple Alliance formed in 1788 with Prussia and the United Provinces (Holland) was a step towards regaining diplomatic leverage on the Continent. It was Britain's obligations under this alliance that brought it closer to war when France invaded the Austrian Netherlands in November 1792. In the same month, France's promulgation of a decree promising assistance to peoples of all nations who sought to reclaim their liberty raised fears that it was now in the business of exporting revolution. In the event, France declared war first on 1 February 1793; but, according to Clive Emsley, 'given the growing expectation of war they probably pre-empted similar action by Britain'.[11] The long conflict (1793–1815) that followed has been described by one historian as Britain's greatest crisis of national security between the Spanish Armada and World War II.[12]

The progress of the war against France was marked by a series of volatile alliances between Britain and the crowned heads of Europe, and a massively expensive string of subsidies and loans to other states – over £46m between 1793 and 1814 – without whose assistance a successful land war was deemed impossible. Britain was ill prepared for war when hostilities broke out. Its standing army numbered only 40,000 men (of which just 15,000 were in Britain), and, when combined with the fragility of the First Coalition, could do little to stem the tide of French military successes on the Continent, buoyed up as these were on the pioneering *levée en masse* (mass conscription). The capitulation of the Austrians in October 1797 was perhaps Britain's darkest hour in this first phase of the war, leaving it isolated and in serious danger of invasion. The country's lifeline, as always, was its navy, which maintained the security of its borders and achieved significant victories over France in the West Indies and the Mediterranean. Defeat on land coupled with dominance at sea produced a stalemate that led to the controversial Peace of Amiens in March 1802, which ceded nearly all Britain's territorial gains with little in return by way of French concessions.

Britain was in better shape when it took France by surprise and renewed hostilities in May 1803, but the long second phase of the campaign was in some respects more difficult than the first, dominated as it was by Napoleon's new policy of economic blockade, which produced high prices and unemployment. Britain retaliated with its own blockade, and the resulting full-scale economic warfare was damaging to both sides, although the strength of its navy gave Britain a decided advantage. On land the situation was very different: Pitt's Third Coalition, an alliance with Russia and Austria, proved incapable of halting the march of Napoleon's troops – the humiliation of the Austrians at Austerlitz in December 1805 is regarded as his greatest military achievement – or the expansion of the French empire. However, the conquest of Britain was the elusive final piece in Napoleon's new geographical jigsaw of Europe. A second major invasion scare of 1803–05 was exorcised by Nelson's crushing victory at Trafalgar, and the French blockade was unsuccessful at starving Britain into submission. The Peninsular War which followed Napoleon's invasion of Spain in 1808 proved a turning point: Wellington's campaign there took Britain's policy of offering limited armed support to coalition partners onto a wholly new level, and by severely overstretching Napoleon's forces contributed significantly to his downfall. With the French army crippled by a catastrophic invasion of Russia in 1812, a fresh bout of coalition-building and a further huge injection of men, money, and armaments allowed Britain and its allies to press the war to the final defeat of Napoleon – first at Paris, and then, after the Hundred Days in which he briefly regained control of France, at Waterloo.

Just as British response to the Revolution rapidly changed complexion and divided on ideological lines, so did public opinion on the war against France show a restless conflict of ideas and feelings. This conflict was at its most extreme in the very early months. The anonymous author of one uncompromising tract begins by summarising the iniquities of the *ancien régime* in France, then berates the injustice of persecuting those labouring for the advancement of truth. For him, the war is one of political principles and systems, and he lashes the people of England for their feeble-minded collusion with the tyranny of wealth and hereditary privilege:

> It is therefore evident that you are now forbid even to exercise your understandings; you are driven on to Slaughter in the very mockery of power, and are to be loaded with fresh taxes, that Kings and Ministers may hereafter sleep in security, and Aristocracy continue to gorge itself on the industry of the Nation and not at the public expence. The truth is, YE ARE SLAVES, the most abject Slaves. . . .[13]

The author also argues that war will greatly increase the national debt and have a ruinous effect on industry and commerce. Among radicals of this ilk, opposition to the war went hand in hand with their domestic reform agenda: as George Dyer warned with grim precision, 'Should an evil day arrive, may it be remembered that those who have been friends to a reform, have been enemies to a war!'[14] In print, however, they more commonly opposed the war on economic grounds than from pro-French or pro-republican sympathies, highlighting the sufferings of the poor and the plight of those press-ganged into the army and navy. There was also a wide body of middle-class liberal opinion, the self-styled 'Friends of Peace', who maintained consistent opposition to the war on both moral and pragmatic grounds but could scarcely be accused of Jacobinism. They organised numerous petition campaigns for peace and their protests 'reached a crescendo in 1812, ironically just as the tide of war at last turned and victory suddenly loomed'.[15]

Right from the start, radical and liberal opponents of the war were countered by conservative and loyalist writers who emphasised the unique nature of the French Revolution and the need to combat the spread of disorder. According to John Bowles, the welfare of Europe, perhaps of the world, depended on the outcome of the war:

> upon its success depend the important questions, Whether Government shall exist – Whether Religion shall retain any influence in social life – Whether laws shall continue to bind, and Justice be anywhere administered – Whether, in short, any link of the social chain shall be preserved unbroken? – or, Whether mankind shall be uncivilized, and reduced to a state of more than Gothic barbarism, and the whole of this Quarter of the Globe, like France, become at once the licensed Theatre of every crime?[16]

When Pitt negotiated unsuccessfully for peace in 1795–7, the ageing Edmund Burke summoned his waning rhetorical energies to denounce a 'regicide peace', defending the war as 'a just war . . . to prevent the tearing of all crowns from all heads which ought to wear them' and 'to preserve national independence, property, liberty, life, and honour, from certain, universal havoc'.[17] In 1803, with Britain under renewed threat of invasion, the Association for Preserving Liberty and Property against Republicans and Levellers (see the section on 'Reform' below) addressed the people in typically rousing fashion: reminding Britons that they were fighting for their 'very existence as a nation', it hurled defiance at an enemy whose rapacious cruelty it painted in the most vivid colours:

Let them then attempt to come when they will, they will find us ready to receive them. They will find the British Lion as terrible as ever. They will find that there is one nation at least, which has spirit and energy to repel their attacks, and to make them repent of their insolence and presumption.[18]

The rhetoric here is matched across a wide range of popular pamphlets and broadsheet propaganda. In one local pamphlet that scarily imagines the French marching into Birmingham, the British lion rises and 'shakes his shaggy mane' in a final patriotic verse appeal:

> And those we don't Sink, we'll do over by Land,
> So let them come on, Boys, on Sea, or on Shore,
> And we'll drub them again, as we've drub'd them before.[19]

The reminder here of former victories against the French, drawing on centuries of hostility to the Catholic foe, is typical of such literature. Such propaganda did not fall on deaf or unwilling ears, as Linda Colley's analysis of the volunteer movement, using data derived from government surveys undertaken in 1798 and 1804, makes clear. Despite big regional disparities, mixed motives, and some surprising findings regarding the greater disposition of urban Britons to volunteer, her overall conclusion is that the home front was secure: the evidence of half a million volunteers, and the government's willingness to trust them with arms, suggests that 'the unreformed British state rested on the active consent of substantial numbers of its inhabitants'. Nor should the participation of women be overlooked: an unquantifiable number were involved in organising or contributing to subscriptions to the expense of the war, demonstrating 'that their concerns were by no means confined to the domestic sphere'.[20]

As Colley also convincingly argues, by encouraging a patriotism that cut across classes, genders, political and religious affiliations, the British authorities ran the risk of stimulating demands for social and political change that the peculiar circumstances of war could not defer forever. This raises the question of both the immediate and longer-term consequences of war. The human cost was not great by the obscene standards of the twentieth century, but very significant in individual terms, with few extended families unaffected by loss. The financial cost exceeded £1,500,000,000, an astronomical figure that tripled the pre-war national debt. Economic historians disagree profoundly about the overall impact of the war on the British economy, but there is no doubt that the post-war depression in industry and agriculture had a devastating effect on working people, exacerbated by the demobilisation of some 200,000 soldiers. At the other end of the social scale, there was a sense in which victory at Waterloo allowed the ruling class to strengthen its hold on power: the fact that Britain was the only major country not to experience invasion or a change of government in the period burnished the institutional curriculum vitae of its leaders. But the elite's fear of change was not universally shared, and it was not long before men who had fought for their country began to insist on the right to have more say in how it was run, if not a greater share of its wealth.

Rights

Aspects of the bitterly divided British response to the French Revolution as it progressed from constitutional monarchy to Jacobin republic have already been described in broad historical perspective. It is now time to look in more detail at the fierce debate – the war of words – that the Revolution occasioned, because of its long-term effects on political and cultural life and the way in which its concepts and vocabulary inflected discussion on topics quite remote from the original centre of controversy. I shall pursue this enquiry by focusing on the concept of 'rights' or 'natural rights'.

The earliest, and most influential, voice to denounce the Revolution was that of Edmund Burke, in his *Reflections on the Revolution in France* (1790), which was to become a benchmark for modern conservatism. The occasion for Burke's treatise was a sermon given by the leading Dissenter, Richard Price, in November 1789, which portrayed the Revolution as the legitimate heir of the Glorious Revolution of 1688 and gave enthusiastic witness to 'a general amendment beginning in human affairs; the dominion of kings changed for the dominion of laws, and the dominion of priests giving way to the dominion of reason and conscience'.[21] Although addressing the main points of Price's sermon and indulging in something of a character assassination of its author, the *Reflections* vastly outgrows this initial stimulus. Burke sets against Price's view of what has happened in France – an arbitrary monarch being cashiered for misconduct by his subjects – a 'monstrous tragi-comic scene' in which a flawed yet fundamentally sound and reformable system of government has been torn down by the vulgar machinations of the 'new monied interest', the fanatical conspiracies of atheistic men of letters, and the unrestrained barbarities of a 'swinish multitude'.[22] What Burke sees, and deplores, in France is an attempt to remake a government on the basis of abstract ideas and theoretical speculations, ignoring circumstances, history, and the lessons of experience; such ideological constructions, in his opinion, are violations of nature, which itself provides a model for wise governance predicated on conservation, inheritance, and organic development. Such continuity and stability are all the more important since human beings are complex, sinful creatures, and those entrusted with political leadership need to show a deep understanding of human nature and of the institutions that have evolved over time to manage the natural inequalities and destructive passions of society's members. For Burke, it stands to reason that the men best qualified to undertake this awesome task will come from the landed classes, since only in that situation are they free from the hurly-burly of getting and spending and able to cultivate an exalted objectivity. Rejecting the French revolutionaries' belief in human perfectibility, Burke rejects also their veneration of the dignity of natural man: on the contrary, 'the defects of our naked shivering nature' need to be fully clothed to make private and public life morally respectable and emotionally satisfying, and this 'decent drapery' comes from custom, tradition, religion, and the whole wardrobe of manners and sentiments that Burke romantically identifies with a lost 'age of chivalry' (pp. 170–1).

Burke's *Reflections* was the catalyst for a vigorous political debate that lasted about six years, conducted through a variety of media to a large and heterogeneous audience. First to respond was Mary Wollstonecraft, in the less well-known of her two 'vindications', which offers an indignant defence of natural rights and shrewdly turns Burke's rhetoric upon himself, aiming to hunt down his 'pernicious opinions' and 'shew you to yourself, stripped of the gorgeous drapery in which you have enwrapped your tyrannic principles'.[23] The following year, James Mackintosh celebrated the Revolution as a 'grand experiment' to find the limits of attainable freedom and happiness, and praised the National Assembly's courage and determination in seizing the moment: 'Their reform was total, that it might be commensurate with the evil, and *no part of it was delayed*, because to spare an abuse at such a period was to consecrate it.'[24] The weightiest contribution to the Revolution controversy was William Godwin's *Enquiry Concerning Political Justice* (1793), which actually relegates direct engagement with Burke to a few footnotes; it delighted radical intellectuals with its systematic critique of aristocratic government and the forms of political imposture, although it deplores revolution, prefers rational anarchy to any kind of representative democracy, and envisions an ideal future achieved through the accumulated power of enlightened individual minds rather than collective action: 'Truth will bring down all her forces, mankind will be her army, and oppression, injustice, monarchy and vice, will tumble into a common ruin.'[25] However, the most important reply to Burke, and the iconic text of British radicalism of the 1790s, was Tom Paine's *Rights of Man* (1791–2). Part I of this work contested Burke's interpretation of events in France, argued for the sole legitimacy of governments founded upon universal natural rights, and insisted that no generation had the right to legislate for all posterity; Part II, which brought upon Paine a prosecution (*in absentia*) for seditious libel, was more concerned with setting out Paine's own republican political theory, leaning for inspiration more on the American than the French example, and proposing reforms that amount to a blueprint for a modern welfare state.

The central reference point for natural rights theory in Britain in the eighteenth century was the second of John Locke's *Two Treatises of Government* (1689). Locke crucially distinguishes between a 'State of Nature' and a 'State of Society'. In the former, a state of freedom and equality, human beings enjoy the rights to life, liberty, and (perhaps oddly) property, and, in the event of an infringement of one of these rights, are judges in their own cases. In a state of society, humans recognise the precarious nature of their privileges and 'unite for the mutual *Preservation* of their Lives, Liberties and Estates'; they relinquish a certain portion of their natural rights to the regulated power of the community, always on the understanding that 'no rational Creature can be supposed to change his condition with an intention to be worse'.[26] The broad outlines of this theory are recognisable in Rousseau's *The Social Contract* (1762), a work of huge import for the history of revolutionary France; Rousseau, however, does not recognise property as a natural right and puts severe constraints on natural liberty in his analysis of civil society, which involves 'the total alienation by each associate of himself and all his rights to the whole community'.[27] In his *Reflections*, Burke has little time for natural rights (those rights belonging to all humans by reason of their existence), but is passionate in support of civil rights (those rights that pertain by reason of inclusion in a society). Whereas for Paine (as for Locke) civil rights are a means of better securing natural rights in an unsafe world, for Burke the very fact of joining together in civil society means that natural rights are overridden by a new set of conventional rules, for which the test of experience provides the only true legitimacy. All 'metaphysical' talk of entitlements is so much hot air alongside the deep and complex practical art of politics: thus, although he regards such things as equality before the law, property, and inheritance as valuable civil rights, the question of what share, if any, individuals are to have in how their society is governed is 'a thing to be settled by convention'; furthermore, Burke wishes to include among civil rights the right to have one's passions 'restrained' and one's inclinations frequently 'thwarted' (pp. 149–52), and in his defence of this position the distinction between rights and responsibilities appears hopelessly blurred.

Paine cuts through Burke's orotund discourse with a plain, forthright argumentative style that was political dynamite when circulated in a cheap sixpenny edition. His response to the last-mentioned passage of the *Reflections* is a good example of this. He employs Burke's own definition of government as a 'contrivance of human wisdom' against him as part of a sustained assault on the principle of monarchy:

> Admitting that Government is a contrivance of human *wisdom*, it must necessarily follow, that hereditary succession, and hereditary rights (as they are called), can make no part of it, because it is impossible to make wisdom hereditary; and on the other hand, *that* cannot be a wise contrivance, which in its operation may commit the government of a nation to the wisdom of an idiot.[28]

Compounding this absurdity, according to Paine, is Burke's wish to set apart 'the nation as fools on one side' and his mysteriously-constituted 'government of wisdom' on the other (p. 117), and then declare it a right of the people to have their deficiencies made good by the latter bogus entity. *Rights of Man* is committed to exposing such fraud and demystifying the rhetoric with which it typically cloaks its intention: a crown is just a fancy hat, Paine tells us, and whereas Burke had ridiculed the notion (suggested by the Revolution's disregard of the privileges of rank) that 'a king is but a man', Paine insists that he is *no less* than a man.

The essence of *Rights of Man* is that 'all men are born equal, and with equal natural right' (p. 66), natural right being construed along the lines of the American and French Declarations; civil rights grow out of natural rights and only supersede them in cases (such as the right to security) where the individual's means of enforcement are inadequate; and the sole legitimacy of government lies in the sovereign will of the people, who have an 'inherent right' to participate, through their representatives, in the processes of lawmaking and taxation (p. 89). Repudiating Burke's attempt to argue that the Revolution Settlement of the seventeenth century settled the constitution of England for all time, Paine insists that human rights are passed down not by any form of legal transmission but as if by genetic endowment, and 'wrongs' cannot be so passed down; consequently, if 'the present generation, or any other, are disposed to be slaves, it does not lessen the right of the succeeding generation to be free' (p. 124).

The rights of man became so much part of the table talk of the period that the phrase was readily appropriated to articulate the claims made on behalf of particular groups within society. The French context is instructive. Although the Declaration of the Rights of Man is nominally a universal statement, with 'man' used as a general noun in the fashion of the day, it rapidly became clear after the Revolution that none of its key provisions applied to women. Representations were made to the National Assembly between 1789 and 1793 demanding the extension of the rights of man to the other half of the human race, and the playwright Olympe de Gouges (later guillotined) produced a rival declaration, *Droits de la femme*, in 1791 to correct the omissions of the first; but, despite their active contribution to the Revolution, women ended being completely excluded from the political process.[29] De Gouges's feminist manifesto pre-dates Mary Wollstonecraft's much better known *Vindication of the Rights of Woman* (1792). Wollstonecraft argues that women should only be 'excluded . . . from a participation of the natural rights of mankind' if it can be proved that they 'want reason';[30] but this is impossible to maintain in a society which holds women legally and morally accountable for their actions, for if women can take ethical decisions they must possess souls and the capacity to think, and if women possess such capacities it should be society's duty to educate them to their maximum potential. It is on this basis that she grounds her appeal for the equal education of women, which would remove them from the state of 'perpetual childhood' they currently inhabit, increase the national stock of knowledge and virtue, and, at the very least, make women more able and responsible wives and mothers – still, she acknowledges, their likely destiny for the foreseeable future. In addition to asserting a close alliance between the rights of woman and national education, Wollstonecraft argues for women to be politically enfranchised, to be given individual property rights, and to have access to a variety of occupations. As Anne Mellor points out, if her demands appear self-evidently reasonable to today's readers, 'it is only because the educational reform she demanded actually happened'.[31]

Wollstonecraft repeatedly and tendentiously compares the situation of women with that of slaves. With public attention focused intently on universal human rights, it is hardly surprising that the campaign to abolish slavery and the slave trade brought this powerful new ideology to bear on the institution that most flagrantly denied such rights to whole classes of humanity. William Fox was just one campaigner who urged British readers to consider slaves as their fellow-subjects and afford them the protection of the law, denying that the rights of men were 'limited to any nation, or to any colour'.[32] The example of France was again not encouraging: although the Revolution might be assumed to have given unstoppable force to the abolitionist cause, commercial interests meant that the National Assembly ignored pressure from the newly-created

Society of Friends of the Blacks and voted to retain slavery in 1790 and 1791. Many in Britain who favoured abolishing the slave trade were unwilling to scrap slavery itself, arguing that slaves were not yet ready for liberty: 'Like children,' according to one such reasoner, 'they must be restrained by authority, and led on to their own good.'[33]

Women, slaves, and children tended to be grouped together as categories to which the principle of natural rights did not apply. However, in the agrarian reformer, Thomas Spence, even children found their champion. In *The Rights of Infants*, Spence compares the rights of animals 'to provide from the elements the proper nourishments of their young' with the lack of such rights on the part of most mothers. The radical redistribution of land to parochial ownership that he urges would see farmers paying rent to the people rather than to aristocratic ruffians, as the 'imprescriptible right of every human being in civilized society, as an equivalent for the natural materials of their common estate, which by letting to rent, for the sake of cultivation and improvement, they are deprived of'.[34]

Spence's reference to the rights of animals may be rhetorical, but this final evolution of the discourse of natural rights, namely its extension to the non-human world, was indeed made in the period. Thomas Taylor's *A Vindication of the Rights of Brutes* (1792) was largely satirical in intent – it anticipates future treatises on the rights of vegetables and minerals – but its argument concerning the capacity of animals to feel and suffer, and their signs of intelligence and ability to communicate, seems genuine to some extent. More to the point, John Oswald's *The Cry of Nature* (1791) is a serious document linking political liberty to the nascent animal rights movement, and contributing strongly to contemporary vegetarian propaganda and the campaign against vivisection. Oswald deploys a range of historical, scientific, and ethnological arguments to condemn the anthropocentric pride that makes 'civilised' man 'an enemy to life and happiness through all their various forms of existence'.[35]

Reform

It is now time to take a closer look at British radicalism and reform – and their opponents – in the period, focusing on the two main 'waves' of activity in the 1790s and the 1810s. Although 'reform' is an umbrella term for political agitation on many fronts, including Catholic emancipation, poor relief, and education, I shall concentrate on the parliamentary reform and anti-slavery campaigns.

The Britain that reformers set out to change was very hierarchical, overwhelmingly rural, and, despite overlapping of the worlds of agriculture and business, dominated by the landed interest. Although many towns grew rapidly in the eighteenth century, at the start of the period only London, Glasgow, Edinburgh, and Bristol had more than 50,000 inhabitants, and little more than a quarter of the population of England and Wales (less in Scotland) lived in urban conditions. Land was still a major source of wealth, and the unrivalled source of social status. At the top of the social pyramid were some two hundred immensely powerful aristocratic families; beneath them, a landed gentry around 12,000 families strong. This privileged minority, apart from owning over half the country's land, controlled government at local and central levels. Local government was a more important reality in people's lives than it is today, and enjoyed almost total independence from Westminster. Among the key roles, Lord-Lieutenancies were powerful positions controlling a ladder of patronage stretching down to posts like parish clerk, and Justices of the Peace were their executive arm and the leaders of their local communities. In central government, patronage and rivalry amongst the great families were the order of the day, and patronage began with the king himself, whose power to appoint ministers and set the political direction was reined in only by the House of Commons' control of finance and taxation. Election to the Commons was itself determined to an astonishing extent by patronage: in 1793, an estimated 308 out of 513 seats for England and Wales were decided by either nomination or influence by peer or wealthy commoner; the newly-formed reform society, the Friends of the People, pointed out that a majority of MPs were elected by just over 11,000 men from a population of around ten million. The electoral system had no logic or consistency, with voting qualifications varying widely, gross regional imbalances in representation, and the emerging industrial towns disenfranchised. In over fifty of the borough seats the electorate numbered fewer than fifty; to take just one choice statistic, in the borough of Gatton two electors had the awesome responsibility of returning two MPs. In a parliamentary system that lacked political parties in the modern sense, where much more depended on family loyalties and informal alliances, the two hundred or so independent MPs, who voted according to conscience rather than the whim of their patrons, could not be ignored by the government of the day.

The struggle to reform this manifestly corrupt political system began in earnest in the 1780s, both inside and outside Parliament. The formation of the Yorkshire Association and other county reform organisations, and the establishment of the Society for Constitutional Information, were examples of middle-class reform activity that cooperated with parliamentary sympathisers, despite significant variation in aims and objectives. The failure of Pitt's reform bill in 1785 left the movement moribund. As suggested above, the French Revolution was responsible both for the reinvigoration of reform and for its eventual suppression. Of most concern to the authorities was the emergence for the first time of popular radicalism, channelled through bodies like the Sheffield Society for Constitutional Information and (most famously) the London Corresponding Society, with their low subscriptions, efficient organisation, and memberships that reached out to skilled artisans and tradesmen. The London Society's first *Address to the Public* in May 1792 called for universal male suffrage and 'a fair, equal and impartial Representation of the People in Parliament', and complained of 'oppressive taxes, unjust laws, restrictions of liberty, and wasting of the public money',[36] but steered clear of overt republicanism. The corresponding societies were committed to political

15

education and propagandising, and were keen to maintain standards: in Jennifer Mori's account, their leaders 'sought to replace a traditional popular culture of drink, custom and community with a reformed artisan culture emphasizing reason, the rights of the individual and a non-deferential plebeian respectability'.[37] Nevertheless, there was also an 'unrespectable' side to British radicalism, associated in particular with Thomas Spence and his followers, with their open advocacy of an agrarian utopia and their predilection for alternative media such as graffiti, broadsides, and fake coins countermarked with radical slogans. After the government crackdown in 1794–5, moderate elements fell away from the corresponding societies and a more revolutionary subculture developed, influenced in part by the United Irishmen who had begun recruiting on the mainland. In 1798 the leaders of the London Corresponding Society and the United Societies were arrested and an Act the following year terminated their existence. Thomas Hardy, radical shoemaker, concluded that fear of revolution had torpedoed the cause of reform: a word that 'may *now* be blotted out of the vocabulary'.[38]

From its first appearance, popular radicalism met a loyalist backlash that proved equally skilful in the art of propaganda and in cultivating new media of mass communication. John Reeves, a London police magistrate, formed the Association for the Preservation of Liberty and Property against Republicans and Levellers in November 1792, stimulating the creation of copycat organisations up and down the country and rapidly attracting government backing for its comprehensive anti-Jacobin programme. The associations were responsible for vigilante action against radicals in their local communities, but their cultural significance lay in the production and dissemination of loyalist propaganda, which took various forms including pamphlets, broadsides, prints, mugs, and tokens. This material characteristically melds the French Revolution and the aims of radical reformers into a single body of 'mischievous opinions' that threatens 'Established Law' and 'peaceable Society'.[39] The associations had variable lifespans, in some cases rapidly dissolving once they had squashed the local radical movement, but conservative propaganda stayed very much alive through the 1790s, as the success of Hannah More's popular pamphlets amply testifies. Her *Village Politics* (1793) was produced in vast quantities, and is notable for its use of a kind of architectural analogy to defend the British constitution that is common (though sometimes wielded with opposite ideological intent) in literature of the period:

> When Sir John married, my Lady, who is a little fantastical, and likes to do every thing like the French, begged him to pull down yonder fine old castle, and build it up in her frippery way. No, says Sir John, what shall I pull down this noble building, raised by the wisdom of my brave ancestors; which outstood the civil wars, and only underwent a little needful repair at the Revolution . . . shall I pull it all down, I say, only because there may be a dark closet or an inconvenient room or two in it? My lady mumpt and grumbled; but the castle was let stand, and a glorious building it is . . . so now and then they mend a little thing, and they'll go on mending, I dare say, as they have leisure, to the end of the chapter, if they are let alone. But no pull-me-down works.

Such an attitude seems to allow for only the most moderate and gradual reform. However, its main speaker's conclusion that England has 'the best laws in the world, if they were more strictly enforced; and the best religion in the world, if it was but better followed' shows that More's conservatism was far from complacent.[40] It demonstrates, moreover, that an important part of the loyalist message involved acknowledging that success in the war on French principles required putting one's own political and moral house in order. This was certainly the burden of the bestselling *Cheap Repository Tracts* that More went on to produce between 1795 and 1798, which generally avoid direct political comment in favour of strong evangelical themes of hard work, self-responsibility, and acceptance of one's lot.

The fortunes of reform were blighted, but not destroyed, by the passage of the Corresponding Societies Act in 1799. The mainly extra-parliamentary stirrings of the movement in the early 1800s escalated into a full resurgence of radical politics in the context of a severe post-war economic depression, aggravated by the 1815 Corn Laws (imposing a high tariff on imported grain and guaranteeing high bread prices) that were seen as self-serving legislation on the part of a landowners' parliament. This reinvigorated campaign manifested itself in mass petitions for parliamentary reform; the re-emergence of an aggressive radical press, fully capable of engaging with different audiences within an increasingly heterogeneous reading public; and the new phenomenon of the huge political rally, culminating in the notorious 'Peterloo' massacre in Manchester in August 1819, in which over 400 casualties (including eleven fatalities) resulted from the local magistrates' decision to use troops to disperse 60,000 peaceful protesters. There were also a few uncoordinated attempts at insurrection, in which Spencean revolutionaries, who had never gone quiet, played a notable part: the Cato Street Conspiracy, in which about forty urban guerrillas sought to assassinate the Cabinet and establish a provisional government, was the disastrous flowering of their ambitions. The response of Lord Liverpool's government to this new wave of radicalism mirrored that of Pitt in the 1790s: imprisonment without trial, strict new legislation on public order offences, a crackdown on the radical press. One key aspect of this press's activity was the effort to mobilise support for reform across class divides, to appeal to a nation of right-minded people against the effluvia of 'Old Corruption': in his twopenny *Political Register*, the labouring-class radical journalist William Cobbett claimed that an alliance between the middle and labouring classes in any provincial town would bring about reform immediately.[41] This ideal unity did not materialise, and improved economic prosperity in the 1820s buried the cause of reform, but it moved rapidly back up the political agenda following the passage of highly controversial legislation on Catholic emancipation in 1828. Severe electoral turbulence in 1830–2 issued finally in the historic first Reform Bill of 1832, which redrew the political map of Britain, redressed the worst biases of the old representative system, and began the process of widening the franchise – though keeping it firmly in the hands of property-owners.

Like the parliamentary reform campaign, the campaign to abolish the slave trade and slavery began in earnest in the 1780s, motivated in part by a desire to regain the moral high ground after the loss of the American war had instilled a mood of national self-questioning. The Society for Effecting the Abolition of the Slave Trade was founded in 1787, and the first anti-slavery debate was held in Parliament in 1789, led by William Wilberforce. Tactical concerns about not appearing to attack colonial business interests meant that abolition focused in its first phase on the slave trade alone (by the 1780s, Britain was transporting an average of 23,000 slaves annually to America and the West Indies); this campaign, supported by a broad coalition of Anglicans and Nonconformists, was derailed for a while by its association with Jacobinism in the general recoil from the French Revolution, but reached fruition in 1807 under the short-lived administration of Lord Grenville. In the second phase, abolitionists turned their attention to the institution of slavery itself, and Wilberforce lived just long enough to see an Act passed in 1833 outlawing slavery in British territories abroad. Throughout the period abolition attracted more public support than parliamentary reform: successive mass petitions attracted hundreds of thousands of signatures, while the petitions preceding the 1833 Emancipation Act were signed by a formidable one and a half million people. Abolitionism permeated the culture of the period, helping to define the tenor of evangelical Christianity, influencing consumer behaviour, and generating a diverse body of propaganda. Abolitionist literature was a remarkable genre, defined by harrowing accounts of the Middle Passage and uncompromising assaults on the prejudices of its audience. Leading campaigner Thomas Clarkson constantly harangues his readers, urging them to see the contradictions between slavery and the principles of their professed religion: 'how can any man be justly called to an account for his actions,' he says, 'whose actions are not *at his own disposal?*'[42]

There is disagreement among historians as to whether slavery was ended because it was uneconomic, or for humanitarian reasons. Linda Colley favours an ideological interpretation somewhere between these extremes, suggesting that abolition 'supplied the British with a powerful legitimation for their claims to be the arbiters of the civilised and the uncivilised world', which would be of great importance in the subsequent development of the Empire and of the 'Victorian culture of complacency'.[43] Whatever the reasons, the success of abolition, along with Catholic emancipation in 1828 and the Reform Bill of 1832, meant that, despite the overall conservatism of post-Revolutionary Britain, the period ended with three major victories for radical reform.

Industrialisation

In terms of economic philosophy, the period's agenda had already been set by Adam Smith's *Inquiry into the Nature and Causes of the Wealth of Nations* (1776). Smith pioneered the cause of free trade, challenging the received wisdom that economic strength flowed from a healthy balance of payments achieved through the elaborate machinery of protection (import tariffs, monopolies, and so forth) embedded in eighteenth-century Britain. An early proponent of the labour theory of value, he believed that increased productivity resulted from division of labour and specialisation of function, and that the most efficient use of labour within an open, competitive market would create a virtuous circle benefiting producers, labourers, and consumers alike. The hostility between protectionists and free trade advocates was a key feature of economic debate in the Romantic period, and the final victory of the latter was not won until later in the nineteenth century. Despite his reputation as the prophet of capitalist free enterprise, Smith did not see economic growth as limitless: he assumed that growth achieved through investment – first in agriculture, then industry, then domestic and international trade, as the rate of return successively declined – would eventually plateau out, creating a low-profit, low-wage environment where competition for work would be fierce. It was this rather grimmer aspect of Smith's thesis that was picked up in the economics text that had the greatest impact in the period, Thomas Malthus's *Essay on the Principle of Population* (1798). The polemical thrust of this work is against Godwin's serene view of human perfectibility and his vision of a future based on complete equality of property and sexual freedom. Whereas Godwin ascribed the prevailing misery to human institutions that were eminently replaceable, for Malthus the real culprit is 'the laws of nature, which human institutions, so far from aggravating, have tended considerably to mitigate, though they never can remove'. By this he means a basic imbalance between population growth and food supply. From the premises that food is necessary to human existence, and that sexual passion is here to stay, Malthus argues that 'the power of population is indefinitely greater than the power in the earth to produce subsistence for man', the former increasing in geometrical ratio, the latter only in arithmetical ratio.[44] Faced with this desperate scenario, the alternatives are for the balance between population and food resources to be periodically restored by the 'positive checks' of famine, disease, and war, or for society to take more seriously the 'preventive checks' of celibacy and delayed marriage and childbirth. Unsurprisingly, Malthus preferred the latter solution – hence his controversial opposition to poor relief, which, he felt, encouraged families to have children without increasing the resources available for their support.

Malthus's alarming prophecies received confirmation from David Ricardo, whose *Principles of Political Economy and Taxation* (1817) also saw people exhausting the land's capacity to provide, with the shift to ever more marginal and labour-intensive land producing larger rents for landowners but reduced profits for farmers and falling wages for labourers. Ricardo became (unlike Malthus) an apostle of free trade and saw the advantages of investment in machinery, but he still believed that the dreaded 'stationary state' could only be postponed. The view of modern economic historians seems to be that there was indeed compelling evidence for a Malthusian/Ricardian crisis at the end of the eighteenth century, a period when population growth was accelerating, food prices were rising, and real wages stagnating, but that at some point the cycle was broken as the operations of capital and new technology allowed for a sustained increase in productivity: 'The restraints of the Malthusian economy were released, and growth became cumulative.'[45] This fundamental gear change as the country threw off the shackles of a traditional 'organic' economy is what is still sometimes referred to as the 'industrial revolution'.

The orthodox picture of the industrial revolution is of a rapid economic take-off after 1780, neatly corresponding with the age of political revolutions and, for our purposes, the birth of Romanticism. The process is taken to have involved a mass movement of labour from the countryside to towns to work in industrial employment, especially in large factories characterised by mechanised production and the application of steam power; this 'revolution' is said to have been driven by a 'leading sector', the cotton industry, enabled by high levels of capital formation, and facilitated by major improvements in transport and communications. Eric Hobsbawm's definition of the industrial revolution as 'self-sustained economic growth by means of perpetual technological revolution and social transformation' fits into this paradigm.[46] Once the revolution has been accepted as a reality, the next question is why it happened in Britain first. Explanations focused on natural resources, demography, developments in science and technology, the unique Protestant work ethic, or the situation of Dissenters excluded from public office who had to find alternative outlets for their energies, are among those put forward. For Hobsbawm, who sees the industrial revolution very much as synonymous with factory-produced cotton goods, the crucial factor was 'monopolizing the export markets of a large part of the world in a sufficiently brief period of time' (p. 26), a process involving war, colonisation, and a government in Britain prepared 'to subordinate *all* foreign policy to economic ends' (p. 27).

Historical revisionism has progressed so far in this area that it is now possible for the industrial revolution to be dismissed as a 'fictitious entity'.[47] The validity of the data, and their interpretation, that form the basis of such claims, and the inevitable counter-claims, is impossible for the layman to adjudicate; but there seems a broad consensus that economic growth was not the volcanic phenomenon it was once taken to be, and that British industrialisation was thus more evolutionary than revolutionary. The more measured approach, as pursued by M.J. Daunton, appears to be one which recognises the coexistence of slow growth and major structural change, and which gives much fuller attention to regional differences in the pace and modality of industrialisation. The importance of exports is nevertheless conceded, and it is argued that this contributed to a 'skewed pattern of industrialization' narrowly based on cotton and iron and on low investment in education and training, which would come back to haunt Britain in the future.[48]

For much of the eighteenth century London was the most important industrial centre in the country, and there was significant industrial activity across southern and eastern England (textiles in East Anglia and the West Country, for instance, and iron production in Kent); small towns were growing rapidly elsewhere, often becoming the centre of specialised local industries that could access the national or international market given improvements in transport, marketing, and distribution. During the Romantic period a major change in the industrial map of Britain was completed: London retained its importance, but southern England deindustrialised and growth became firmly centred on the west Midlands, the West Riding of Yorkshire, Lancashire, south Wales, north-east England, and Lanarkshire in Scotland. This growth took different forms in different parts of the country and in different industrial sectors. In the classic model of industrialisation, an initial stage in which artisans produce goods on their own account is succeeded first by a system of 'outworking' or 'putting out', in which home-based workers receive raw materials from a merchant (such as yarn for weaving) and return the finished product for payment; then by centralised factory production in which labourers are reduced to 'hands' in the service of machinery. However, this tidy narrative only suits certain cases, and misrepresents the structural diversity of industry in the period: in some industries growth occurred through an expansion of domestic manufactures, in others domestic and factory production coexisted healthily for some considerable time. Neither did mechanisation, and the application of steam power, take hold as early, or as widely, as is sometimes imagined: by 1830 most industrial activity was still small-scale, and 'except for cotton, and the large-scale establishments characteristic of iron and coal, the development of production in mechanized factories . . . had to wait until the second half of the nineteenth century'.[49]

Nevertheless, just as literary periods become identified with writers who were thoroughly untypical of their age, so a period's economic activity may be popularly known only for its spectacular exceptions. Even under revisionist eyes, cotton was king at the turn of the eighteenth century. The success of this industry was built on raw material from slave plantations, first in the West Indies then later the southern USA; it was also made possible by early (and cheap) mechanisation, first of the spinning process (in the 1780s), then, after the Napoleonic wars, of weaving. These technological innovations made factory production viable, and accommodated the later introduction of steam. Cheap cotton goods were supplied to an increasingly consumerised domestic market, but the export market (located first in Europe, then in the underdeveloped world), which grew over thirty-five times in annual value between the 1780s and the 1820s, gave the industry its main propulsion.

Steam power implies coal, and it was the exploitation of Britain's vast coal reserves that allowed it to escape the 'organic' constraints of human, horse, wind, and water power at the end of the eighteenth century. (By a nice irony, it was the problems of extracting coal, in particular draining water out of deep mines, which themselves provided the inspiration for the invention of the steam engine.) Output increased tenfold between 1700 and 1830, and by 1800, when industry was the major consumer, was five times that of the rest of Europe. Urbanisation supplied the early stimulus; then came its application to the capital-intensive processes of smelting and refining iron, and to generating steam to power furnaces and forges. However, although war was good news for the iron industry by increasing demand from the military and keeping foreign iron out of the market, it was not until the coming of the railways in the 1840s that metal manufactures really 'took off'.

The broader social and cultural balance sheet of industrialisation is a huge subject that can only briefly be touched on. In materialistic terms, the question of whether the overall standard of living rose or fell in this period is, as always, a matter of dispute; but there is little doubt that, while the aristocracy and gentry, and the professional and business classes, either prospered or suffered no adverse effects from industrialisation, the labouring poor got at least relatively, and perhaps absolutely, poorer. Apart from agricultural labourers, the worst losers were dispossessed artisans such as handloom weavers and framework knitters, as well as those caught up in the exploitative growth of a range of non-factory and 'sweated' trades, which included large numbers of women and children.[50] The new industrial towns and cities, built without regard for the workers who had to live in them, began in the period a process of reckless expansion that far outstripped the provision of adequate housing or basic services and produced recurrent epidemics of cholera and typhus. Industrialisation also entailed profound changes to established ways of life, including the imposition of an alien time and work discipline and 'a mechanized *regularity* of work which conflicts not only with tradition, but with all the inclinations of a humanity as yet unconditioned into it'.[51]

As these highly condensed remarks indicate, the problems of industrialisation cannot be divorced from the transformation of rural Britain in the period, itself sometimes referred to as an 'agricultural revolution' (for some, yet another spurious revolution). This was not a matter, as it was in France, of the destruction of an ancient feudal system of land tenure, since the basic capitalist structure of landownership – great landlords, tenant farmers, and hired labourers – was already in place by the mid-eighteenth century. Nor was it a matter of mechanisation, which made little headway until the 1850s. Instead, it involved the progressive consolidation of land in fewer hands in the creation of great estates; a sharpening of the distinction between owning and renting property (previously blurred in legal arrangements such as 'customary tenure' and copyhold tenancies); a major redistribution of income from farmers to landlords; and the immiseration of the rural poor who were stripped of their common rights and reduced to increasingly insecure forms of waged labour. The most notorious vehicle of these changes was 'enclosure' – or, more precisely, the parliamentary enclosure movement, the culmination of a much longer process of consolidation or 'modernisation'. Under enclosure, open fields typically divided into strips belonging to individual villagers (rather like today's 'allotments'), together with surrounding areas of common waste, all of which was cultivated on an agreed communal basis, were rationalised into larger holdings under a stricter definition of ownership, later to be physically enclosed by fences or hedgerows. A vital stage in the process was the abolition of 'contingent use rights' of gleaning, grazing, and foraging enjoyed by all villagers, which provided vital subsistence for those with no land to cultivate and valuable supplementary income for others. Enclosure had taken place uncontroversially since the Middle Ages, but parliamentary enclosure was a more contentious and accelerated phase of activity, with 3,828 separate Acts being passed between 1750 and 1819. It was a complex, negotiated process, but one which was weighted heavily in favour of large landowners, and E.P. Thompson's description of it as 'a plain enough case of class robbery, played according to fair rules'[52] receives plenty of support from contemporary testimony. The alleged greater efficiency and productivity of the newly enclosed land, said by some commentators to be necessary to address the Malthusian crisis of output, is still argued over; but landlords and large tenant farmers were the main beneficiaries of enclosure, while its victims were the ordinary villagers who lost their meagre independence and customary way of life to become part of a structurally underemployed labour pool subsidised by poor relief.

Enclosure was only one aspect of the period's agrarian distress: rural labourers suffered in all possible ways, whether from high prices and intermittent bad harvests in the war years, or from wage cuts after 1815 when the workforce was swollen by demobilisation. Successive waves of food riots throughout the period, and the proliferation of poaching in defiance of a tightening of the game laws, tell their own story of desperation and resentment. While it is easy to romanticise the so-called 'moral economy' of a traditional countryside invaded by the hostile forces of capitalism, it is hard not to conclude that this resentment was strengthened by what was perceived as the degradation of an entire inherited culture. Indeed, the Swing riots of 1830–1 (named after their mythical leader, 'Captain Swing') have been interpreted as a last-ditch protest against the decline of the old, paternalistic rural order.

Notes

1. The phrase is E.J. Hobsbawm's. See *The Age of Revolution: Europe 1789–1848* (London, 1962).

2. *The French Revolution* (London, 1988), p. 31.

3. D.G. Wright, *Napoleon and Europe* (London and New York, 1984), p. 94.

4. *Interpreting the French Revolution*, trans. Elborg Forster (Cambridge, 1981), pp. 20, 23, 26.

5. 'What was Revolutionary about the French Revolution?', in *The French Revolution in Social and Political Perspective*, ed. Peter Jones (London and New York, 1996), pp. 18–29 (pp. 27, 29, 28).

6. *Thoughts on the Probable Influence of the French Revolution on Great Britain* (London, 1790), pp. 1, 6.

7. *A Letter from Earl Stanhope to the Right Honourable Edmund Burke* (London, 1790), p. 34.

8. Cited in F. O'Gorman, *The Whig Party and the French Revolution* (London, 1967), p. 46.

9. 'Ireland and the French Revolution', in *Britain and the French Revolution, 1789–1815*, ed. H.T. Dickinson (Basingstoke and London, 1989), p. 100.

10. *Britons: Forging the Nation 1707–1837* (London, 1992), pp. 247, 237.

11. *British Society and the French Wars 1793–1815* (London and Basingstoke, 1979), p. 18.

12. Eric J. Evans, *The Forging of the Nation: Early Industrial Britain 1783–1870* (London and New York, 1983), p. 77.

13. *Extermination, or an Appeal to the People of England, on the Present War with France* (London, 1793?), pp. 11–12.

14. *The Complaints of the Poor People of England* (London, 1793), p. 222.

15. H.T. Dickinson, 'Introduction: The Impact of the French Revolution and the French Wars 1789–1815', in *Britain and the French Revolution*, ed. Dickinson, p. 11.

16. *The Real Grounds of the Present War with France* (London, 1793), p. 68.

17. *The Portable Edmund Burke*, ed. Isaac Kramnick (Harmondsworth, 1999), p. 517.

18. *An Address to the People of the United Kingdom of Great Britain and Ireland on the Threatened Invasion* (London, 1803), pp. 10–11.

19. *England in Danger! And Britons Asleep* (Birmingham, 1798), p. 8.

20. *Britons*, pp. 328–9, 276.

21. *A Discourse on the Love of our Country* (London, 1789), p. 50.

22. *Reflections on the Revolution in France*, ed. Conor Cruise O'Brien (Harmondsworth, 1968), pp. 92, 211, 173.

23. *A Vindication of the Rights of Men*, in *The Works of Mary Wollstonecraft*, ed. Janet Todd and Marilyn Butler (London, 1989), V, 37.

24. *Vindiciae Gallicae: Defence of the French Revolution and its English Admirers against the Accusations of the Rt. Hon. Edmund Burke* (Dublin, 1791), pp. 49, 48.

25. *Enquiry Concerning Political Justice*, ed. Isaac Kramnick (Harmondsworth, 1976), p. 462.

26. *Two Treatises of Government*, ed. P. Laslett, 2nd edn (Cambridge, 1967), pp. 368, 371.

27. *The Social Contract*, trans. Maurice Cranston (Harmondsworth, 1968), p. 60.

28. *Rights of Man*, ed. Eric Foner (Harmondsworth, 1984), p. 116.

29. See Jane Abray, 'Feminism in the French Revolution', in *The French Revolution*, ed. Jones, pp. 236–52.

30. *Vindication of the Rights of Woman*, ed. Miriam Brody (Harmondsworth, 1975), p. 88.

31. *Romanticism and Gender* (London, 1993), p. 35.

32. *A Call to the People of Great Britain, to Refrain from the Use of Sugar and Rum* (London, 1791), p. 11.

33. James Ramsay, *Objections to the Abolition of the Slave Trade, with Answers* (London, 1788), p. 2.

34. *The Rights of Infants* (London, 1797), pp. 5, 9.

35. *The Cry of Nature; Or, an Appeal to Mercy and Justice, on Behalf of the Persecuted Animals* (London, 1791), p. 78.

36. Quoted in Albert Goodwin, *The Friends of Liberty: The English Democratic Movement in the Age of the French Revolution* (London, 1979), p. 195.

37. *Britain in the Age of the French Revolution* (London, 2000), p. 67.

38. Quoted in J.R. Dinwiddy, *Radicalism and Reform in Britain, 1780–1850* (London and Rio Grande, 1992), p. 193.

39. *Liberty and Property Preserved Against Republicans and Levellers. A Collection of Tracts Recommended to Perusal at the Present Crisis. Part the First* (London, 1793), pp. 2, 6.

40. *Village Politics. Addressed to all the Mechanics, Journeymen, and Day Labourers, in Great Britain* (Canterbury, 1793), pp. 6–7, 15.

41. 'To the Middle Classes of England, on the Benefits which Reform would Produce to them', *Political Register*, 13 November 1819, in *William Cobbett: Selected Writings*, vol. 4, ed. Leonora Nattrass (London, 1998) pp. 151–64.

42. *An Essay on the Slavery and Commerce of the Human Species*, 2nd edn (London, 1788), p. 162.

43. *Britons*, pp. 380, 381.

44. *An Essay on the Principle of Population*, ed. Geoffrey Gilbert (Oxford, 1993), p. 81.

45. M.J. Daunton, *Progress and Poverty: An Economic and Social History of Britain 1700–1850* (Oxford and New York, 1995), p. 8.

46. *Industry and Empire*, revised edn (Harmondsworth, 1999), pp. 12–13.

47. J.C.D. Clark, *English Society, 1688–1832* (Cambridge, 1985), p. 4.

48. Daunton, *Progress and Poverty*, p. 379.

49. Hobsbawm, *Industry and Empire*, p. 50.

50. Evans, *Forging of the Nation*, pp. 122–4, 152–3.

51. Hobsbawm, *Industry and Empire*, p. 64.

52. *The Making of the English Working Class*, 2nd edn (Harmondsworth, 1968), pp. 237–8.

Chapter Two

Travel, Exploration, and the Geographies of Mind

Constantin François Volney's *Ruins* (1791), a passionate yet forensic examination of the sources of human misery in arbitrary political and religious
tyranny, was one of the key texts of the French Enlightenment and a major
influence on British radicals and freethinkers in the early nineteenth century.
An interesting aspect of the text is that its narrator presents himself as a
traveller, and the entire political education which takes place in *Ruins*, through
both a sweeping review of history and a vision of future general emancipation,
is rooted in the observations and reflections excited by a foreign landscape.
The first chapter, 'The Tour', describes a visit to the ruins of Palmyra, the
ancient city supposedly founded by Solomon in biblical times and later a
major city-state in the Roman Empire. The narrator spends days contemplating
such monuments as the Temple of the Sun and the famous Colonnade,
re-creating the living city in his mind's eye and comparing it to the 'miserable
skeleton' before him:

> The silence of the tomb is substituted for the hum of public places. The opulence of
> a commercial city is changed into hideous poverty. The palaces of kings are become
> the receptacle of deer, and unclean reptiles inhabit the sanctuary of the Gods. –
> What glory is here eclipsed, and how many labours are annihilated! – Thus perish
> the works of men, and do nations and empires vanish away![1]

He is disturbed at the thought that the same fate may await (his native) France
as befell Palmyra. He is minded to refer such doubts to the inscrutable wisdom
of the Almighty, but at this point is confronted by an 'apparition' who advises
him to stop blaming God or Fate for every calamity and listen instead to the
'voice of reason' (p. 15), which instructs him in the causes of historical change
and the principles of good society.

Addressed as the 'Genius of tombs and ruins' (p. 23), the apparition might
also be dubbed the Genius of Travel, for the process of self-education in
natural law and secular rationality that the narrator undergoes is a theatrically
amplified version of the benefits of foreign travel as commonly expressed in
eighteenth-century travel literature. Usually referred to as 'philosophical travel'
or 'scientific travel', this mode of discourse emphasises the value of distancing
oneself from the 'natural' language of one's own culture and developing a
facility for observation and comparison, a more comprehensive and objective
view of the world. It remains a powerful discursive mode in the Romantic period,
but alongside it, in various complementary and contradictory formations,

are other vocabularies and narrative styles that help shape and colour the increasingly global perspectives of the Romantic reader. It is the purpose of this chapter to explore some of the complexity of this cultural conversation through brief surveys of a number of the most important geographical areas to which a voluminous travel literature was devoted.

The literature of travel and exploration was hugely popular throughout the Romantic period. A reviewer of one anthology of travel literature published in 1805 says that 'Next to novels, voyages and travels constitute the most fashionable kind of reading'.[2] In fact, crude quantitative bibliography indicates that the largest single category of books published at this time was religious literature, but given the peculiar circumstances surrounding the production of such literature (enormous quantities were produced by evangelical and missionary groups for free distribution at home and abroad) this commentator is undoubtedly right in stating that in terms of the books people actually *wanted to read*, narratives of travel and exploration were surpassed in popularity only by novels. The records of Bristol Library, patronised by Coleridge and Southey, for example, show that borrowers' favourite loans were travel books; while a prospectus for William Lane's circulating library published in 1798 lists 102 items to whet the appetite of potential subscribers, of which approximately one third are works of travel and exploration. My own searches for the years 1795, 1805, 1815, and 1825 suggest that the annual output of new titles in the field, excluding anthologies and collections, averaged over 30 – few by today's standards, but very significant at a time when new book titles numbered several hundred per year at most. There is a mass of anecdotal evidence that readers' appetites for travel literature remained strong throughout the period 1789–1830, and that literature is the single most powerful resource for understanding how the rest of the world was constructed in the eyes of British Romantic readers.

Britain and Europe

The foreign, from the point of view of the Romantic tourist or traveller, was not necessarily very far away. In certain respects, journeying to the remoter parts of Wales, Scotland, and to a lesser extent (because there were fewer visitors) Ireland, could seem like venturing abroad. A reviewer of one tour of North Wales published in 1804 says that the expedition

> might be described as a kind of *foreign* travel which may be performed *at home*: for without crossing the water, we are introduced to a country presenting singular aspects, a rich variety of scenery, and a state of society dissimilar from our own; inhabited by a people altogether distinct from ourselves, speaking a different language, and distinguished by peculiar qualities, habits, and manners . . .[3]

The foreignness of the Celtic periphery, associated in particular with communities of people 'altogether distinct' from the educated metropolitan and urban readers who constituted the reviews' target audience, is a common theme in

Romantic travel literature. Here that foreignness is appraised in a broadly positive way, although in describing the Welsh as a 'remnant' of an ancient people he suggests a population in decline from earlier glory. Another traveller to North Wales in this period is complimentary about the 'original character' he claims they have preserved, including a 'love of liberty and independence . . . implanted by nature in their breasts', which he identifies with the rugged natural environment they inhabit. He sees this primitive strength and simplicity of character as the mark of a people who resisted subjugation by the English under Edward I, and as a positive contrast to the modern vices of luxury and corruption of the 'commercial people' from whose ranks the writer himself comes.[4]

There is thus a tendency to perceive the Welsh- or Gaelic-speaking inhabitants of the British Isles as singularly different to – in some sense, historically remote from – the educated, urban population of the politically, economically, and culturally dominant 'centre' of the kingdom. A more extreme version of this process of 'othering', again not untypical of Romantic travel writing, can be illustrated from Dorothy Wordsworth's journal of her tour of Scotland in 1803. It involves comparing the inhabitants, or their country, to indigenous peoples and landscapes from far-flung parts of the world, and known to the authors only second-hand, usually from printed texts. Thus Dorothy Wordsworth finds that a simple hut close to the Falls of the Clyde 'resembled some of the huts in the prints belonging to Captain Cook's Voyages'; the view of Loch Lomond from the highpoint of Inch-ta-vannach is an 'outlandish scene' comparable with the North American wilderness; and the skill of their Highlander guide on the mountains above Glenfalloch reminds her 'of what we read of the Hottentots and other savages'.[5] In passages like this, Wordsworth imports geographical and ethnographical distance into what one critic has called 'Britain's own internally colonized Celtic backyard'.[6] The effect is to amplify the self-confidence and sense of superiority with which the British middle classes confronted the strains and divisions within their notionally united kingdom. The civilised centre seems to delight in a regular supply of images of the 'savages' on its own shores as a way of mentally dominating those spectres of its bloody history.

The obvious alternative to domestic tourism for middle- and upper-class men or family groups in this period was Continental travel. In the second half of the eighteenth century, the traditional Grand Tour changed its character as the upwardly mobile and expanding professional and commercial classes began to usurp and refashion this aristocratic custom. The long war against France starting in 1793 interrupted travel, but it resumed in earnest after Waterloo, and differences are apparent between the writings of this new generation of tourists and those of their eighteenth-century predecessors. One thing that is noticeable is a less crudely Anglocentric view of foreigners and foreign ways of life. Traditionally, Grand Tourists, who were supposed to be broadening their mental horizons by an immersion in different cultures, tended with uncanny regularity to return home with a confirmed sense of the superiority of their own country. This degree of naive prejudice, often accompanied by crude national stereotyping of Europeans, fierce anti-Catholicism, and a good helping of old-fashioned British prudery, was mitigated by the democratisation of the Grand Tour. Political open-mindedness was in most quarters one of the first casualties of the war against France, but when the Continent reopened the British plunged into foreign travel with a great relish for unfamiliar scenes and new experiences. The huge cultural influence of rebellious figures like Byron, and of the literary vogue for Romantic heroes who put themselves at odds with society, made it unfashionable to assume an uncritically patriotic and conformist stance. Although there is still a lot of preference shown for the British way of life in post-1815 travel writing, the lazy and complacent national pride of earlier generations of Grand Tourists has largely disappeared.

For this new generation of tourists, Romantic tastes and values led to reconstruction of the imaginative geography of the Grand Tour. This geography had always had as its deep structure the passage from North to South[7] – it was this that guaranteed the encounter with difference that was indispensable to the experience and writing of Continental travel – and for eighteenth-century Grand Tourists all roads did, indeed, lead to Rome. In the Romantic period travellers overlay their conventional respect for Rome as a centre of Western civilization with distinctive new responses: in particular, there is a more acute awareness of the contrast between the city of the (historical) imagination and the actual city that tourists contended with daily.[8] Italy's lamentable political degradation – recently returned to Austrian domination after more than ten years as a satellite territory of France – compounded the impression of many travellers that modern-day Italians were unworthy of their glorious past.

But at the same time that the gap between imagination and reality was complicating travellers' reception of Rome, the spiritual centre of the Grand Tour was undergoing a displacement. The growth of scenic tourism in the second half of the eighteenth century had been so spectacular that the Alps were now a serious rival to Italy and its cultural heritage: what were once a natural barrier on the route to the South, to be crossed or circumvented as swiftly as possible, were now a principal source of interest. Inspired by the powerful new aesthetics of the sublime (see Chapter 8), the Mont Blanc region became the new spiritual home of writers and artists. At the same time, increasing numbers of travellers began venturing further east – to Greece, Turkey, the Levant generally – in a quest for novelty and authenticity that had no logical termination.

America

As the site of the only large-scale European (including British) colonisation prior to the nineteenth century, no part of the world was of more interest to the reading public in the period than America – North and South. Here I shall focus solely on North America. As noted in Chapter 1, the loss of its American colonies after the War of Independence of 1775–83 was of huge political, economic, and psychological significance to Britain, and the poor relationship resulting from this traumatic conflict worsened into fresh crisis in the

Anglo-American War of 1812–14. Within the period the territory of the United States grew enormously, notably with the Louisiana Purchase of 1803, by which 800,000 square miles of land west of the Mississippi, bought from Napoleon for a paltry $15m, doubled the size of the infant republic. A constant flow of publications fuelled British interest in the so-called 'New World', and these can be loosely divided into three types: the literature of exploration, the literature of tourism, and the literature of emigration.

Anthony Pagden has compared the profound impact of the European 'discovery' of America with that of the Copernican revolution in astronomy: it was recognised from the first that it was 'unthinkable . . . that a culture should remain unchanged by the recognition that for centuries it had lived in ignorance of the very existence of half the globe it inhabits'.[9] One effect was to legitimise curiosity and boost the claims of empirical science over religious tradition: looking to the West became a potent symbol of new horizons of knowledge. It also came to signify realms of gold. For some these realms were decidedly literal, in the sense that opening up the New World was seen to offer commercial opportunities and material riches on an incalculable scale. For others they were more of a poetic conceit, in that America was seen as some kind of terrestrial paradise, where natural bounty and spiritual reward awaited the meritorious settler. Material aspirations and Utopian yearnings came together in the 'westering' impulse that accompanied the ever-moving frontier through the Romantic period and beyond. Needless to say, all these acquired ways of seeing the New World were entirely Eurocentric, and ignored the history, experience, and even the existence of the native peoples who had continuously inhabited the continent for at least twenty thousand years prior to the voyages of Columbus and Cabot, and who numbered an estimated ten million (in North America) at the time of first contact. Europeans were not alone in regarding their own culture as superior, but the particular cast of their beliefs – notably the belief that nature should be controlled and transformed by technological means – and the kinds and quantities of resources available to them gave them unique power to wreak havoc among those they perceived as savage or at best pre-civilised.

To give some reality to these general themes, I shall look first at two works of exploration literature. William Bartram's very popular *Travels* (1791) were those of an American citizen working on behalf of a British naturalist, as evidenced by the quality of his botanical descriptions and drawings. Bartram's overall response to the wilderness of the south-eastern states is an interestingly complex one. His opening evocation of the magnificent coastal scenery on his voyage to Charleston, which gives 'an idea of the first appearance of the earth to man at the creation', points to an idealising strand in the contemporary imagining of America.[10] But such imagery usually rubs against a more scientific vocabulary: there is, for example, a memorable word-picture of Six Miles Springs in East Florida and its surrounding 'aromatic groves', which Bartram presents as 'inexpressibly admirable and pleasing', indeed as positively 'Elysian'; yet the deep pellucid basin in which all manner of creatures seem to enjoy life without threat to each other, and which suggests 'the peaceable and happy state of nature which existed before the fall', is admitted to be an illusion, the animals' behaviour explained by the peculiar conditions of their environment (pp. 149–50).

In his frequent observations on the Indian peoples he has had contact with, and their interaction with white settlers, Bartram is open-minded and a firm advocate of the politics of treaty, mutual understanding, and peaceful coexistence. His description of savannah cranes which, on landing by a lake, 'approach the kindred band, confer, and treat for habitation', then 'confederate and take possession' (p. 136) is easily read as an idealising allegory of relations between Native Americans and European colonisers. He is also capable of casting Indians as 'noble savages', possessors of an instinctive morality uncontaminated by a corrupt civilisation: thus the Siminoles are 'blithe and free as the birds of the air' (p. 182), naturally affectionate and honest, perfectly content with what they have and what they are. The Indian social system generally is seen as maintained by the natural promptings of individual conscience, and their benign, universally esteemed monarchs are contrasted favourably with the schism and intrigue endemic in European courts. What really seems to be happening here is that Bartram is projecting onto Indian society a defence of the rational constitution of the new United States against the political iniquities of the Old World. Even though his travels do not have an explicitly colonial purpose, therefore, Bartram still brings colonial eyes to bear on the places and peoples he encounters; indeed, the entire scientific frame of his endeavours has an imperial dimension to it, in bringing the flora and fauna and human inhabitants of a part of America within the classificatory regimes of European science.

Another popular work of exploration literature was Samuel Hearne's *Journey* in the northern territories, first published in 1795. Hearne, an employee of the Hudson's Bay Company, the British corporation that enjoyed proprietary rights over a vast territory draining into Hudson's Bay, was commissioned to locate a river in the far north of the territory where native people had access to very pure copper. He did indeed successfully complete the round trip from Churchill on Hudson's Bay to the Coppermine River, making a significant contribution to geographical knowledge and establishing that the copper was not at that time commercially exploitable. However, the success of his book was probably due not to these factors or to what it revealed of the intricacies of the fur trade, but to Hearne's personal narrative of survival and adventure in extreme conditions, and for his intimate account of the Chipewyan Indians with whom he lived for two years.

The evidence provided by modern critical editing of Hearne as to what he added to his original journal for the purpose of book publication shows a keen awareness of what would gratify the appetite of readers addicted to sentimental comedies and Gothic romances. He focuses cannily, for example, on the treatment of Indian women: his description of the fate of one member of a travelling party, who is required to move on almost immediately after giving birth, is clearly filtered through the contemporary discourse of sensibility that made a fetish of images of suffering women. Still more strikingly 'literary' an interpolation in his journal is a graphic account of an ambush carried out by his Indian companions on an Eskimo encampment. At the heart of this episode is a voyeuristic description of the slaughter of a young girl:

> she fell down at my feet, and twisted round my legs, so that it was with difficulty that I could disengage myself from her dying grasps. As two Indian men pursued this unfortunate victim, I solicited very hard for her life; but the murderers made no reply till they had stuck both their spears through her body, and transfixed her to the ground. They then looked me sternly in the face, and began to ridicule me, by asking if I wanted an Esquimaux wife; and paid not the smallest regard to the shrieks and agony of the poor wretch, who was twining round their spears like an eel![11]

It is not just the emotive account of violence that requires comment here, but the fact that it is embedded in a representation of people who are regarded as backward and inferior with respect to Europeans. The violence is seen as the behaviour of cultural primitives, whose tribal brutality is expected to fascinate and appal the book's implied sentimental readers. The incorporation of such sensational, novelistic elements in a work of travel literature consolidates a process of 'othering' by restricting indigenous people to a repertoire of emotions and gestures typical of negative fictional character types, and reinforces a pact of civilised values between narrator and reader.

One of the remarkable features of travel within America was how rapidly land opened up by exploration became accessible to tourism. American tourists, in common with their British counterparts, had a taste for landscape appreciation and an interest in the literary or historical associations of place. These concerns were hardly relevant to explorers and early settlers, but as the frontier moved steadily westward, tourists, with their more aesthetic values, moved quickly to fill the spaces left behind. Writers and artists frequently led the way, then, assisted by the pace of transport innovations, the 'masses' followed, and a rapid process of commodification of sights and attractions ensued. Thus the Niagara Falls, though first visited in the seventeenth century, was still a pioneering destination in the 1790s, but the construction of the Erie Canal accelerated development and by the 1830s the area was attracting thousands of tourists a year. Similarly, the Ohio valley was first settled in the 1740s, and by the early nineteenth century European and American tourists were arriving *en masse* and the packaging of the very recent frontier past as tourist spectacle had already begun.

In general terms, tourists in America, either European travellers or members of educated elites on the eastern seaboard, did everything they could to mitigate the newness of the New World, and this entailed trying to assimilate the landscapes they set out to admire to the aesthetic categories familiar from the Old World. In certain areas, such as the Hudson Valley north of New York City, this was reasonably successful, but in many other areas the endeavour was doomed. The rules of picturesque beauty simply had no relevance to the prairies or the Badlands or the Rockies, and merely to categorise such vast landscapes as 'sublime' seemed a feebly mechanical response. What happened later was that the wilderness came to be regarded as a symbol of national identity, as something not to be visually contained and controlled but to be valued and preserved for what it intrinsically was – different and indifferent to civilised man.

The literature of American travel therefore comprises works of exploration arising from the progressive opening up of the continent to European settlers, and, hard on the heels of these, works of a more touristic nature dedicated to non-utilitarian perspectives on those parts of the country that had been 'discovered'. Somewhere between the textual domains of these two genres lies a third: the literature of emigration. This was every bit as important for British audiences; indeed, Stephen Fender, in his major study of the phenomenon, argues that 'Hardly a British book of travels in America published in the first half of the nineteenth century . . . failed to include the question of emigration among its observations on the new country'. As Fender shows, the case for North American settlement had been put from the late sixteenth century onwards for a variety of political, economic, and ideological reasons, but the official British line varied in the late eighteenth and early nineteenth centuries according to changing political and economic conditions in the mother country. Thus anxiety was raised at the inroads being made into the labour pool when emigration reached a quarter of a million between 1775 and 1783, but the combination of a rising population and economic rationalisation in the early decades of the next century produced renewed governmental encouragement for the exodus. Further complicating the situation were the legacy of British resentment at American Independence, the war against France, and the embarrassment of having a democratic republic prospering across the Atlantic at the same time as ideological (as well as military) war was being waged against its Continental successor: as Fender puts it, 'the United States remained an inconvenient disconfirmation of Tory jeremiads against jacobinism'.[12] For this reason, the British government increasingly coupled support for emigration to its colonies (Canada, Australia, New Zealand) with propaganda against 'defection' to the United States, and the rough data available suggest that to some extent it was successful in marshalling patriotic sentiment: of over half a million emigrants between 1815 and 1832, only two-fifths went to the United States.

But just as official British attitudes towards America were conditioned by a domestic agenda, so the discourse of emigration at sub-governmental levels was closely shaped by reflections on the state of the nation that emigrants would be forsaking. The deplorable situation of the disenfranchised labourer or tenant farmer forced to bear an inequitable burden of tithes and taxes and faced with an uncertain future is repeatedly put forward as an inducement to leave, and private letters from emigrants themselves regularly draw the same contrast between a corrupt Britain and a socially liberating America: 'You could not desire the New World without rehearsing your distaste for the Old.'[13] A typical emigration tract thus contains a narrative of the journey to be undertaken, a range of factual information about the new territory and the opportunities for settlers, and a collection of positive testimonies from those who have made the passage already.

One of the most influential such works was Morris Birkbeck's *Notes on a Journey in America* (1818). Birkbeck had a vested interest in the cause he was espousing, since he had recently bought 1,440 acres of land in Illinois which he intended to resell in lots, in order to build an 'English colony' called 'Prairie Albion'. Because of these pecuniary motives, his book became the target of numerous fierce attacks, including Henry Bradshaw's *Sketches of America* (1819), William Savage's *Observations on Emigration* (1819), and comments by William Cobbett (who later changed his mind) in his *Year's Residence in the United States of America* (1819). However, there is considerable overlap in terms of argument and rhetoric between Birkbeck's *Notes* and demonstrably non-propagandist handbooks such as John Noble's *Instructions to Emigrants* (1819), which carefully defines the character of the successful emigrant and promises the industrious that the fruits of their labour will not be taken from them to 'support arbitrary and oppressive measures, to supply the extravagance of a Court, and the rapacity of Sinecurists and Pensioners'.[14]

Noble quotes a number of the same settlers' letters in praise of emigration as Birkbeck does, and Fender observes that not only is there no evidence that such letters were fabricated, but that archives uncovered in modern times show marked similarities in language between the promotional tracts and the private letters of real emigrants. It is a style that mixes reassuringly precise inventories of the prices of goods or livestock bought and sold and a plain rhetoric of steadily growing prosperity, with occasional atavistic recurrences of Golden Age imagery. The lure of such imagery was so powerful, and the need to affirm the validity of their choices so strong, that even settlers experiencing the rigours of the new way of life could be drawn into constructing an American version of pastoral at the same time as they provided facts and figures to bring it down to earth. Such were the conflicting messages that British readers received about America in the Romantic period. The literatures of travel and emigration both waver between realism and romance; indeed, for Morris Birkbeck, the distinction between traveller and settler is an unreal one, because Americans are a 'migrating people', always ready to contemplate a change of situation even in prosperous circumstances – regarding travel, indeed, as no less than an 'exertion of their liberty'.[15]

Africa

In the Romantic period Africa was not the feared 'dark continent' or 'heart of darkness' that it was to become later in the nineteenth century, although the seeds of that development are visible. At the beginning of the period knowledge of Africa was limited almost entirely to the coast, and to a large degree the interest of works of travel and exploration to British readers lay in seeing parts of the interior opened up to Western eyes for the first time. In 1788, Sir Joseph Banks founded the Association for Promoting the Discovery of the Interior Parts of Africa (popularly known as the African Association), giving the new agenda institutional backing. However, over the years 1789–1830

Africa also featured in the mental map of British readers as the base of the Atlantic slave trade, in which Britain had been a major player since the mid-seventeenth century. The campaign to abolish this trade was one of a number of factors adversely affecting the commercial interest in west Africa in the late 1790s and early 1800s, and the first three decades of the nineteenth century were a period of fluctuating interest and confused policy on the part of the British government in regard to the continent – a situation not helped by a series of disastrous expedition failures. But although Africa's role in Britain's development from a protectionist colonial system to an expansive free-trade empire was put on hold until later in the century, the imperatives of economic growth meant that interest never disappeared completely, and there was a broader public interest that was largely independent of the debates around trade. A brief look at three popular travel books on different parts of Africa, published over a ten-year period, will show how the literature of exploration keys into this intricate and unstable context.

One of the most talked-about travel books of the period was James Bruce's monumental *Travels to Discover the Source of the Nile* (1790). In finding his way to the fountains of the Blue Nile in central Abyssinia (present-day Ethiopia), Bruce, in fact, mistook the object of his quest, although his tracking of this major tributary to its confluence with the White Nile was still a significant achievement. At the time of his visit Abyssinia had not suffered significantly from the attentions of Europeans, although by his own account it was in a state of political anarchy, with its nominal hereditary ruler hard-pushed to maintain supremacy against a bewildering number of provincial warlords. Bruce's dealings with these rulers and their hangers-on constitute a substantial part of his sprawling narrative.

In true romantic fashion, Bruce is completely the hero of his own narrative, not only in the manner he overcomes formidable accidents and hardships during his travels, but also in the improbably spectacular actions through which his reputation among his native hosts is enhanced: he shoots hawks out of the sky with consummate ease, and fires a tallow candle through three shields and a sturdy wooden table. While Bruce's deeds and deportment seem sure to raise his standing in the eyes of readers back home, his detailed ethno-logical portraits contain sufficient sensational or culturally alien material to confirm their belief that Abyssinia, albeit a bastion of primitive Christianity, harbours barbarous and immoral customs. One of the most notorious passages in the *Travels* – which cast doubt on Bruce's reliability, despite being true – describes a banquet at which the raw meat of a living animal is cut and consumed. His descriptions of semi-public couplings of men and women, of male and female circumcision, and of the varieties of capital punishment, would also have had sensationalist appeal. Although there are strands of considerable respect and admiration in Bruce's individual characterisations, usually where there are grounds for strong masculine self-identification, there is also a good deal of Orientalist stereotyping, the warlords being depicted as quick-tempered, resentful, cunning, and suspicious, the lower orders more frequently as cowardly and dissimulating.

In the dedication to his book Bruce speaks of the reign of George III as one in which exploration has distanced itself from a history of piracy and cruelty and become an enterprise uniting 'humanity and science'; its heroes, he says, are men inspired with the belief that all men, though unequal, are brethren, creating a need for Britons to set an example of benevolence and compassion to weaker and less enlightened peoples. Accordingly, the *Travels* present a narrator-hero who is a worthy representative of his society and culture – typically in contradistinction to the people he is journeying among. The climax of Bruce's travels is, of course, the 'discovery' of the springs of the Nile (which actually consists in Bruce being led to the spot by his native guide and having the source pointed out to him):

> Though a mere private Briton, I triumphed here, in my own mind, over kings and their armies; and every comparison was leading nearer and nearer to presumption, when the place itself where I stood, the object of my vain-glory, suggested what depressed my short-lived triumphs. I was but a few minutes arrived at the sources of the Nile, through numberless dangers and sufferings, the least of which would have overwhelmed me but for the continual goodness and protection of Providence; I was, however, but then half through my journey, and all those dangers which I had already passed, awaited me again on my return. I found a despondency gaining ground fast upon me, and blasting the crown of laurels I had too rashly woven for myself.[16]

Joy and pride in success are swiftly replaced by despondency, for which the proffered explanation seems inadequate. It seems more likely that Bruce's disappointment springs from having an inspiringly ideal object offered to his gaze as a paltry 'hillock of green sod' (III, 596). Nevertheless, he drinks from the spring and toasts George III, and the serenity of the night later quells the 'torrent' of his grief. He comforts himself with the thought of divine super-intendence, and of his accomplishment of a goal entailing both personal and national rivalries: 'a trophy in which I could have no competitor, for the honour of my country, at the feet of my sovereign, whose servant I was' (III, 641). The message is that God has secured this triumph for Britain through the agency of James Bruce: a seemingly innocent conquest – a mental rather than military victory, as Bruce makes explicit in his celebratory remarks – but one which all the same subordinates this stronghold of African independence to a form of Western domination.

Equal in popularity to Bruce's *Travels* was Mungo Park's *Travels in the Interior of Africa* (1799). Park's expedition was of a different order. For a start, it was directed to west Africa, where Britain's commercial interests and activities principally lay. Added to that, it was funded by the African Association, and played a key role in the development of government-sponsored exploration which increasingly had ulterior economic motives: Park's statement of his ambition of 'rendering the geography of Africa more familiar to my countrymen, and . . . opening to their ambition and industry new sources of wealth, and new channels of commerce'[17] clearly indicates the symbiotic link between scientific travel and commercial development. Indeed, in the year Park's book appeared, Banks put forward a proposal for 'annexation of the whole coast from Arguin to Sierra Leone, seizure of the Senegal Valley, and formation of a chartered company to carry the march of empire into the interior'.[18] Only the continuing war against France prevented implementation of this plan.

Different as Park's expedition was in conception and context, his written narrative exhibits many of the same characteristics as Bruce's. There is a similar emphasis on the author's physical hardships and suffering, and a similarly strong line in native 'curiosities'. Park is capable of maintaining ethnographical neutrality, though this is occasionally modified by Rousseauesque observations on Africans as 'children of nature', and invariably abandoned when dealing with the Moors, 'those merciless fanatics' (pp. 82, 212). Park matches Bruce in being completely the central interest of his own narrative, his purgatorial journey and eventual deliverance absorbing more imaginative energy than his celebrated 'discovery' of the true course of the Niger. However, whereas Bruce is typically portrayed as a man of action, Park is a man of feeling to whom things unrelentingly happen, whose heart bleeds for others but who pleads for sympathy himself via a narcissistic, self-regarding style of narration. His vulnerability is dramatically rendered on the occasion when Park is taken prisoner by Moors and treated as something of a circus freak by native women, who 'counted my toes and fingers, as if they doubted whether I was in truth a human being' (p. 122). Yet even reduced to the most pitiful state of physical and mental dereliction, Park still has an ace up his sleeve: Providence. He is rescued for the first time, when faint from thirst, by the coming of rain in the desert, and by the generosity of a poor villager: he gives thanks to 'that gracious and bountiful Being' who has 'spread for me a table in the Wilderness' (p. 181). Later in his long walk back to the safety of the coastal trading post he is robbed, and stripped naked, and brought close to despair. The agency of his restoration on this occasion is again natural – he catches sight of a beautiful small moss:

> Can that being (thought I) who planted, watered, and brought to perfection, in this obscure part of the world, a thing which appears of so small importance, look with unconcern upon the situation and sufferings of creatures formed after his own image? – surely not! (p. 244)

The dramatic irony here is that, while Park reads his comforting theological lesson from the apparently wasteful benignity of God's creation, he seems to have forgotten the plight of the many black slaves he has seen, with whom he has acknowledged the bond of a common human nature, but whose 'situation and sufferings' seem of no concern to the Creator. His failure to make the connection betrays his assumption that as a representative of Western Christendom he is entitled to special privileges. God, in fact, would seem to have taken a personal interest in every aspect of Park's mission, and in the larger British imperialist project of which it is a part: in the famous earlier 'discovery' scene, in which Park catches sight of the Niger flowing – this was what he had set out to confirm – eastwards, he prays in gratitude to the 'Great Ruler' for having 'crowned my endeavours with success' (p. 195), thus putting a divine seal of approval on the huge project of the European production of (commercially exploitable) knowledge about Africa.

The third book of African travels I want to examine is by John Barrow, who acted as private secretary to Lord Macartney on a trip to South Africa in 1797–8. At the time of his visit the Cape Colony had only recently come into British hands, having been taken from the Dutch by force in 1795. The Dutch had had a presence on the Cape since 1652, and interior colonisation had progressively expanded against resistance from the native Khoikhoi (the so-called 'Hottentots'), who by the end of the eighteenth century were thinned in numbers and largely reduced to the status of indentured labourers. Macartney despatched Barrow into the interior to resolve border conflicts between the colonists (Afrikaners) and the Nguni (or 'Kaffirs') to the east, to provide a display of British authority, and to complete the charting of the colony through its remoter areas.

Compared to Bruce's action-hero posturing and Park's sentimental excesses, Barrow's narrative is generally flat, objective, and professionally detached. It is not entirely purged of the travel writer's fascination with the marvellous or extraordinary, but mostly his style exhibits the severe decorum one would associate with someone in an official diplomatic position. A deeper analysis suggests that this style represents a subtle form of taking control through discourse that complements Barrow's more explicit views on the politics of conquest and colonial administration. This is best seen in the way his account assumes dominance over the region's inhabitants, Afrikaners included but more especially indigenous Africans. His ethnographical portraits of the Khoikhoi, the Nguni, and the San (in Barrow's terminology, 'Bosjesmans' or Bushmen) are wide-ranging, detailed, and, by the standards of his time, liberal-minded. They are, however, predictably Anglocentric in their treatment of alternative ways of life, and the negative attributes assigned to the different peoples sharply reduce them with respect to the implied civilised norm of Barrow's readers: thus the Khoikhoi are incapable of thinking temporally, and their language lacks the evolutionary sophistication of an alphabetic sound system; the Nguni are not bothered by notions of love in relations between the sexes, nor have they 'bewildered their imaginations' with metaphysical ideas; while the San, a nomadic people living on the northern frontier in continual conflict with both the Khoikhoi and Dutch settlers, are represented uncomplicatedly as 'savage'.

More than the other indigenous peoples, the San are made the object of a quite prurient bodily voyeurism, focused on their genitalia. While the men are described as having had their testicles pushed up into 'the upper part of the root of the penis',[19] the women are said to have the even more remarkable feature of elongated 'nymphae' or inner labia:

> Their color is that of livid blue, inclining to a reddish tint, not unlike the excrescence on the beak of a turkey, which indeed may serve to convey a tolerable good idea of the whole appearance both as to color, shape, and size. (I, 279)

The purpose of this feature, Barrow speculates, must be to protect against rape, since it makes non-consensual sex impossible. Taking this together with other traits, such as 'extended posteriors' (I, 281), Barrow, unencumbered by modern notions of the cultural relativity of beauty, concludes that 'Nature seems to have studied how to make this pigmy race disgusting' (I, 279).

The ethnographic material in the *Travels* is largely set aside from the main narrative in separate chapters. It is heavily idealised, subsuming individuals within a collective third-person pronoun, as though to speak of one group member is necessarily to speak of them all; and it is characteristically written in a kind of timeless present, denying the possibility of any kind of historical development. The different indigenous peoples are thus more readily incorporated into the coloniser's system of knowledge: incapable of producing meaning for themselves, they have it imposed on them. In essence they are assimilated to the imperturbable stability of the landscape, the slow mutations of which fire Barrow's geological imagination on his final journey around the western Cape.

In the African travel literature I have discussed, there are striking similarities in the way each author diligently services what he takes to be his audience's intense fascination with the exotic, the extraordinary, and the domestic taboo-breaking aspects of foreign cultures. It is tempting to fashion a term like 'ethnopornography' to cover this ethically dubious fixation on whatever is most likely to repel, titillate, or horrify the reader. Also in common is the three texts' projection of the author or narrator as an exemplar of national character and national destiny. Whether the context is Abyssinia (a region remote from British influence), or west Africa (where Britain's major trading interests lay), or the Cape (where it had recently secured a hold), the home audience is rarely led to question the country's fitness for the purpose of bringing this continent, if not under its rule, then at least under the rule of knowledge. Even in dire extremity, the 'unaccommodated' white British male is shown as indomitable, emissary of the highest state civilisation has reached.

The South Seas

Because of continuous maritime exploration by the Dutch, French, and English from the seventeenth century onwards, at the start of the period the South Seas were in some respects better known than some regions much closer to home. As in other parts of the world, it was simply assumed that these territories were available for European exploitation. On his first voyage in 1768–71, for example, James Cook had carried secret instructions from the Admiralty relating to the possible discovery of a southern continent: these advise him to establish friendly trading relations with the natives, but also, with their 'Consent', to 'take possession of Convenient Situations in the Country in the Name of the King of Great Britain'.[20]

There is a sharp divide in Romantic representations of the South Seas between accounts of Tahiti, on the one hand, and those of Australia and New Zealand, on the other. As Bernard Smith has convincingly argued, these differences relate to contradictory Enlightenment views of nature:

On the one hand it was claimed that all our misfortunes are due to our departure from nature's laws, while on the other it was claimed that man could only raise himself above the brute creation by improving upon nature. . . . Whereas the discovery of the Society Islands [including Tahiti] ministered . . . to the first attitude, the discovery of Australia (and New Zealand) ministered rather to the second.[21]

A related distinction, also sketched by Smith, is between 'soft primitivism' and 'hard primitivism', of which the Society Islanders, on the one hand, and the Maoris and Australian Aborigines, on the other, were used as evidence. Both forms of primitivism share a belief in the natural virtues of a pre-civilised state, but differ sharply in the aspects of character and way of life that they emphasise. Soft primitivism found in Tahiti a version of earthly paradise, where nature was kind and bountiful, while hard primitivism found in Australia an environment that newcomers adapted to their needs only through hard work and determination.

Cook was not the first European to visit Tahiti, nor was he the originator of the myth of an island paradise, but he shows a definite weakness for the idea of noble savagery – the idea that man in his natural state was spontaneously happy and virtuous, living an easy and uncomplicated life, superior to his civilised counterpart burdened with the knowledge of good and evil. In his journal of his first voyage, he catalogues a variety of fruits and vegetables produced almost without labour, and says that the indigenous people seem 'exempt from the curse of our fore fathers; scarcely can it be said that they earn their bread with the sweet of their brow' (I, 121). Even more sensationally, Cook describes sexual practices among the islanders that seem paradisal in their complete freedom from shame. One 'scene' in particular, in which a young man has sex with a girl no more than twelve years old in full view of both natives and visitors, was to be cited countless times, whether approvingly or satirically, in subsequent literature. It encouraged speculation on the arbitrary and conventional character of sexual mores, suggesting a natural morality that was attractive to some but was at odds with Christian teaching, and fuelled the resolve of evangelicals in Britain to intervene in Tahiti for the purpose of saving native souls. This resolve took effect in 1796 with the departure of a ship financed by the recently-formed London Missionary Society. The expedition was a disaster: no conversions were made, whereas many defections from the missionary party to the side of the natives took place.

Tahiti was at the heart of another South Seas drama that enthralled Romantic readers – the mutiny on the *Bounty*. The mission of Captain Bligh's ship, which set sail in December 1787, was one characteristic of colonial travel: instead of merely enjoying paradise, Bligh was to appropriate its resources – namely, its breadfruit, which Banks had persuaded the government could be used to feed slaves on West Indian plantations at greatly reduced cost. The mutiny, led by Fletcher Christian, that scuppered his expedition, was later attributed by Bligh to the 'allurements of dissipation' on Tahiti. Some of the mutineers were caught and repatriated, but Christian and a breakaway community of sailors escaped. They left Tahiti in 1789 along with six native men and a rather larger number of native women, whom they effectively kidnapped, and established a community on Pitcairn Island that remained undiscovered until 1808. In what seems a fittingly ironic dénouement, a series of mutinies by the islanders culminated in a massacre in which Christian was among the Britons killed. When the island retreat was eventually found, the sole remaining Briton had undergone a conversion and had begun instructing the children in Christianity. The whole story proved of immense interest to the British public. In John Barrow's opinion (as summarised by Neil Rennie), it was 'a story of paradise lost by "the disobedience of our first parents", an act of disobedience symbolically repeated by the mutiny, followed by paradise regained on Pitcairn'.[22] In a typical piece of doublethink, this appraisal is sufficiently romantic to see the Europeans as violators of paradise, but sufficiently imperialist to affirm the value of the alien religion that had, by that time, been imposed on Tahiti.

As already stated, representations of Australia in travel narratives pursued a different track from those of Tahiti. The 1790s witnessed a stream of publications centring on New South Wales following the establishment of the Port Jackson settlement in 1788 as a penal colony to remedy the loss of the American colonies as a dumping-ground for transported criminals. Cook's first voyage had already established many of the perpectives from which the country would be viewed: the perception, for example, that it was not a bountiful Eden like the Society Islands but would richly repay labour if European crops and livestock were introduced. His observations of the indigenous people were recorded with a degree of objectivity that later visitors rarely matched. Despite the hostile reception accorded to his first arrival at Botany Bay, Cook's final judgement is that the Aborigines are 'a timorous and inoffensive race, no ways inclinable to cruelty' (I, 396), and he admires their hunting skills. His perceptions of the natural environment and of the Aborigines' efficient adaptation to it produce a leaning towards the 'hard primitivism' characterised above, which comes to the fore in a rare passage of philosophical reflection:

> From what I have said of the Natives of New-Holland they may appear to some to be the most wretched people upon Earth, but in reality they are far more happier than we Europeans; being wholy unacquainted not only with the superfluous but the necessary Conveniencies so much sought after in Europe, they are happy in not knowing the use of them. They live in a Tranquility which is not disturb'd by the Inequality of Condition. (I, 399)

Cook's responses can be compared with those expressed in one of the more colourful and popular of the Botany Bay narratives of the 1790s, the *Voyage to New South Wales* (1793) nominally authored by George Barrington. Barrington was a notorious pickpocket transported to the penal colony for a term of seven years, but rewarded for his good behaviour by a series of official positions culminating in the role of superintendent of convicts. His narrative, widely assumed at the time to be authentic, is now known to be a masterly 'publishing forgery', produced by 'a team of players, clever and devious editors and illustrators who skilfully cut, précised, pasted and copied' from a variety of less accessible sources.[23] Treading a fine line between fiction and reality, it tells us as much about what readers were prepared or wanted to believe about the new colony as about the actual conditions down under. (In what follows, 'George Barrington' is merely a term of convenience.)

Barrington provides a vivid account of the horrors of the voyage and of the life of the colony from the prisoners' perspective. Aside from the long days labouring at brick- and tile-making, house-building and road-making, it is an eventful life of mutinies, escape attempts, and robberies, with additional conflict arising from uneasy relations between settlers and natives – usually as a result of unprovoked aggression on the part of settlers. Barrington's concluding observation that 'our early years of toil, famine, and difficulty, were now exchanged for an era of plenty, ease, and pleasure'[24] reflects the hard primitivist attitude displayed by Cook.

One feature of Barrington's account that was of great interest to contemporary readers was its detailed account of Aboriginal life and the interaction between colonists and natives. He describes vividly the colonists' dealings with one particular native, known as Banalong, who was effectively kidnapped by the Governor in an attempt to train up interpreters and was later transported to England and presented to George III. Barrington describes Banalong as a keen mimic of English manners and customs – rapidly learning, for example, how to behave at the dinner table that he shares with the Governor's family. However, when allowed complete liberty again after a year's semi-captivity, Banalong disappears. Contact is eventually re-established and trust built up again, but tension flares up from time to time. When he returns from his English sojourn, Banalong is apparently much changed, treating his family and acquaintances with a new hauteur:

> He was much offended at some little indelicacies which he observed in his sister, who came in such haste to see him, with his little nephew at her back, that she left all her paraphernalia behind her, and literally appeared in her birthday suit. (p. 112)

But it soon becomes plain that Banalong is no less attached to his 'birthday suit': he gets tired of artificial restrictions at the Governor's house, and returns to his native settlement for long periods – 'always taking care to leave his clothes behind him, and to resume them when he reappeared before the Governor' (p. 113). This was a kind of adroit and unselfconscious cultural switching that perplexed and troubled actual and armchair travellers of the time in their encounters with 'primitive' peoples. It raised problems for a Western audience accustomed to thinking of cultural progress as a one-way escalator moving from a primitive to a civilised state: for savages to easily reframe themselves within different cultural contexts put the whole notion of improvement and European superiority in doubt. 'George Barrington' was not the writer to theorise its significance, but Banalong's 'fancy-dress' approach to Western clothes and culture was one item in an accumulating series of observations and impressions that worked to destabilise Western assumptions about the nature and development of civilisation.

Disturbing and controversial as its implications might be, the overall trend towards a scientific understanding of Australia and other territories in the

South Seas was irresistible, and indeed Pacific exploration was in the long run of considerable importance in the history of European thought. For example, the many samples of Australia's flora and fauna brought back to Britain exposed the inadequacies of current systems of biological classification and helped to discredit the traditional concept of the Great Chain of Being (which rested on the immutability of individual species). Long before the voyages of the *Beagle*, Charles Darwin's grandfather Erasmus drew on evidence from Australasia, including John Hunter's *Journal of the Transactions at Port Jackson and Norfolk Island* (1793), to produce the first fully developed theory of organic evolution.[25] In the longer history of European encounter with the South Pacific, therefore, science emerged a clear victor over myth, but one reason why Romantic writing on the region is so interesting is that the confrontation between science and myth is at its most temperamental and ambiguous.

The East

Asia, or more imprecisely 'the East', exerted a strong pull on the imaginations of readers and writers in the period. This owed something to the long-standing fascination with a generalised, idealised Orient conflating everywhere east of Suez in a series of stereotypical oppositions to Western order and rationality. More important was the serious scholarly production of knowledge about Asian countries and cultures for which the late eighteenth and early nineteenth centuries were remarkable, and which Raymond Schwab has memorably dubbed the 'Oriental Renaissance'. Britain's commercial relations with Asia, and, increasingly, its political involvement in the region, developed rapidly and controversially. British consumers, long familiar with fine Indian textiles and Indonesian spices, grew dependent on Chinese tea, while the fashion for *chinoiserie* in architecture and furniture reached new heights under George III. However, actual Asian visitors, as opposed to their products, were few and far between, and opportunities for cultural interaction were limited. In this context, the literature of travel and exploration again served as window on the world and played a key role in shaping and reinforcing attitudes and perceptions in regard to these vast and remote territories. I shall focus in this section on India, because of its importance to subsequent British colonial history, while glancing too at representations of China.

In his pioneering study, *Orientalism*, Edward Said defines a general sense of his keyword as a way of thinking predicated on a sharp and simplified distinction between East and West – sensuality, splendour, and barbarism being among the conventional attributes of the former. In a narrower historical sense, Orientalism arises in the late eighteenth century as 'the corporate institution for dealing with the Orient – dealing with it by making statements about it, authorizing views of it, describing it, by teaching it, settling it, ruling over it: in short, Orientalism as a Western style for dominating, restructuring, and having authority over the Orient'.[26] As this highly compressed sentence makes plain, Said perceives a straight and smooth path from having ideas about the East to exercising political power over it. The Oriental Renaissance documented by Schwab covered a broad field of linguistic and anthropological research undertaken by British, French, and German scholars, facilitated in particular by the rediscovery and translation of Sanskrit texts, which led to the realisation that biblical or classical antiquity was not the most ancient past that could be known – that the languages and culture of Europe were not foundational but had more distant Asiatic origins. For Schwab, this revelation that the world could no longer be divided between a Mediterranean 'center of civilization' and a 'vast and contemptible unknown' was primarily 'one of the great events of the mind'.[27] For Said, the production of knowledge about the Orient could never be merely that: it would have to have been tied intimately to the growth of colonial power. Said views travel literature as just another armament in the arsenal of the Western will to power, all the more useful in that it appears so 'natural': such literature encourages what he calls a 'textual attitude' to the foreign and unfamiliar, in which books can '*create* not only knowledge but also the very reality they appear to describe'.[28] Many of Said's critics have objected to the relegation of literature (of all kinds) to such a passive ideological function, and condemned furthermore what they see as the insidious generalising of all colonial discourse into 'a monolithically powerful and unchallengeable system of domination'.[29]

While it is defensible to claim that travel writing of the period, along with other literary forms, was more complex in its representational practices and more varied in its political expression than Said allows, the relentless expansion of British power and influence in Asia means that his thesis needs taking seriously. In China, diplomatic efforts were made to loosen the restrictions hampering the operations of the East India Company, which at the start of the period still enjoyed a national monopoly of all Asian trade. An embassy led by Lord Macartney in 1793, the first to this highly protective state, was unsuccessful, although detailed first-hand accounts of the expedition by Sir George Staunton and John Barrow brought the reading public face to face with 'the calm dignity and sober pomp of Asiatic grandeur, which European refinements have not yet attained'.[30] Eventually Chinese protectionism was breached forcibly by the Anglo-Chinese war of 1839–41: instigated by the Chinese government's attempt to crack down on the unofficial and illegal traffic in opium which had come to dominate the Company's trade with China, the war resulted also in Britain's acquisition of Hong Kong.

Relations with India were altered even more profoundly in the period. The East India Company took advantage of the dissolution of the Mughal Empire and the emergence of violent inter-regional conflict to complete its transformation from a chartered trading company to a full-blown governing body backed by its own armies in Bengal, Madras, and Bombay. As Anthony Farrington describes it, the Company's personnel evolved 'from merchants into administrators, judges, revenue collectors and soldiers', in a process that ensured that 'the whole economic structure of the sub-continent came to serve the needs of the new rulers'. In doing so, they also 'eagerly adopted the manners and lifestyles of their Mughal predecessors',[31] and this was a cause of increasing concern to the British government back home. An Act of 1784 placed the political and military affairs of the Company under closer Parliamentary supervision, while the long-drawn-out impeachment of governor-general Warren Hastings on charges of mismanagement and corruption ended in acquittal in 1795. The Company's trading monopoly in India was finally ended in 1813, though its administrative functions were revalidated.

Deepening political responsibilities in India demanded a greater knowledge of the languages and cultural traditions of its indigenous peoples, and this was where the work of Orientalists, the most prestigious of whom were gathered in the Asiatic Society of Bengal, was of more than academic importance. Sir William Jones, the founder of the Asiatic Society (and who worked as a judge in the Bengal Supreme Court), is best known for his series of hymns to Hindu deities, cross-cultural fusions of Indian and European sources,[32] and for his research into the similarities between Sanskrit, Greek, and Latin that grounded his thesis of an Indo-European family of languages and laid the foundations of modern historical and comparative linguistics. However, in the context of his working life in India from 1783 onwards, he was just as notable for his project of establishing a digest of Muslim and Hindu laws to assist the administration of justice in territories controlled by the East India Company. Reflecting his belief that native people should be tried as far as possible according to their own custom and practice, this project, as Javed Majeed argues, typified a concern to legitimise British rule 'in an Indian idiom'.[33] Although it could be seen, perhaps anachronistically, as an attempt to educate the British public in a kind of 'multicultural' broadmindedness, Jones's work was accused by his contemporary James Mill of inventing an India 'that was a land of happy children, by contrast with Europe as the continent of sad grown-ups, yet another reason for Westerners to take Indians over for their own good'.[34] However, Mill, whose *History of British India* (1817) was a monumental attempt to apply the new secular philosophy of utilitarianism to the Indian context, himself supported the 'vernacularist' position against those who favoured (and successfully advocated) the promotion of English in public life.

The travel literature that furnished most Britons with their main ideas of India was of several distinct kinds. Perhaps the most important variety in the early part of the period consisted of books that catered for the taste in exotic scenery, manners, and costume. Nigel Leask has provided an excellent account of such literature, stressing its pretensions to a disinterested contemplation of the landscape, its antiquarian curiosity, and its associative habit that constantly fills the present scene with visual memories of home.[35] An influential early work was William Hodges's *Travels in India* (1793), which is anything but uniform in texture. It has a strong narrative thread detailing the author's tour of Bengal and northern India in the company of Warren Hastings, during which he witnesses scenes of conflict in the Company's war against the Marathas. Interspersed with these episodes are passages more representative of the kind of tranquillised appreciation of scenic effects associated with the emergent vogue of the picturesque: in a classic twilight moment, for example, Hodges is arrested by the sight of Muslim women carrying lamps to the tombs of their dead relations, and finds this both beautiful and sentimentally pleasing.[36] In Thomas and William Daniell's sumptuous series of annotated landscape views, *A Picturesque Voyage to India* (1810), aesthetic motives are paramount. 'View with Cocoa Nut and Betel Trees', for instance, has all the classic ingredients of a Claude landscape, with cocoa and areca trees refreshing the menu as framing devices; however, the Daniells' commentary draws an implicit distinction between the 'simple natives', for whom nature – in the shape of the cocoa tree – provides food and drink and is 'a constant benefactor', and the Western visitor who admires the 'soft romantic beauty' of a coastal scene readily filtered through fashionable artistic conventions. A more intriguing case is 'Near Gangwaucolly, on the Hoogly', which presents a curious disjunction of picture and commentary:

> This view is bounded by impenetrable forests; trees of gigantic growth rise among the underwood which overhangs the banks of the Hoogly, and forms a safe covert for the most fierce and formidable animals. . . . To an European it is difficult to conceive that such an Eden should be tenanted by creatures so destructive. . . . The banian puts forth shoots, which having reached a certain length, strike into the ground, and produce a rapid succession of younger trees, destined in their turn to become the parent stocks of a numerous progeny. The banian is a symbol of pastoral peace and patriarchal longevity. . . .

In fact, there are no animals, destructive or otherwise, visible in the picture, nor any recognisable banyan trees. The romantic quality of the description is perhaps explained in the remarkable introduction to the volume: here the Daniells suggest that the 'oriental scenery' they are transporting to Europe is interesting to the 'philosophic eye' because it contains so many ruins of India's ancient civilisation:

> Happily for curiosity, these vestiges are often elucidated by the manners of the present inhabitants, who with unexampled fidelity have preserved their primitive customs unimpaired by time or conquest; and in their domestic institutions still present the image of a remote and almost obsolete antiquity.

The allusion to 'conquest' hints that the qualification present in 'almost obsolete' may soon be redundant: that is, there is a sense in which the primitiveness of what is recorded serves as a justification for modernising British intervention, which the exquisite charm of oriental pastoral nostalgically conceals. The introduction speaks of the eighteenth century as a period in which 'the passion for discovery, originally kindled by the thirst for gold', became linked to higher aims of science and philanthropy, and the Daniells align their artistic endeavours with these 'guiltless spoliations'.[37] Without a gesture to the colonial violence that Hodges was forced to witness, they give their readers a conscience-free stake in their country's faraway eastern possessions: as Nigel Leask puts it, the Indian picturesque 'commodifies British India for a metropolitan public, but without partaking in the "guilty" private interest of the nabobs of Hastings's generation'.[38]

The picturesque 'conquest' of India was pursued with equal enthusiasm by women writers, who came in increasing numbers in the early nineteenth century as the wives or daughters of Company employees or military men. These women were empowered by removal from their home environment to take on the full range of topics normally reserved for male travel writers, and to offer social and moral reflections on what they saw. Maria Graham's *Journal of a Residence in India* (1812), for example, contains a critical perspective on Anglo-Indian community life, seen as monotonous and country-townish; picturesque accounts of visits to the cave temples of western India, coupled with confident Orientalist digressions on the Hindu, Jain, and Buddhist religions; and some faltering steps towards 'scientifically' neutral ethnographical description. While avoiding sensational topics like suttee (widow-burning), which William Hodges witnessed with voyeuristic disgust, Graham does not hesitate to complain about the moral weaknesses of Indians, whom she sees as having once been simply virtuous but now as 'cunning, and incapable of truth'; and she qualifies her admiration (at Elephanta) for 'the works of a people far advanced in the arts of civilized life' with contempt for the 'crafty priesthood, who kept science, affluence, and honour for their own fraternity, and ... preached a miserable and degrading superstition to the multitude'.[39] Her implied reader would feel respect for the rich sophistication of Indian antiquity, but would be reassured of the need for the rational reform and Christian re-education that Britain was well placed to supply. Later Romantic Indian travel narratives, such as that of Reginald Heber (1828), the liberal second bishop of Calcutta, are more explicit in their endorsement of this self-applaudingly 'civilising' role. Heber, commenting on the Free Schools established for native children, says there is 'not even a semblance of opposition to the efforts which we are now making to enlighten the Hindoos', and on his tour of western India observes plentiful evidence of 'zeal and liberality ... in the improvement of the country, the construction of roads and public buildings, the conciliation of the natives and their education'. Although critical of the arrogant exclusivity of Anglo-Indian society, and forward-thinking on issues of skin colour and toleration of local customs and religion, Heber voices concern about the growing half-caste population – 'a great source of present mischief and future danger to the tranquillity of the Colony' – and is in many ways an uncomplicated apologist for British rule.[40]

It should not go unnoted that there were literary occasions in the period on which the 'imperial gaze' of British travellers was returned. Din Muhammad, a subaltern officer in the Company's Bengal army, who later emigrated to Ireland and married a Protestant Anglo-Irish woman, then moved to London where he worked in alternative medicine and started a coffeehouse, and finally set up as a therapeutic masseur in Brighton, published an account of his travels which was the first book written by an Indian in English. His life story suggests a relative openness in British society at this time, as yet untainted by the more extreme forms of racial bigotry characteristic of Victorian times. Just as importantly, as Michael Fisher argues in his excellent edition of the *Travels*, Din Muhammad's book is a vital instance of an Asian claiming the right to narrate his own experiences to the dominant culture – 'drawing upon an English form to represent his Indian background for an elite anglophone audience'.[41] As such, his account is subtly challenging throughout to Western conceptions of India: no British traveller, for example, could have contrived such a detailed and neutral description of the Muslim ceremonies of circumcision or (arranged) marriage as Din Muhammad provides.

While living in Ireland, Din Muhammad encountered another Indian traveller, Mirza Abu Taleb Khan, who later wrote a Persian-language account of his travels that was rapidly translated into English.[42] This book, which covers a stay of two and a half years in England between 1800 and 1802, is much more critical of the host culture than Din Muhammad's: there is praise for the British constitution and for British manufactures, but also a lengthy disquisition on the defects of the English character. One of its most interesting features is an appendix called 'Vindication of the Liberties of the Asiatic Women', which bullishly defends the greater social and cultural advantages of Indian women vis-à-vis their European counterparts. It is another useful reminder that the ethnocentric assurance that increasingly marked British perspectives on Asia in the period did not go entirely unqualified or uncontested.

Notes

1. C.F. Volney, *The Ruins, or a Survey of the Revolutions of Empires* (London, 1795), p. 7.

2. *Monthly Review*, 51 (1806), 419.

3. *Monthly Review*, 48 (1805), 185–6.

4. J. Hucks, *A Pedestrian Tour through North Wales* (London, 1795), pp. 59, 61.

5. *Journals of Dorothy Wordsworth*, ed. E. de Selincourt, 2 vols (London, 1952), I, 224, 252, 373.

6. Elizabeth A. Bohls, *Women Travel Writers and the Language of Aesthetics, 1716–1818* (Cambridge, 1995), p. 195.

7. Chloe Chard, *Pleasure and Guilt on the Grand Tour: Travel Writing and Imaginative Geography 1600–1830* (Manchester and New York, 1999), pp. 14–15.

8. See Timothy Webb, '"City of the Soul": English Romantic Travellers in Rome', in *Imagining Rome: British Artists and Rome in the Nineteenth Century*, ed. Michael Liversidge and Catharine Edwards (London, 1996), pp. 20–37.

9. *European Encounters with the New World: From Renaissance to Romanticism* (New Haven and London, 1993), p. 113.

10. *Travels through North and South Carolina, Georgia, East and West Florida* (New York, 1988), p. 30.

11. *A Journey from Prince of Wales's Fort, in Hudson's Bay, to the Northern Ocean* (London, 1795), pp. 153–4.

12. *Sea Changes: British Emigration and American Literature* (Cambridge and New York, 1992), pp. 38, 37.

13. Fender, *Sea Changes*, p. 45.

14. *Noble's Instructions to Emigrants* (Boston, 1819), p. 3.

15. *Notes on a Journey in America, from the Coast of Virginia to the Territory of Illinois* (Philadelphia, 1817), pp. 38–9.

16. *Travels to Discover the Source of the Nile, in the Years 1768, 1769, 1770, 1771, 1772, and 1773*, 5 vols (Edinburgh, 1790), III, 597–8.

17. *Travels in the Interior of Africa*, 3rd edn (London, 1799), p. 2.

18. Philip D. Curtin, *The Image of Africa: British Ideas and Action, 1780–1850* (London, 1965), p. 148.

19. *An Account of Travels into the Interior of Southern Africa, in the Years 1797 and 1798*, 2 vols (London, 1801), I, 278.

20. *The Journals of Captain James Cook on his Voyages of Discovery*, ed. J.C. Beaglehole, 4 vols (Cambridge, 1955–67), I (1955), cclxxxiii.

21. Bernard Smith, *European Vision and the South Pacific*, 2nd edn (New Haven and London, 1985), p. 177.

22. Neil Rennie, *Far-Fetched Facts: The Literature of Travel and the Idea of the South Seas* (Oxford, 1995), p. 177.

23. 'Introduction', in *George Barrington's Voyage to Botany Bay*, ed. Suzanne Rickard (London and New York, 2001), pp. 5, 55.

24. *A Voyage to New South Wales* (London, 1793; repr. Sydney, 1985), p. 116.

25. See Smith, *European Vision*, pp. 168–9.

26. *Orientalism* (London, 1978), p. 3.

27. *The Oriental Renaissance: Europe's Rediscovery of India and the East, 1680–1880*, trans. Gene Patterson-Black and Victor Reinking (New York, 1984), pp. 17, 13.

28. *Orientalism*, p. 94.

29. Bart Moore-Gilbert, 'Introduction: Writing India, Reorienting Colonial Discourse Analysis', in *Writing India 1757–1990: The Literature of British India*, ed. Moore-Gilbert (Manchester and New York, 1996), p. 6.

30. Sir George Staunton, *An Authentic Account of an Embassy from the King of Great Britain to the Emperor of China*, 2 vols (London, 1797), II, 237.

31. *Trading Places: The East India Company and Asia 1600–1834* (London, 2002), pp. 100–1.

32. See John Drew, *India and the Romantic Imagination* (Delhi, 1998), pp. 70–7.

33. *Ungoverned Imaginings: James Mill's 'The History of British India' and Orientalism* (Oxford, 1992), p. 22.

34. Marilyn Butler, 'Orientalism', in *The Penguin History of Literature, Vol. 5: The Romantic Period*, ed. David B. Pirie (Harmondsworth, 1994), pp. 395–447 (p. 406).

35. *Curiosity and the Aesthetics of Travel Writing, 1770–1840* (Oxford, 2002), pp. 166–78.

36. *Travels in India, during the Years 1780, 1781, 1782, and 1783* (London, 1793), p. 33.

37. *A Picturesque Voyage to India; by the Way of China* (London, 1810), pp. i–ii. The remainder of the volume, from which the above quotations from plate descriptions are taken, is unpaginated.

38. *Curiosity*, p. 170.

39. *Journal of a Residence in India* (London, 1812), pp. 27, 58.

40. *Narrative of a Journey through the Upper Provinces of India, from Calcutta to Bombay, 1824–1825*, 2nd edn, 3 vols (London, 1828), I, 56; III, 91; I, 42.

41. *The Travels of Dean Mahomet: An Eighteenth-Century Journey through India*, ed. Michael H. Fisher (Berkeley, 1997), p. xx.

42. Mirza Abu Taleb Khan, *Travels of Mirza Abu Taleb Khan in Asia, Africa, and Europe, during the Years 1799, 1800, 1801, 1802, and 1803*, trans. Charles Stewart, 2 vols (London, 1814).

Chapter Three

The Literary Marketplace

The period 1789–1830 was one in which the activities and relations of publishers, authors, and readers underwent significant and lasting change – change associated, in broad terms, with the larger economic process of industrialisation, and which continued through the nineteenth century and into the twentieth. In this chapter I shall give some account of this local revolution from the viewpoint of each of the three major players in the production, reproduction, and reception of books and periodicals. The rapid evolution of the periodical press in the period is of sufficient importance to deserve separate consideration.

Publishers and publishing

All the available evidence indicates that the eighteenth century saw a steadily rising output of printed material of all kinds, but with a particularly vigorous upturn in the 1780s. Figures compiled by James Raven using the digital resources of the *Eighteenth-Century Short Title Catalogue* show annual publication totals (which include a wide variety of ephemera like handbills, catalogues, and advertisements as well as conventional books) increasing from around 1,900 in 1740 to around 3,000 in 1780, then escalating to well over 6,000 by the end of the century. In Raven's words:

> From 1740 to 1780 the growth rate was 1.58 per cent, but from 1780 to the end of the century this rate more than doubled to 3.37 per cent, a take-off in publication totals reflecting the expansion of the country distribution network, increased institutional demand, and new productivity based on financial and organizational innovation.[1]

Raven's explanation excludes a variety of factors that other commentators might wish to put forward to account for this explosion of printed matter, some of which will be noted below, but the 'take-off' he describes is indeed striking.

The production of new book titles would have represented only a fraction of these totals, but it is safe to assume that it followed a similar pattern: the figures collected by Raven for the output of new novels, his specific field of interest, show that new titles were three times more numerous in 1790 than in 1750. The upward trend continued through the first three decades of the nineteenth century: the figures for new books recorded in *Bent's Monthly Literary Advertiser*, as collected by Simon Eliot, rise from 395 in 1802 to

1,061 in 1830.[2] Newspapers and periodicals mirrored this unstoppable growth. The circulation of newspapers, essentially an eighteenth-century invention, increased eightfold between 1712 and 1757; then, helped by the arrival of such influential papers as *The Morning Chronicle* (1769), *The Morning Post* (1772), and *The Times* (1788), total circulation of London papers rose from 9,464,790 copies sold in 1760 to 29,387,843 copies in 1820.[3] (To put this in context, the population of England in 1821 was 11,405,000.) A contemporary treatise on the periodical press gives the total number of newspapers (daily, bi-weekly, and weekly) published in Britain and Ireland as 79 in 1782, 146 in 1790, and 284 in 1821, and notes that it is *outside* London that most of the growth has taken place.[4] This was in a period when the stamp duties on newspapers – 'taxes on knowledge', as they were denounced at the time – were severe enough to put them beyond the reach of the majority of individual citizens. When the many new monthly and quarterly magazines and reviews are added in too, the importance of the periodical press to the publishing boom is underlined. The essential point is that even prior to the full industrialisation of the press there is every reason to speak of a 'circulation revolution' – in terms of the circulation of news, ideas, and opinions – in concert with the industrial revolution that was gathering pace.

As that last sentence indicates, only to a limited extent was this revolution technology-led, though significant developments did take place in the period. Printing, the basic methods of which had remained virtually unchanged for three hundred years, finally began a long and relentless process of modernisation. Wooden hand-presses not dissimilar to those used by Johann Gutenberg in the fifteenth century were superseded first, around 1800, by Earl Stanhope's iron platen press, which allowed a complete forme of type to be printed with one pull of a lever and therefore increased output; then, more momentously, by the steam-driven cylinder press, four or five times faster than a hand-press, pioneered by a German, Friedrich Koenig. Such a press was secretly installed at the offices of *The Times*, and the first issue to be printed on it appeared on 29 November 1814. However, steam printing remained largely restricted to newspapers (where the economics of large print runs favoured mechanisation) until well after 1830, and even Koenig's invention seems with hindsight no more than a staging-post to the rotary press, which eliminated the inbuilt limitation of hand-feeding of paper by feeding paper continuously from a reel between an impression cylinder and the printing surface. When such presses were introduced in the 1860s, ten thousand complete copies of *The Times* could be printed in an hour, and the printing industry was on the road to full mechanisation. Other significant innovations at the beginning of the century were stereotyping, which involved taking lead casts (flat or cylindrical) of complete formes of type and which allowed easy reprinting of popular books without recomposition; and the introduction of mechanised papermaking, by which a single piece of machinery was able to produce paper in a continuous web rather than in individual sheets, developed first in France then put on a commercial footing by the Fourdrinier brothers in London in 1807. The latter was especially significant at a time when the cost of paper contributed up to two-thirds of the total cost of book production. However, the full benefit of this development was delayed while various substitutes were tried for the linen rags which were then the raw material of papermaking, and which were in increasingly short supply; and the impact of stereotyping was limited in proportion to the reluctance among publishers to commit themselves to large and frequent print runs of individual works.

The most significant innovation in printing in the period, at least in the long term, was lithography, pioneered by the Munich-based Alois Senefelder. Up to this point, all printing had depended upon differences in relief on the printing surface: either, as with conventional typesetting, the marks to be printed were raised higher than the rest of the surface (relief printing), or, as with engraving, the marks to be printed were inscribed in the surface (intaglio printing). Lithography used an entirely different principle: chemical differences – in simple terms the mutual antipathy of grease and water – between the printing and non-printing areas. Although slower than relief printing and requiring a completely new kind of press, lithography aroused much interest in the early years because it facilitated the combination of words and images and allowed the artist to retain control over the finished product; in the long run, it would be the method which eliminated letterpress almost completely from commercial printing. There were other important technological steps taken in illustration during the period: wood engraving, an improvement on the longer-established technique of woodcut, was brought to perfection by the Newcastle-based naturalist Thomas Bewick, and provided a viable basis for a mass-market illustrated press by the 1820s; and mezzotint and aquatint, two forms of colour illustration based on engraving and etching respectively, were perfected by the end of the eighteenth century and used for more elite products.

Despite these important gains in technological progress, it was not until much later in the nineteenth century that publishing fully entered the industrial age: naturally conservative publishers were slow to grasp the opportunities presented by the rapidly expanding market, specialised (and relatively well-paid) print workers resisted proletarianisation and the associated decline in status and rewards, and working methods remained largely artisanal throughout the Romantic period. Other factors therefore played a part in the circulation revolution. The evolution of the political and legal framework in the eighteenth century was particularly important. Up to the end of the previous century printing in England was effectively state-controlled, albeit through the agency of a chartered professional body, the Stationers' Company, but the non-renewal of the Printing Act in 1695 put an end to pre-publication censorship and to the tight limit on the number of printing-houses permitted. The liberties that this entailed were not wholly welcome to the vested interests of the book trade, and leading booksellers (who at this time also exercised the functions of today's publishers) began to lobby Parliament for action to restore their traditional monopoly. The Copyright Act of 1710 gave them most of what they wanted, establishing mechanisms for the protection of copyright and thus securing their investment in the books they published. Although the Act set the maximum term of copyright at twenty-eight years, ambiguities of interpretation meant that the trade continued to act for much of the century as though copyright was perpetual. On this assumption, publishers inevitably favoured a healthy backlist of popular works rather than risking new titles: in effect, the only good author was a dead author. This complacency was destroyed by a decision in the House of Lords in 1774 that destroyed the principle of perpetual copyright: as John Feather puts it, this was 'a decisive turning-point in the history of the English book trade', marking 'the end of the long era of protectionism which had begun with the granting of the Stationers' charter in 1557'.[5] Henceforth publishers had a clear incentive to cultivate authors, explore new markets, and diversify their products, and the most successful among them were those who became more entrepreneurial and competitive in their outlook. The increasingly free climate in which publishing operated was dealt a severe blow by the French Revolution and the resulting governmental intolerance of dissent, and over the next thirty years legislative measures such as the Seditious Societies Act of 1799 and the Blasphemous and Seditious Libel Act of 1819 were designed to muzzle the press and restrict the flow of information and ideas to the populace at large. However, the demand for reading matter was so high in these turbulent times that overall, as already demonstrated, the circulation revolution was strengthened and the publishing curve remained upward.

In terms of its general organisation, the book trade in the period 1789–1830 completed a long process of transformation into something recognisably modern. Whereas at the beginning of the eighteenth century it was common for the various processes of book production, distribution, and sale to be undertaken by the same firm, by the end of the Romantic period a specialisation of the publishing, wholesaling, and retailing functions (printing having already evolved into a separate trade) was well advanced. Leading firms like Rivingtons, Longman, and Murray largely or wholly withdrew from retailing and became publishers in the modern sense. Book publishing was still based heavily on London, but Edinburgh and Dublin were becoming notable centres, and, although provincial publishing was still a backwater, the provincial trade was gaining in importance on the back of a greatly improved distribution network. The old protectionist system whereby associations of bookseller-publishers (known as 'congers') bought shares in the copyright of particular titles, which were sold at the traditional high prices and ensured a tidy income for all shareholders, was consigned to history. Publishers did not embrace cut-throat competition overnight: in general they tried to prosper by other means than entering price wars. There was, however, an irreversible trend towards a free-trade publishing environment, one aspect of which was an increased attention to methods of attracting new readerships.

Growing differentiation of readerships meant, of course, that there was still a healthy demand for books at the top end of the market. Book prices in general rose, rather than fell, between 1789 and 1830, and in 1825 books in the middle and high price brackets (from 3s. 7d. upwards) still constituted an overwhelming 85 per cent of the total. The consumers satirised in Thomas Dibdin's *Bibliomania* who evince 'a passion for possessing books; not so much to be instructed by them, as to gratify the eye by looking on them',[6] exemplify a vogue for luxury books which is no more than an extreme manifestation of the small but dependable pool of wealthy purchasers on whom many publishers preferred to rely: it was so much easier than trying to create new audiences. Contrary pressures were at work, however. One source of disturbance was bookseller James Lackington, a shoemaker's son from Somerset who graduated to a country house in Surrey on annual profits of around £4,000. Among his revolutionary trading practices was the cut-price sale of what are now called 'remaindered' books (then commonly destroyed, or auctioned within the trade and sold at full price, by other booksellers). In his blatantly self-aggrandising memoirs, Lackington gives a public service defence of this commercial ruse: 'it affords me the most pleasing satisfaction, independent of the emoluments which have accrued to me from this plan, when I reflect what prodigious numbers in inferior or *reduced* situation in life, have been essentially benefited in consequence of being thus enabled to indulge their natural propensity for the acquisition of knowledge'.[7] Lackington was one of the first to realise that selling large numbers of books at marginal profits could be equally, or even more, lucrative than trading in small numbers of expensive works. The pioneers of cheap reprint series, such as John Bell, who published *The Poets of Great Britain* in 109 volumes at 1*s.* 6*d.* a volume, and John Cooke, who produced editions of British poets, novelists, and dramatists in 6*d.* weekly numbers, were others who saw the potential for higher-volume sales to middling-class readers. Publishers also saw a huge growth market in new fiction, typically produced in multi-volume duodecimos (a small, portable format – of some cultural significance in an age when book size, as well as quality of print and binding, connoted taste and status). These novels were not priced in such a way as to build a large market of fiction-buyers: the average price varied from about 4*s.* up to the absurdly elitist level of 10*s.* 6*d.* at which some of Walter Scott's novels were set. This was at a time when wages for those in the lower and lower-middle classes could be well under a pound a week. Richard Altick points out that in the 1770s 'A woman in one of the London trades . . . could have bought a three-volume novel in paper covers only with the proceeds of a week's work',[8] and this salutary observation is all the more applicable to the period after 1780 when prices began to climb. What publishers realised, however, was that the secret to success in the fiction market, above all others, lay not in increasing individual book purchase but in increasing novel reader-ship: hence the symbiotic relationship between the take-off in novel production after 1780 and the equally rapid growth in commercial circulating libraries. These institutions (often attached to booksellers), which allowed subscribers access to all the new books published during the year, might appear to be damaging publishers by depleting the pool of potential buyers, but in fact performed an essential service for them. Publishers could continue churning out novels in small editions of around a thousand copies, at high prices, confident that the libraries would take the lion's share of the edition and that rapid circulation among clients would mean constant demand for more of the same. The man who most completely mastered the economics of this situation was William Lane, a bookseller and publisher whose Minerva Press, operational between 1790 and 1820, was synonymous with the pulp fiction (Gothic and sentimental) of the day. Lane, however, also ran his own London circulating library, which at its peak stocked up to 17,000 titles, and actively promoted the spread of such libraries to the provinces, offering to supply complete libraries of up to 5,000 volumes together with a printed catalogue and professional advice. As Dorothy Blakey tersely observes, all this cultural enterprise was essentially 'to furnish a wider market for his novels'.[9] Controlling both supply and demand, Lane was able to amass a fortune amounting at his death to £17,500.

Before the 1820s, the only significant new attempts to reach out to lower-class readers either came in the form of political propaganda or were the vehicle of religious proselytising. The much-quoted example of Tom Paine's *Rights of Man*, which shifted hundreds of thousands of copies in its cheap 6*d.* format in the early 1790s, demonstrated the phenomenal sales that could be achieved if workers' interests were engaged. Equally remarkable as a mass-circulation venture, on the side of political and religious orthodoxy, were Hannah More's *Cheap Repository Tracts* (1795–98), a series of moral tales and ballads designed to stem the tide of seditious feeling epitomised by Paine. With subsidies from evangelical backers allowing prices to be set as low as 1/2*d.* to 1 1/2*d.*, the *Tracts* sold two million copies in the first year alone. Evangelicals were also responsible for major initiatives in the production and distribution of bibles and religious tracts, most notably the activities of the Religious Tract Society (founded in 1799) and the British and Foreign Bible Society (1804). The former produced 314,000 copies of tracts in 1804 alone.[10] Much of this literature was either charitably disseminated or hard-sold to recalcitrant workers by an army of volunteers, but it provided an ample revenue stream for printers. Competing healthily with all this material were the chapbooks (illustrated pamphlets) and ballads, the traditional popular literature, which dealt in old fairy-tales and romances, or abridgements of the most sensational contemporary fiction, or 'true life' stories of a macabre or licentious nature. The presses that manufactured this literature, described by Altick as 'the squalid fringes of the trade',[11] found a huge market among the semi-literate labouring classes in big towns and cities, and were a significant feature of the provincial trade.

It was disgust at the vulgar excesses of this popular literature, and alarm at the spread of cheap propaganda 'almost exclusively directed to the united object of inspiring hatred of the Government and contempt of the Religious Institutions of the country', that prompted the journalist-turned-publisher Charles Knight (1791–1873) to take a leading role in the development of a secular and progressive mass-market literature. Describing himself later in life as 'a sort of Communist' at the age of seventeen, Knight was very far from one by the time he made his first forays in journalism in the troubled years leading up to Peterloo. While loathing radical politics, he admired the facility with which 'infidel writers' made their pitch to lower-class readers, and admitted that his own early publications made the same mistake as most of the Christian propaganda in giving the air of writers coming down 'from their natural elevation to impart a small portion of their wisdom to persons of very inferior understanding'. Increasingly convinced that cheap books were fundamental to a scheme of national education by which the personal and social beliefs and values of the middle classes would percolate down to the lower orders, Knight jumped at the chance of becoming first editor, then publisher, of the works produced by the Society for the Diffusion of Useful Knowledge, newly formed by the Whig politician Henry Brougham. The rather forbidding contents of the Library of Useful Knowledge (1827), issued in fortnightly instalments at 6*d*., and the misleadingly titled Library of Entertaining Knowledge (1829), were motivated by the belief that educating the poor would promote social cohesion rather than disorder. The general cause of cheap books – an idea that had previously 'stank in the nostrils' of the trade, according to Knight – was signally advanced by his endeavours.[12]

The restructuring and modernisation of the book trade that I have sketched, along with the technological developments that were beginning to industrialise the press, and most conspicuously the remarkable circulation revolution of the late eighteenth century, helped create an environment in which, as Henri-Jean Martin says, by 1800 'everyone – but city dwellers in particular – felt surrounded by written culture'.[13] Clifford Siskin has argued that the proliferation of writing – essentially a 'new technology' – in the eighteenth century was accompanied by an anxious self-consciousness and a good deal of self-reflexive concern with the material force of that technology, its capacity to effect change. At the same time, he suggests, the spread of writing was intimately connected to the rise of English nationalism: whereas nationalism typically assumes a social group aspiring to political sovereignty, Britain (after union with Scotland in 1707, and Ireland in 1800) was in the unusual position of a sovereign state 'aimed at forming a group', and it was through writing that the imagining of this community took place. By the end of the Romantic period a taming of the new technology had occurred in parallel with the stabilisation of ideas of nationhood: 'writing was domesticated at the same time as that society whose coherence was, in important ways, dependent upon it'.[14] Equally importantly, the spread of writing was inseparably entwined with sweeping changes to the social and economic order, in particular the increasing economic and cultural power of the middle classes (industrial, commercial, and professional) and the growth of an urban working class. The very fact that by 1830 the vocabulary of class was beginning to be used as a means by which British society represented itself to itself is significant. As these changes took place an instinctively conservative publishing industry was forced to recognise that its potential audience was no longer homogeneous; it grew more adept at identifying and addressing different market segments, gauging and manipulating shifts in public taste, and, by the end of the Romantic period, was beginning to perceive and exploit the potential of a mass market for literature. Just as publishers became more consumer-oriented, it was inevitable that readers came to think of themselves as consumers too: by 1830 a process was in train whereby, in Kathryn Sutherland's words, 'Buying identity through reading [became] an act of self-purchase in a world of mass production and anonymous relations'.[15] In the next section I shall examine all these developments from the point of view of the consumers, rather than producers, of print culture.

The reading public

How many readers were there in the Romantic period? In trying to answer this apparently simple question one soon gets bogged down in claim and counter-claim, complicated by competing definitions, disputed premises, and multiple qualifications. Edmund Burke allegedly estimated the size of the reading public in 1790 at around eighty thousand persons, a calculation that Altick damns with faint praise as 'interesting'.[16] The following year, in a much-cited passage of his *Memoirs*, James Lackington proclaimed that 'all ranks and degrees now READ'.[17] This remark is treated with a good deal of scepticism by modern commentators. In Lackington's defence, his statement does not imply universal or mass literacy, merely that the 'reading habit' has permeated all levels of society. Doubtless his wish to underline his own achievements in cheapening books and popularising reading weakens his sociological case, but there is a range of anecdotal evidence to give support to this limited proposition. A different kind of estimate was put forward by Francis Jeffrey, editor of the *Edinburgh Review*, in 1812: Jeffrey put the audience for journals at some twenty thousand members of the gentry and upper middle classes, but saw the prospective total readership enlarged by some two hundred thousand members of the 'middling classes'.[18]

The crucial factor in the constitution of the reading public is literacy. Research on this issue is a minefield by itself, with historians differing profoundly on questions of methodology as well as on their estimates of historical and regional patterns in the spread of literacy. In one school of thought, literacy was indeed widespread in the eighteenth century, even among the labouring classes, and was acquired informally at home, reinforced to some extent by such schooling as was available. The evidence for this view is gathered from a study of educational facilities and of circulation figures for popular literature. A contrasting approach is based on statistical analysis of documents like marriage registers, where the ability to sign one's name (rather than make a mark) is taken to indicate basic literacy. No one claims that this is infallible: there is no way of knowing what level of reading competence is implied by the ability to sign one's name, still less is there a clear relation between the latter and the ability to communicate effectively in writing. (It is possible that some brides and grooms learned to sign specifically to avoid the humiliation of making a mark.) In a much-cited article, Lawrence Stone admits the imperfections of the method but insists that 'any change in the numbers capable of signing their names may be taken to indicate a parallel, but not necessarily entirely proportionate, change in the numbers able to read'.[19] Stone's own analysis of two sets of marriage licences leads him to conclude that the conquest of illiteracy took about four hundred years, with a period of significant advance in the early seventeenth century followed by a century or more of stagnation, then another upward curve beginning in the last quarter of the eighteenth century. More particularly, between 1780 and 1840 literacy among the rural middle classes (yeomen and husbandmen) rose from 75 to 95 per cent, among artisans and shopkeepers from 85 to 95 per cent, and among the labouring classes from around 40 to around 60 per cent. In general literacy in the towns was higher than in rural areas, but this pattern was reversed in the first third of the nineteenth century when an influx of people to the big industrial cities stretched educational resources to breaking point; the huge overall increase in population during the period also means that the actual number of illiterates went up. Nevertheless, if Stone's figures are anything like accurate, it is clear that by the end of the Romantic period, with national averages for male literacy of around 65 per cent, and female literacy of around 50 per cent, the potential audience for printed matter of some description ran into several millions, which makes the sluggish approach of publishers towards embracing the mass market all the more striking. In Scotland, it should be noted, literacy was much higher, with something like 90 per cent adult male literacy by the end of the eighteenth century.

The means and incentives behind these positive trends in literacy require further comment. To the degree that basic education took place outside the home, the availability and quality of primary (then called 'elementary') schooling is plainly the most important factor. It was the fact that Scotland had set up a national compulsory elementary educational system, and had in addition secondary and university systems that were among the best in Europe, that put it far ahead of England and Wales in the literacy stakes in the eighteenth century. South of the border there was nothing resembling a primary education *system*, and after 1780 it was not the chaotic nature of educational provision – the bewildering mix of charity schools, dame schools, endowed schools, private schools, Sunday schools, and so on – that improved, nor in most cases the quality of teaching and learning, but the energy and seriousness with which popular education was pursued. In some quarters the French Revolution and associated 'Jacobin panic' in Britain fuelled interest in educating the lower orders, on the grounds that this would 'wet down the smoldering embers of discontent' and 'safeguard men's minds against thoughts of rebellion'.[20] (In the minds of others, exactly the opposite opinion took hold.) Closely tied in with this political argument was an impetus from religion. From its inception, Protestantism had been, as Stone puts it, a 'culture of the book', insisting that 'God's people were to be a literate people, taking in God's Word from the printed page'; it was this passionate belief that engineered the big rise in literacy during the Puritan ascendancy in seventeenth-century Britain. In Stone's view, at the beginning of the nineteenth century 'the rise of popular elementary education was very largely an incidental by-product of the struggle between Anglicans and Dissenters for the allegiance of the lower classes',[21] Dissenters having led the way and the Anglican establishment becoming concerned to preserve its influence. What this meant was that in most schools indoctrination in a particular form of religion took precedence over any more considered educational policy, but the rudiments of reading were acquired by many children nonetheless. The picture is somewhat less bleak in respect of secondary education, of which admittedly only the children of the upper and middle classes were beneficiaries. Here a similarly diverse range of schools, including the Dissenting academies which offered the most progressive education in the country, catered for the needs of different social groups and improved the *quality* of the literacy of the middle classes at all levels. It was men and women in this expanding sector of society who were the likeliest new members of the reading public.

Becoming fully literate does not necessarily infuse one with a love of reading. If one looks at things from the point of view of potential readers, rather than that of the political and religious establishment, it is clear that incentives are needed to turn latent into actual readers. Religious enthusiasm was certainly sufficient motivation in some cases: in James Lackington's, it was Methodist zeal that directed his early forays into literature, and the small private library he built up prior to setting up in business consisted almost entirely of religious books. For others it was the more understandable lure of fantasy and romance, the otherworldliness of narrative, that turned them into readers: Charles Knight refers to the 'seductions' of the *Arabian Nights*, *Robinson Crusoe*, *Gulliver's Travels*, and ballads like 'Peter Wilkins', contrasting them favourably with 'the tamer fictions in which moral and religious truths are inculcated'.[22] This kind of escapist motive, serviced at the simplest level by the chapbooks sold by street hawkers, became stronger for the growing numbers of urbanised workers living in squalid conditions, with few other recreational possibilities, and subjected to the stultifying routines and discipline of factory work. The desire for self-improvement encouraged some members of this class to read, as it did also numbers of the middling classes above them. As the professional and businesses classes expanded, and scientific and technological developments made an impact on diverse spheres of life, the demand for practical knowledge increased; as Altick says, the kinds of literature that responded to this need at the very least 'kept men's literacy in good repair and accustomed them to the everyday presence of books'.[23] As for the leisured female audience that consumed the novels popularised by the circulating library, in the eyes of their anxious male minders these women were seeking mental diversion at untold cost to their future well-being; more positively, through reading a literature produced dominantly *by* women *for* women, women readers found the satisfactions typical, in Alberto Manguel's account, of members of a socially excluded group: seeing their own lives 'lived or unlived, idealized or fantasized', rescuing 'from between the lines the presence of their fellow outcasts'.[24]

A huge stimulus was given to reading in the Romantic period, especially among the middling and lower classes, by intense interest in political affairs generated by the two main phases of radical activism, in the early 1790s (in response to the Revolution) then again after the coming of peace in 1815. The huge sales of Paine's *Rights of Man*, assisted like much other radical propaganda by free distribution through the offices of the London Corresponding Society, is the established high-water mark of this surge in popular reading. The book was said by contemporary observers to be 'in almost every hand' and to be 'as much a Standard book in this Country as Robinson Crusoe & the Pilgrim's Progress'.[25] It was significant that workers would congregate in pubs and elsewhere to hear Paine read to them, and to discuss his ideas, since activity like this demonstrates the importance of reading in this era as a social experience instrumental in the formation of group consciousness. Many artisans who were thus introduced to print culture developed a permanent reading habit: Francis Place, leading light of the London Corresponding Society, says that politics 'induced men to read books', compelled them to 'find reasons for their opinions, and to tolerate others', and 'elevated them in society'.[26] A similar phenomenon occurred in the years of radical agitation after Waterloo, which again witnessed a vigorous radical press achieving high circulation figures, a mushrooming of cheap political books and pamphlets, and the related phenomena of shared purchase, communal reading, and public disputation.

However, just as radical politics can be accounted one of the principal factors in the growth of the reading public in the period, it was by the same token responsible for most of the opposition to popular education, cheap publishing, and the spread of the reading habit, on the part of the dominant classes. Although, as I have indicated, there was growing acceptance towards the end of the period that educating the poor was essential to improve standards of morality and thus enhance social discipline, the reverse attitude prevailed in the 1790s under pressure of events. Altick again eloquently summarises:

> Suddenly, in the supercharged atmosphere of a nation plunged, unprepared and bewildered, into a general war, the potentialities inherent in the press spread alarm among the people who prized above all the settled stability of the nation. . . . Compared with the threat of internal subversion, that of military invasion was small.[27]

To contain this threat, the ruling classes had two options: either to restrict access to basic education and thus stifle the circulation revolution on the demand side, or to pursue a supply-side policy and exercise much tighter control over what was written, published, and distributed. The first option was to some extent a case of shutting the stable door after the literacy horse had bolted; and although anti-educational attitudes held back the mental emancipation of the working classes, the uneven yet long-established trend towards universal literacy proved irresistible in the long run. The second option entailed both direct government censorship of the press, earnestly pursued in the Revolutionary decade and with renewed vigour in response to the post-war troubles (and which included taking whatever steps were necessary to keep the price of books and periodicals high), and action on the part of the conservative and religious establishment to promote more ideologically sound reading matter, of which the spectacularly successful example of More's *Cheap Repository Tracts* has already been noted. William Hazlitt wrote scornfully in 1818 that it was the 'fear of the progress of knowledge and a *Reading Public*' that 'made the Church and State so anxious to provide us with that sort of food for our stomachs, which they thought best'.[28]

There were, of course, many barriers to reading in the lower echelons of society. The restricted availability of leisure time, the physically draining effects of long working days and weeks, the overcrowding of homes and consequent lack of private space, and the abysmally bad lighting in most homes, were all important material factors. The notoriously poor quality of most elementary schooling, which was based on mechanical rote learning from books that the poor could scarcely understand, let alone enjoy, also needs mentioning. But the barriers which probably surprise and shock today's students most are the ideological ones that were erected by cultural elites who saw the existing distribution of knowledge as essential to maintaining the existing favourable distribution of wealth and power. In this respect the intense alarm aroused by the spectre of Paine did no more than sharpen the focus of ideas concerning social hierarchy and social control that had a much longer history. Francis Place describes an incident in 1812 that vividly illustrates the depth of hostility there was towards lower-class reading and, by extension, the democratising culture of print:

> One day when I was from home on business, a customer came to try on a pair of pantaloons, and my foreman, incautiously took him into my room; he expressed much surprize at the number of books, the fitting up, and the library table though there was nothing in the least expensive but it was all neat and in keeping. his remarks were sarcastic and he was evidently displeased, I waited upon him in a few days when some trifling omission being discovered, he told me, he supposed I was thinking more about my books, than about his orders. . . . Other somewhat similar instances occurred as some of my customers learned from time to time, that I was a 'bookish man', and had made acquaintance with other 'bookish men'. . . . To accumulate books and to be supposed to know something of their contents, to seek for friends, too, among literary and scientific men, was putting myself on an equality with themselves, if not indeed assuming a superiority; was an abominable offence in a tailor, if not a crime.[29]

As this story makes abundantly clear, there was an intimate connection between levels of reading (both the amount of reading, and the kinds of literature consumed) and the social distinctions that privileged minorities wanted to see preserved. The attitudes of Place's customer are largely unvoiced, but there were no inhibitions attaching to expressing such views in public. A bill to establish parish schools out of local taxes brought before the Commons in 1807 was opposed by Davies Giddy on the grounds that it

> would teach [the poor] to despise their lot in life; instead of making them good servants in agriculture or other labourious employments, instead of teaching them subordination, it would render them fractious and refractory, as was evident in manufacturing counties; it would enable them to read seditious pamphlets, vicious books and publications against Christianity; it would render them insolent to their superiors and in a few years the legislature would find it necessary to direct the strong arm of power towards them.[30]

Here we see the full arsenal of middle- and upper-class prejudices and concerns: the zeal for preserving social distinctions and the structures of deference which accompanied them; the worry that all occupations, especially the most 'laborious' ones, should continue to be filled by adequate numbers of men; and the now recognisable fear that any written material that smacked of sedition should be prevented from reaching those most likely to be manipulated by it. Education, and the reading habit that it established, were the demons of this mindset. The process of exorcising those demons only began when sufficient numbers of people were persuaded that education was a way of averting their worst nightmares – was part of the solution, not part of the problem.

Both middle-class and lower-class readers alike, albeit to very different degrees, faced additional barriers to reading in the form of price deterrence: the high cost of books in relation to incomes for much of the period has already been noted, as has the government's fondness for using taxes on newspapers, advertisements, and paper to restrict the circulation of periodicals. It was for this reason that the reading public in this period has to be seen as a very different entity to the book-buying public, and that the various facilities for communal access to books and periodicals were so important in spreading the reading habit. Of these the most culturally significant, as well as the most controversial, were the commercial circulating libraries. These multiplied rapidly in the second half of the eighteenth century, and by 1800 there were said to be 'not less than one thousand' in England alone.[31] They typically offered a range of subscription options, depending on the subscriber's place of residence and the number of books allowed at any one time. At Thomas Hookham's library, for instance, the top subscription of three guineas a year entitled one to borrow twelve books as a town-dweller, or twenty-four as a country-dweller; for the lowest subscription of one guinea, the equivalent allowances were four and eight books. The library was similar to its competitors in being open from 8 a.m. to 8 p.m. (except Sundays), and in setting down various rules (no sub-lending, for instance) to regulate use of the facilities. Hookham's catalogue is divided into 'History, Antiquities, Voyages, Travels', 'Lives, Adventures, Romances, and Novels', 'Poems and Plays', 'Miscellanies' (including literary criticism, essays, and philosophy), 'Tracts', 'Surgery and Physic', 'Divinity', and 'Addenda' (a catch-all category for late additions), giving some idea of the range of literature available. Of the 8,866 entries, 1,187 belong to the category that includes novels, but Hilda Hamlyn has argued that in this respect extant catalogues are unrepresentative, and that smaller libraries may well have been dominantly fiction.[32] Certainly, in contemporary discourse their reputation was closely linked with that of the pulp fiction manufactured by the Minerva Press and others, just as their users were invariably perceived as young and impressionable. These assumptions were responsible for much of the negative publicity they attracted from the gatekeepers of polite culture. The anonymous author of *The Use of Circulating Libraries Considered* (1797) defends them as 'depots of learning, and stores for rational amusement', and argues that 'Proper books are proper companions, and often keep us from improper ones', including even modern novels among those works that 'improve the morals of the age'.[33] The opposite view is represented by Edward Mangin, whose *Essay on Light Reading* (1808) fulminates against '*novels, romances, and poems of a particular class*: in other words . . . the ordinary contents of a circulating library'. He fears the effects of this literature on its audience, namely 'the YOUTH of both sexes, and of the middle ranks of the state'; and is most exercised about the dangers for leisured young women who are rendered incapable of distinguishing fiction and reality – who are led to believe '*intrigue* to be natural, *falsehood* and *filial disobedience* venial, and the passion of *love* absolutely invincible'.[34] What these contrary arguments have in common is their recognition of the growth of recreational reading in the 'middle ranks' of society, and of the circulating libraries' key role in this; but whereas one is positive and optimistic about this trend, the other is apprehensive. As for all those emergent or potential readers below the middle ranks, even the modest subscriptions of these libraries were beyond their means. For this sector of the reading public, private book clubs and mutual improvement societies and other forms of cooperative purchase or book-sharing, and, later, the Mechanics' Institutes' libraries, played a more important part.

For all the information available about the expansion of reading and access to print culture in this period, one of the hardest things to find out about are actual reading practices. By this I mean not only what people read, but also (in a variety of senses) *how* they read and how their reading affected their lives. A range of deceptively simple questions such as Alberto Manguel explores in his *History of Reading* teases the scholar: What was the difference *then* between being read to in company (as was common) and reading to oneself? Between reading aloud and silent reading? In what physical settings did people read – outdoors? indoors? – and for what reasons? Were different types of books read in different locations, such as the living room and the bedroom? What effect did the size, shape, and feel of a book have? How did readers connect word and image, in the infancy of the illustrated press? Answers to these questions await the outcome of modern research collating reading experiences wherever they are found in diaries, autobiographies, annotations to books, creative literature and so on – a monumental undertaking to which every reader and student is capable of making a contribution.

Authors and authorship

In terms of the position of authors in the literary marketplace, the period 1789–1830 should be seen as one consolidating, at best accelerating, changes that had been taking place for much of the eighteenth century. What it meant to be an author, and the opportunities available to practise authorship and to earn a living from writing, altered profoundly during this period. In the crudest possible terms, the story is one of the final withering of patronage, the growth and increasing respectability of authorship as a profession, and the subjection of authors to what many in the Romantic period would see as the tyranny of public taste, as expressed in the economics of publishing.

'The professional author', John Feather asserts, 'is a product of the age of the printed book', and even by the end of the fifteenth century 'books were being written which would not have been written had there not been a press on which to print them and a book trade through which to sell them'.[35] Nevertheless, as Feather himself acknowledges, patronage, an institution whereby writers received material support from high-ranking, wealthy, and influential members of society, remained a vital factor in literary history for at least another two hundred years. While the monarchy enjoyed absolute power, it was to nobles and courtiers that aspiring writers looked for support, and in return they were expected to toe the required ideological line and to become in some fashion useful accessories to the Court. When Parliament gained the ascendancy, such patronage as continued was more narrowly political in character, with compliant writers serving as propagandists for the Whig or Tory cause. The supply of patrons dried up under the Hanoverian dynasty, and in any case a burgeoning commercial press was already making provision for writers who could meet the demands of publishers and the book-buying public rather than dance to the tune of an aristocratic patron or political master.

It is a cliché of literary history that Alexander Pope (1688–1744) was the first writer to make a living from literature alone, his verse translations of Homer's *Iliad* and *Odyssey* bringing him around £10,000 by themselves. Few could approach Pope's success, and most literary authors in the eighteenth century had to subsidise their work with journalism or were dependent on other sources of income; but as the book trade expanded opportunities for writers multiplied, and the acceleration of print production in the last quarter of the eighteenth century and beyond, married to other changes which increased the status of the author, enhanced those opportunities proportionally. Terry Belanger encapsulates this trend when he points out that most of the options available to writers at the end of the eighteenth century – publishing in a local newspaper or journal; publishing in a London newspaper or journal; contracting with a local or London printer for self-publication, perhaps on a subscription basis; or finding a local or London publisher willing to speculate on the commercial prospects of a book – were not on offer a hundred years earlier.[36]

A major event in eighteenth-century publishing history, as noted earlier in this chapter, was the legal decision in 1774 abolishing perpetual copyright. Traumatic as this was for the oligarchy of booksellers jealous of their rights to the intellectual property of the dead, it was good news for living authors, who had everything to gain from a more urgent commercial incentive on the part of publishers to seek out new material. Another significant milestone was the Copyright Act of 1814, a major provision of which was to extend copyright to twenty-eight years from the date of publication, plus the residue (if any) of the author's natural life. This important qualification made explicit, for the first time, that the purpose of copyright was to protect the interests of the author, rather than those of the book trade. There was intensive campaigning by publishers in the run-up to the 1814 Act for a relaxation of the requirements regarding delivery of free copies of published books to certain libraries. The argument was conducted largely in terms of the financial damage to authors and the potential suppression of literary works published in small editions at marginal profit, but much of it sounds like special pleading on the part of businessmen who resent the imposition on their own account. It is also difficult to take seriously the emotive claims of polemicists like Sharon Turner, who argued in 1813 that the 1709 Act (or rather its reinterpretation in 1774) had 'robbed' authors of 'the permanent enjoyment of the fruits of their labour, which every other class of society is enjoying',[37] since few authors were, even then, in a strong enough position to demand any kind of long-term stake in the sale of their work. (When forced to sell copyright in your work for a paltry lump sum, the term of protection was irrelevant.) After 1814, however, authors became more interested in their rights and more active in seeking to improve their remuneration, and in addition to a campaign for extending copyright that eventually bore fruit in 1842, various forms of profit-sharing agreement between writers and publishers became more common (though the systematic adoption of royalty payments did not come until the end of the nineteenth century).

When earnings started improving, it was long overdue. As James Raven observes, 'authors were the very last participants to benefit from the eighteenth-century book bonanza'.[38] George Dyer, author of the *Complaints of the Poor People of England* (1793), used the occasion of his *Dissertation on the Theory and Practice of Benevolence* two years later to include the plight of authors among the forms of distress he had failed to cover. He welcomed the establishment of the philanthropically-funded Literary Fund Society (later the Royal Literary Fund), set up to alleviate such distress. The situations of a few high-profile, high-earning Romantic authors can easily distort the picture: Byron was paid £2,000 for Canto 3 of *Childe Harold's Pilgrimage* in 1816, Thomas Moore reaped £3,000 for *Lalla Rookh* in 1817, while the very commercially-minded Scott received £4,000 for *The Lady of the Lake* (1810) and was advanced the same amount for *Rob Roy* in 1818. But these were exceptional cases, and the remarkable payments for poetry reflect its then fashionable status and a temporary publishing boom in the genre. The other side of the picture is represented by the disposable novels – the circulating library fodder – produced by the Minerva Press. Although Lane tried to attract manuscripts with promises of up to a hundred guineas, it seems the copyright in these novels was purchased for an average of £30, and sometimes much less. Jane Austen, who records in her novels the disdain with which circulating library fiction was treated, received just £10 for the manuscript of *Northanger Abbey*. An alternative for writers throughout the period was subscription publishing, whereby needy authors collected signatures from sympathetic persons willing to buy a copy of the book when it appeared, but this habitually delayed publication and was only marginally more dignified than contracting for self-publication.

Given the unpredictable and limited rewards to be gained by writing, it is remarkable that so many individuals sought to earn a living by it. It is worth emphasising how many women were included in this number: Stuart Curran highlights how 'there were not mere dozens, nor even hundreds, but actually thousands, of women whose writing was published in Great Britain in the half century between 1780 and 1830'.[39] Many of these women attempted to live by their writing, and some succeeded. Among the obstacles they confronted was the unrespectability of writing as a profession, a stigma that bore more heavily on women than on men: in 1800, half of all the books published by the Minerva Press were anonymous, concerns of female propriety being the most likely explanation. Margaret Oliphant described the first two decades of the nineteenth century as 'the days . . . in which remuneration was suggested with delicacy, as beneath the exquisite feelings and purpose of a writer'; what Lee Erickson says apropos G.H. Lewes around 1850, that 'In the social order the author's status was uncertain and his position as a gentleman less than assured',[40] was even truer of the first quarter of the century, and truer still – with appropriate rephrasing – of the situation of women writers. Only towards the end of the Romantic period, with the rapid growth in the periodical market and significantly improved terms of payment for contributors, was the overall social status of writing for money lifted.

In material terms, therefore, the period 1789–1830 was one in which opportunities and potential rewards multiplied in parallel with the circulation revolution described above, ushering in the prosperous era of mass-market Victorian publishing; but this time of transition was by no means wholly comfortable, nor even entirely beneficial in outcome, for many of the writers involved. The world that was beckoning offered the prospect of greater financial security and access to a considerably enlarged readership. But in seeking to maximise their circulation figures, especially via exploitation of the expanding periodical market, authors had to learn to accommodate their creative talents to the vagaries of public taste. Wordsworth consoled himself for the low sales of his poetry in mid-career by drawing a distinction between the reading public, a 'small though loud portion of the community, ever governed by factitious influence', and an idealised audience, the 'People', which would one day recognise his worth.[41] In reality there were simply different markets, and even during a poetry boom Wordsworth's appeal was too narrowly aesthetic to achieve high sales. The writers to find success with 'the people', or rather larger constituencies of readers, were those who could interpret and manipulate the 'factitious' course of literary fashion, or accept the collaboration and intervention of editors and publishers in such enterprise. This was perhaps the hardest truth to swallow: that in a purely economic analysis authors were becoming mere suppliers to the publishing industry, their labour being to produce books and essays as commodities from which their publishers would extract surplus value before retailing them to anonymous consumers.

Clifford Siskin has written provocatively of how the dangerous proliferation of writing in the late eighteenth century was gradually brought under control through the establishment of separate disciplines (a specialisation of kinds of writing which increases output but hinders socially productive interaction with other discourses) and the growth of professionalism. In this rather scarily sweeping form of conspiracy theory, professionalism has become 'a central form of modern power' monitoring and regulating all aspects of our lives.[42] Insofar as this is persuasive, it can only be our imaginative lives into which professional writers have acquired the right to intrude. But writers themselves are arguably victims in this process too, and Romantic-period authors were well placed to perceive the disadvantages. When writing became predominantly construed as work, or more specifically mental labour, it was open to writers to construct their identities principally *through* their work, with a possible gain in self-esteem; but professionalised authorship also entailed a loss of autonomy, an acceptance of the codes and practices that come with 'membership' of any such body. And in any profession, being a good professional, or simply 'being professional', is often what counts for most. Although many writers in the period would have had no problem with this mental attitude, it was hard to accept for those who held exalted conceptions of the author's role that could not be reduced to a matrix of professional duties.

The periodical press

The huge growth in the periodical press – newspapers and magazines – in this period, matching or outrunning the surge in book production, has already been described in general terms. It remains to provide a fuller picture of the main developments and trends in this important branch of written discourse, and give some sense of its cultural significance.

The distinctive character of the earlier eighteenth-century magazine – a term that originally signified a storehouse or repository, hence a compilation of previously-published items and excerpts, like today's *Reader's Digest* – was crystallised in the monthly *Gentleman's Magazine* (1731–1818), the most successful periodical of the century. Its contents included essays on diverse topics (many in the form of letters from readers), poetry, births, marriages and deaths, commodity prices, lists of new publications, and parliamentary reporting; its spread of interests straddled what would now be thought of as the separate realms of the arts and sciences, appealing to an audience that would unite more progressive members of the gentry with the professional middle classes. With its comprehensive, anti-elitist coverage, and its accessibility to outside contributors, it modelled a public sphere that was more egalitarian than the world outside the text. Its example was followed by numerous other journals, some of a more specialised nature. The *London Magazine* (1732–85) copied its precursor almost exactly, while the *Scots Magazine* (1739–1826) and *Hibernian Magazine* (1771–1810) exported the formula to other parts of the kingdom. The *Traveller's Magazine* (1749) reflected the huge popularity of voyages and travels explored in Chapter 2, while the *Lady's Magazine* (1749–53) was one of several similarly-titled productions which aimed to exploit or construct a leisured female readership. The middle of the century saw the launch of two important literary reviews, the *Monthly Review* (1749–1845) and *Critical Review* (1756–90), which were broadly Whig and Tory, respectively, in their political outlook. Both these journals adopted the format of a number of long reviews followed by a section of briefer notices. They ranged widely in the fields of literature they surveyed, though avoiding anything very abstruse, and the *Monthly* in particular was receptive to Continental works. Like the magazines, they give the impression of speaking to their readers as equals, and of seeing that readership as a steadily and seamlessly expanding community.

The Revolutionary decade proved a major stimulus to the periodical press, as it did to books and pamphlet literature, and it was even more the case for periodicals that readership was far higher than mere circulation figures would indicate. What also occurred at this time was a more profound politicisation of the periodical press that lasted through the Romantic period, and an associated fracturing of the eighteenth-century ideal community of readers. In a searching analysis of Romantic periodicals, Jon Klancher writes that the audience-building enterprise of the eighteenth-century magazines and reviews had reached the point where the public was so diversified as to be unstable; by 1790 the unitary 'public sphere' was a representation rather than a social reality, and under the shock of the Revolution and everything that came in its wake that representation was itself revealed as hopelessly utopian.[43] An anonymous writer (probably the editor, James Anderson), launching the first issue of *The Bee* in 1791, compared a journal to 'a spacious coffee-house, which is frequented by men of all nations, who meet together for their mutual entertainment and improvement',[44] but this seems anachronistic when the 'men of all nations' would shortly be embroiled in a generation-long military conflict. From the 1790s on, as Klancher shows, periodicals became increasingly partisan, addressing and helping to shape and define particular audiences of politically like-minded individuals in contradistinction to other implied constituencies of attitudes and values. Thus the radical (reformist) cause was sustained under increasing pressure in the 1790s by new journals like the *Monthly Magazine* (1796–1843), the *Analytical Review* (1788–98) and the *English Review* (1783–96), all of which were strongly identified with Dissent and were predominantly middle-class and intellectual in complexion, and in a more popular mode by productions like Daniel Eaton's *Politics for the People* (1793–?). They were opposed, satirised, and vilified by journals like the *British Critic* (1793–1843) and *The Antijacobin, or Weekly Examiner* (1797–8), which vigorously promoted the values of the Tory, High Church establishment. Most radical journals were casualties of government repression and a patriotic backlash during the war years, but oppositional politics was kept alive by John and Leigh Hunt's *Examiner* (1808–81), most famous otherwise for its fierce support of the young Shelley and Keats, then fully reinvigorated after peace in 1815 by Cobbett's twopenny *Political Register* and the many other radical weeklies it inspired, such as T.J. Wooler's *Black Dwarf* (1817–24), John Wade's *Gorgon* (1818–19), and Richard Carlile's *Republican* (1819–26). These latter journals, whose publishers, printers, and editors (roles often combined in one person) frequently worked from within prison, are called by Kevin Gilmartin 'as decisive an intervention in the history of print as in the history of politics or class consciousness', through their innovative linking of formal features to political circumstances and their resistance to emerging trends in the consumerisation of the press.[45] As with the popular radical publications of the 1790s, their typical mode of writing is what Klancher calls an 'interdiscourse', a critical, ironic dialogue with the daily press, conservative opinion, and polite culture that demonstrated the irreparable splintering of the public sphere.

On a different stratum of public debate, the war years saw the arrival of some of the most famous titles in periodical history, their own intense rivalries masking a common project of questioning the cultural supremacy of London. Leading the pack was the quarterly *Edinburgh Review* (1802–1929), the most influential journal of its day. One contemporary observer, looking back in the 1820s, says that in the early years of the war the *Edinburgh* was 'almost the only periodical work of talent in Europe', and that the Whigs who superintended its production 'not only ruled the Press in the North, but . . . considered themselves entitled to the sole direction of public opinion'.[46] Certainly the journal's editor, Francis Jeffrey, gives the impression of aspiring to such a role, cultivating a brutally forthright critical style applied to a purposefully selective review of new books. The tone of the *Edinburgh* was high-minded yet secular, its politics liberal and increasingly partisan on the Whig side. Marilyn Butler defines its constituency more precisely when she describes it continuing the tradition of

> delivering advice to the English in tones of moral and intellectual superiority. . . . It spoke for the efficient, meritocratic, and socially progressivist Scottish professional class that increasingly either worked for the government and aristocratic opposition in London or built the empire in Canada and India.[47]

The *Edinburgh*'s rhetorical grandstanding, as well as its generous terms of payment, put paid to any sense of ordinary readers as collaborators, while its literary policy was sternly neoclassical and it did little to encourage or identify new talent. Its success provoked the creation of a Tory rival and regional competitor, the *Quarterly Review* (1809–1967). The *Quarterly* was more gung-ho in its pronouncements on the war and was faithful to the established Church, but its format mimicked that of the *Edinburgh*, its tone was equally magisterial, and it practised a similar cultural elitism. Despite the pivotal role of Walter Scott in its inception and its championship of the so-called 'Lake School' of Wordsworth, Coleridge, and Southey, the *Quarterly*'s treatment of new authors has worn badly because of its hostility to Shelley and Byron and its denunciation of the 'Cockney School' grouped around Leigh Hunt. The journal's literary values were, in Walter Graham's words, always 'subordinated to those of politics', and whatever 'tended to decrease general respect for the established order, the Church, the monarchical form of government, the laws, the King, and the landed aristocracy, was evil'.[48]

Blackwood's Edinburgh Magazine (1817–1980) was Tory and High Church in its sympathies, but more pointedly middle-class and middle-brow in its appeal. It opened its columns to communications from readers in the manner of earlier magazines, published a good deal of original literature and criticism, and gave plentiful if satirical attention to the contemporary Scottish literary scene. With an equally strong investment in modern literature, the *London Magazine* (1820–9) was notable for accommodating some of the best prose of writers like Hazlitt, Lamb, and De Quincey, and for its role in developing an 'autonomous literary sphere' in which writers were becoming more familiar to their readers.[49] The tragic outcome of its first editor's duel with one of the *Blackwood's* reviewers has become synonymous with the literally deadly earnestness with which literary quarrels were conducted at this time. Another key journal was the *New Monthly Magazine* (1814–84), which amply declared its ideological position in an 'address to the public' in its first issue, denouncing the 'political poison', 'ribaldry and irreligion' of its radical namesake.

While journals like *Blackwood's* and the *New Monthly* achieved circulations of five or six thousand, a new generation of cheap mass-readership journals brought circulations up to between fifty and two hundred thousand. The *Mirror of Literature, Amusement and Instruction* (1822–49), an illustrated sixteen-page weekly costing 2*d.* which was essentially a cut-and-paste job on assorted books and periodicals, brought entertainment and easily digestible knowledge to the 'respectable' working class and prefigured the success of Charles Knight's *Penny Magazine* (1832–45) and similar ventures. These record circulations brought the non-radical press up to or beyond the levels achieved by Cobbett's *Political Register* in the post-war heyday of the radical weeklies. The latter productions were halfway between a newspaper and a journal, exploiting as they did a legal loophole whereby they avoided paying penal stamp duties by not directly reporting – instead, providing an ironic or inflammatory commentary on – the news. These taxes, progressively increased in 1789, 1797, and 1815 to bring the price of a paper to a strategically prohibitive 7*d.*, put a severe brake upon the growth of the newspaper press, which nevertheless remained strong in a period when momentous political events and social instability fuelled a constant demand for news. Most newspaper readers were not newspaper purchasers: they read copies in coffeehouses or circulating library reading rooms, or hired a copy from a newsman for a penny an hour (an illegal but widespread practice), or waited their turn as a member of one of the thousands of informal newspaper societies which organised subscriptions on a cooperative basis. Richard Altick estimates that 'Most copies of a daily paper in the first third of the [nineteenth] century passed through a dozen or even scores of hands'.[50] The anonymous treatise on the periodical press cited earlier argues that newspaper taxes have burdened the respectable classes rather than inhibited the 'popular phalanx', and that reduction or abolition of the taxes would lead to increased and more varied production, purchase, and reading of papers, which would in turn counter the perceived political threats more effectively than repression. 'The operative and labouring classes of society', it declares, 'can never read too much.'[51] By 1830, experience as much as conviction had led much of the conservative and liberal establishment to the same conclusion.

In conclusion, the development of the periodical press between 1789 and 1830 offers a valuable yet neglected means of charting the enlargement and disunification of the British reading public and the vicissitudes of literature and literary debate in a highly politicised cultural environment. The press accrued considerable social power, and recognised this power in itself: the treatise just quoted calls it 'the most powerful moral machine in the world', more influential than law, politics, or religion in framing manners and opinions, and roundly asserts that intolerant governments will be defeated by the power of the press – a point that recalls Arthur Young's conviction, as he travelled through France in the early 1790s, that the aberrations and excesses of the French Revolution resulted from the absence in France of the 'universal circulation of intelligence' found in peaceable England.[52] In a related vein, the author of a piece in *Blackwood's* in 1824 argues that periodical publications have improved immeasurably in number, variety, and quality over the past fifty years, and traces this improvement to the Revolution itself:

> The impulse and agitation of such a dreadful crisis cannot rouse and exercise the mind without benefiting it: it produces, indeed, a moral earthquake, bringing to the surface the lava which destroys and overwhelms all in its progress; but this lava itself, in a short time, is converted into a fertile soil, fitted to nourish and rear, not only the common produce, but to cause those seeds to germinate, which, but for this convulsion, would have still lain dormant and useless in the bosom of the earth.[53]

This contributor essentially takes the view that readers get the newspapers and magazines they deserve – that periodicals by their very nature are a more reliable index of the cultural health of the nation than other types of publication because they quickly and constantly adapt to the true state of demand, whether in terms of the numbers of readers or the range of interests seeking mental sustenance. Given the evidence presented earlier in this chapter of publishers' foot-dragging approach to the mass market, this seems a very sanguine belief. It is true nonetheless that periodicals, for all their importance in mediating hostilities in a politically divided country, persisted in espousing grand Enlightenment ideals of progress through knowledge, education, and communication. An article in *The Bee* in 1791 compares their benefits with those of travel:

> What travelling, therefore, and a general acquaintance with mankind, is to man in his private capacity, writing in a periodical work, is to literary persons. . . . It is only when literary men mix with others, in a periodical publication, where liberty is permitted to every one to do what he thinks proper, on a footing of perfect equality, that they can properly feel their own weight, and be compelled to relinquish those ungracious self-sufficient tones, which the fancied superiority that every man is disposed to ascribe to himself, before he has experienced the powers of others, so naturally inspires.[54]

For this writer, truth is a negotiable and provisional quality, determined through a process of estrangement from one's habitual perceptions or mental surroundings. This faith in social dialogue came under great pressure in the Romantic period; but although the flow of conversation bears little resemblance by 1830 to the coffeehouse intimacies of pre-Revolutionary times, and although the industrialisation of society and the press was bringing further changes to author–reader relations, interaction would continue in a different key: writers and readers would continue to need each other and to use their best efforts to 'read' each other, even if this was no longer as citizens of the world but as producers and consumers of a commodified culture.

Notes

1. *Judging New Wealth: Popular Publishing and Responses to Commerce in England, 1750–1800* (Oxford, 1992), p. 35.

2. *Some Patterns and Trends in British Publishing 1800–1919* (London, 1994), pp. 109–11.

3. Figures cited in Henri-Jean Martin, *The History and Power of Writing*, trans. Lydia G. Cochrane (Chicago and London, 1994), pp. 414–15.

4. *The Periodical Press of Great Britain and Ireland: Or an Inquiry into the State of the Public Journals, Chiefly as Regards their Moral and Political Influence* (London, 1824), pp. 92–3.

5. *A History of British Publishing* (London and New York, 1988), pp. 82–3.

6. *The Bibliomania: Or, Book-Madness; Containing Some Account of the History, Symptoms and Cure of this Fatal Disease* (London, 1809), pp. 57–8.

7. *Memoirs of the First Forty-Five Years of the Life of James Lackington* (London, 1791), p. 227.

8. *The English Common Reader: A Social History of the Mass Reading Public 1800–1900* (Chicago and London, 1957), p. 52.

9. *The Minerva Press, 1790–1820* (London, 1939), p. 112.

10. Altick, *Common Reader*, p. 101.

11. *Common Reader*, p. 287.

12. Charles Knight, *Passages of a Working Life during Half a Century*, 3 vols (London, 1864), I, 234, 75, 236, 243, 276.

13. *History and Power*, p. 355.

14. *The Work of Writing: Literature and Social Change in Britain, 1700–1830* (Baltimore and London, 1998), pp. 181, 187.

15. ' "Events . . . have Made us a World of Readers": Reader Relations 1780–1830', in *The Penguin History of Literature, Vol. 5: The Romantic Period*, ed. David Pirie (London, 1994), pp. 1–48 (p. 48).

16. *Common Reader*, p. 49.

17. *Memoirs*, p. 255.

18. *Edinburgh Review*, 20 (1812), 280.

19. 'Literacy and Education in England 1640–1900', *Past and Present*, 42 (1969), 69–139 (p. 98).

20. Altick, *Common Reader*, pp. 141–2.

21. 'Literacy and Education', 78–9, 81.

22. *Passages*, I, 21.

23. *Common Reader*, p. 46.

24. *A History of Reading* (London, 1996), pp. 233–4.

25. From letters cited in E.P. Thompson, *The Making of the English Working Class*, 2nd edn (Harmondsworth, 1968), pp. 117–18.

26. *The Autobiography of Francis Place*, ed. Mary Thale (Cambridge, 1972), pp. 198–9.

27. *Common Reader*, p. 72.

28. 'What is the People?', in *The Complete Works of William Hazlitt*, ed. P.P. Howe, 21 vols (London and Toronto, 1930–4), VII (1932), 259–81 (p. 273).

29. *Autobiography*, pp. 222–3.

30. Cited in Raymond Irwin, *The English Library: Sources and History* (London, 1966), pp. 277–8.

31. Hilda M. Hamlyn, 'Eighteenth-Century Circulating Libraries in England', *The Library*, 5th Series, 1 (1947), 197–222 (p. 198).

32. 'Eighteenth-Century Circulating Libraries', 218.

33. *The Use of Circulating Libraries Considered; With Instructions for Opening and Conducting a Library, Either upon a Large or a Small Plan* (London, 1797), pp. 9, 11, 15.

34. *An Essay on Light Reading, as it May be Supposed to Influence Moral Conduct and Literary Taste* (London, 1808), pp. 2, 11–12, 17.

35. *British Publishing*, p. 26.

36. 'Publishers and Writers in Eighteenth-Century England', in *Books and their Readers in Eighteenth-Century England*, ed. Isobel Rivers (Leicester, 1982), pp. 5–25 (pp. 5–6).

37. *Extract from Mr Turner's Pamphlet on the Subject of Copyright* (London, 1813), p. 3.

38. *Judging New Wealth*, p. 60.

39. 'Women Readers, Women Writers', in *The Cambridge Companion to British Romanticism*, ed. Stuart Curran (Cambridge, 1993), pp. 177–95 (p. 179).

40. *The Economy of Literary Form: English Literature and the Industrialization of Publishing* (Baltimore and London, 1996), pp. 174, 176.

41. 'Essay, Supplementary to the Preface' (1815), in *The Prose Works of William Wordsworth*, ed. W.J.B. Owen and Jane Worthington Smyser, 3 vols (London, 1974), III, 84.

42. *Work of Writing*, p. 106.

43. *The Making of English Reading Audiences, 1790–1832* (Madison and London, 1987), ch. 1.

44. 'On the Advantages of Periodical Performances', *The Bee*, 1 (1791), 10–14 (p. 14).

45. 'Radical Print Culture in Periodical Form', in *Romanticism, History, and the Possibilities of Genre*, ed. Tilottama Rajan and Julia M. Wright (Cambridge, 1998), pp. 39–63 (p. 40).

46. *Periodical Press of Great Britain*, pp. 168, 170.

47. 'Culture's Medium: The Role of the Review', in *The Cambridge Companion to British Romanticism*, ed. Curran, pp. 120–47 (p. 136).

48. *English Literary Periodicals* (New York, 1930), pp. 248, 245.

49. Butler, 'Culture's Medium', p. 145.

50. *Common Reader*, p. 322.

51. *Periodical Press of Great Britain and Ireland*, pp. 26, 29.

52. *Travels During the Years 1787, 1788, and 1789* (Bury St Edmunds, 1792), p. 147.

53. 'On the Reciprocal Influence of the Periodical Publications and the Intellectual Progress of this Country', *Blackwood's Edinburgh Magazine*, 16 (1824), 522.

54. 'Further Remarks on the Utility of Periodical Performances', *The Bee*, 1 (1791), 170.

Chapter Four

Education and the Family

The theory and politics of education

For all their profound ideological differences, most educated observers in the Romantic period shared a belief in both the importance and the power of education – power not only to shape the minds and morals of individual children and adults, but also to influence the health of the wider society to which those individuals belonged. There was a belief that education could triumph over other, negative environmental factors, disproving the view that undesirable traits 'lay in the nature of the children, rather than the condition in which they were placed'.[1] Nowhere is this confidence in the socially progressive power of education more apparent than in the work of pioneer feminist, Catharine Macaulay, whose *Letters on Education* (1790) eloquently dismiss the idea of natural or innate character:

> There is not a wretch who ends his miserable being on a wheel, as the forfeit of his offences against society, who may not throw the whole blame of his misdemeanours on his education; who may not look up to the very government, by whose severe laws he is made to suffer, as the author of his misfortunes; and who may not with justice utter the hardest imprecations on those to whom the charge of his youth was entrusted, and to those with whom he associated in the early periods of his life.[2]

Macaulay asks why there is so little interest among parents in the education of their offspring, but there is plentiful evidence that education was indeed a topic of consuming interest, at least among the middle and upper classes. There was also an intense public concern with education as a force in strengthening – or presumably, if 'wrongly' directed, undermining – the social order: as interest mounted in the prevention, rather than punishment, of crime, soundly-principled education was seen by many as a way of combating a decline in social morality, or alternatively of tending the seeds of reform.

This belief in the power of education drew philosophical support both from the native British empirical tradition and the *philosophes* of the French Enlightenment. The two names most frequently cited in educational discourse of the period are John Locke and Jean-Jacques Rousseau. Locke's *Thoughts Concerning Education* (1693) had asserted that 'of all the men we meet with, nine parts of ten are what they are, good or evil, useful or not, by their education', and, while making necessary allowance for 'native propensities', referred to a small child as a 'white paper' on which ideas were imprinted:[3] by manipulating the power of association which Locke held to be the fundamental principle of mind, for example by applying praise or blame consistently to actions of various kinds, the parent or instructor had extraordinary influence over the child's future development. Locke's treatise was liberal and child-centred in a disconcertingly modern-looking way, notably in its insistence that education should be adapted at all stages to the understanding of the child, but also implied a striking degree of discipline and surveillance, to ensure that the environment which was so determinative of character was strictly controlled at all times.

These complementary libertarian and disciplinarian tendencies were reinforced in Rousseau's *Emile* (1762). For Rousseau, the child was not morally neutral (as in Locke's 'white paper' metaphor) but essentially innocent, and should be educated according to nature in isolation from corrupt social institutions. In practice, this entailed a still more severe supervision of the child's daily environment than Locke had prescribed, and methodical organisation of the child's learning according to Rousseau's rigid conception of three periods of development. The main subject of *Emile* was a boy, but its final Book concerned the education of his future wife, Sophie, who is allowed considerable liberty and more contact with society than Emile but whose upbringing is oriented entirely towards a life of subjection to the male.

The strong continuing influence of Locke's and Rousseau's ideas on education, in various combinations and interpretations, can be seen in most of the progressive educational writing of the Romantic period. A practical application of Locke and Rousseau for the middle-class parent was made by Maria Edgeworth and her father Richard Lovell Edgeworth, in their jointly-authored *Practical Education* (1798). Education is presented here as an experimental science (and Richard, with eighteen children from four marriages, had plenty of raw material at his disposal). The Edgeworths emphasise meticulous control of the child's environment to exclude all educationally unsound impressions and experiences. This leads them to prefer home- rather than school-based education, which leads in turn to a paranoia about possible contamination through the company of servants, who 'should not in any degree be permitted to interfere with the management of children, till their own education has been radically reformed'.[4] Other distinguishing features of their programme of 'rational' education are the principle that the content and method of teaching should be made to fit the child rather than the child being asked to fit into an adult curriculum; an emphasis on self-activity and the educational value of play; an equal stress on the culture of the heart to that of the understanding; a bias against discipline through force and towards the reward of praise ('emulation' is a principle beloved of theorists across the educational spectrum in this period); and a strong preference for useful knowledge and (what would now be called) transferable learning skills over the anachronistic irrelevancies of a classical education. The flavour of the book can be taken from the chapter on 'Books', which advises both a rigorous policing of the child's linguistic environment (for instance, declarative sentences which amount to statements of opinion rather than fact, such as 'Nobody wears a hat in the house', are debarred because they lay the foundation for 'prejudice' in the juvenile mind) and a stern selection of reading: 'Few books can safely be given to children without the previous use of the pen, the pencil, and the scissars', the Edgeworths assert, and certain genres like sentimental stories, adventure books, and poetry are to be introduced sparingly if at all.[5] This suspicion of imaginative literature (which comes partly from a preference for simple words linked to clear ideas, and partly from a fear of stimulating yearnings unlikely to be gratified in most walks of life) made rational education unpopular among many literary authors; nevertheless, the Edgeworths undoubtedly represent progressive educational orthodoxy in the period and their reputation and influence were considerable.

On the national political stage, however, concern was focused more on the plight of the masses than on the most appropriate form of tuition for the pampered offspring of upper-middle-class parents. The case for a national education system – including, for some campaigners, one that would be universal and compulsory – was first seriously made in this period. John Adamson says that at the end of the eighteenth century Britain was unusual in western Europe in its reluctance to accept that the state had any responsibility for the general education of its populace – a position no doubt inexplicable to many students today, but accounted for by a jealous regard for religious liberty and the dominant creed of individualism, which made people averse to public bodies taking responsibility in areas where it was thought individuals should provide for themselves.[6] Further grounds for resisting any major expansion of educational provision – which essentially meant the education of the lower classes – were nervousness about disturbing the social hierarchy and loosening class distinctions, a view that better popular education would lead to difficulties in filling the most menial and unrewarding jobs, hostility to higher taxation, and a post-Revolutionary fear of encouraging the poor to aspire beyond their station. Pioneer socialist Robert Owen's plan for a national system of non-sectarian education, put forward in his *New View of Society* (1816), fell on deaf ears for these reasons. But counter-arguments had increasing weight in public debate: in particular, it was difficult in a Protestant country, where the state religion laid such stress on understanding of the Scriptures, for some Christians to withhold from others the means of their own spiritual instruction; and the view that general education would enhance rather than weaken social (and industrial) discipline finally exorcised the spectre of popular revolt. A typically moderate case for reform was made by P. Colquhoun in 1806. Responding to information that in Westminster around a third of all children of school age were not receiving any kind of education, and were growing up 'in the grossest ignorance and profligacy', Colquhoun urges the necessity of legislative action: 'The prosperity of every state depends on the good habits, and the religious and moral instruction of the labouring people', he asserts, and this demands some training in literacy and the Bible for even the poorest children, provided that their minds are not elevated 'above the rank they are destined to fill in society'.[7] The case for popular education is here based on the resulting benefits to society as a whole, not to the disadvantaged individuals who might be given a better start in life, but at least the case was being made.

Primary education

Not only was there no national education system in England and Wales in the period, there was no *system* of any kind. (In Scotland, with its unique religious and political history, something approaching a national system had developed by the eighteenth century under the aegis of the Presbyterian Church.) Any study of educational provision in the late eighteenth and early nineteenth centuries reveals a confused mishmash of facilities, varying enormously in reach from county to county and town to town, chronically inefficient in its administration, and often of abominably low quality in terms of personnel and the content and method of teaching. These dismal observations apply most forcefully of all to primary (then called 'elementary') education, clearly the most important sector from the point of view of social justice.

It is not even possible unequivocally to distinguish a 'primary' education sector as such. Children of very different ages and levels of attainment were mixed in the same classes even in some of the more progressively-minded schools; indeed, it was not unusual for adults to be taught alongside children in some schools. However, given that most children would rarely attend school for more than two (often interrupted) years, and that few would remain in school after the age of ten, perhaps what primary education means in this context is a minimal programme of instruction aiming to impart the ability to read (after a fashion) and perhaps to write, some simple arithmetic, and a good dose of religious indoctrination.

At the bottom of the pile were the so-called 'dame schools' – run, as the term suggests, by elderly women who charged a weekly fee of a few pence, and described by H.C. Barnard as 'little more than baby-minding establishments'.[8] In the same bracket were the private day schools, again charging a small weekly fee, but staffed by schoolmasters who, in the words of one reformer, were often the 'refuse' of superior schools, or indeed of other employments, and whose 'drunkenness' was 'proverbial'.[9] Of a slightly higher standard were the charity schools found in many towns and villages, which took mainly day pupils but also some boarders. Their curriculum focused largely on reading and religious instruction, but extended to 'vocational' subjects such as spinning, sewing, gardening, and ploughing with a view to the likely destinations of their pupils as labourers and domestic servants. The existence of both Anglican and Nonconformist charity schools points to the 'religious divide' that was to continue to obstruct educational reform through the nineteenth century. This divide was institutionalised in the middle of the period by the establishment of rival national organisations: the Royal Lancasterian Association (1810; later renamed the British Foreign School Society), which supported elementary schools on a nondenominational basis, and the National Society for Promoting the Education of the Poor in the Principles of the Established Church (1811). Both associations pioneered the introduction of training schools for teachers.

Also in the business of providing free education were the Sunday schools, which had two hundred and fifty thousand pupils by 1787 and over a million (many of them adults) by 1831. Staffed largely by volunteers, their aims were religious and philanthropic, with a curriculum again dominated by reading and Bible study – the former taught largely through, and as a preparation for, the latter. Most were attached either to the Church of England or to one of the Dissenting groups, intensifying the religious turf war. Their popularity owed much to the fact that attendance on Sundays would not deprive employers of their child labour, and they attracted many adults for the same reason. Of a very different complexion were the so-called 'schools of industry', which had the apparent aim of clawing back some economic gain from the children of families in receipt of poor relief, and which in some parishes were incorporated with workhouses. Reading, and even religious instruction, took second place in these establishments to the teaching of such skills as spinning, knitting, sewing, cobbling, and gardening, and the profits of the children's labour were used to pay the expenses of the schools. The fact that adult paupers were frequently mixed with the children, and sometimes used as their teachers, gives a measure of the quality of these schools.

Within the higher social classes, it seems to have been more common for girls than for boys to be educated at home – presumably in order to practise closer moral supervision. Girls who were sent to one of the more prestigious female academies spent much of their time acquiring fashionable accomplishments such as drawing, singing, dancing, and embroidery; even the broad, rational curriculum advocated by the leading Nonconformist, Erasmus Darwin, was subordinated to the cultivation of a female character with 'mild and retiring virtues rather than the bold and dazzling ones'.[10] The segregated girls' classes in charity schools had a rather different bill of fare, in keeping with the religious and social agendas they were pursuing. A large free school in Westminster operating the monitorial system (see below) included needlework 'and other *suitable female employments*' in its provision for girls, because its main object was 'to fit them for domestic situations, and to make them good servants, by fortifying their minds against those vices to which they are more particularly exposed – to guard them against seduction, and to impress upon their minds the utmost horror of a state of female prostitution'.[11]

What this rapid survey of primary education demonstrates above all is the extent to which the Church had a stranglehold on the provision of this social good, with opposition coming mainly not from secular reformers but from the Dissenting community. In 1807 an ambitious scheme was presented to Parliament for a national system of parochial schools, but was defeated in the House of Lords because it was insufficiently biased towards the religious establishment. On the other hand, a system more comprehensively under Anglican control would have been unacceptable to Nonconformists and Catholics, so Henry Brougham's Parish Schools Bill of 1820, which proposed a national school system supported from the rates in which the schoolmasters would be members of the Church of England, was eventually withdrawn in deference to the Dissenting lobby. It was not until the political map had altered with the passing of the Reform Bill in 1832 that the first decisive steps towards state control of education were taken.

In terms of the primary curriculum and teaching methods the period's most progressive initiatives were generally small-scale or confined to domestic tuition. In the area of formal schooling, the incorporation of more and more lower-middle-class and lower-class children entailed a shift towards increasingly authoritarian and disciplinary teaching methods. In particular, the catechistic method, a form of repetitive (and competitive) drilling with the stress on religious and moral indoctrination, became entrenched in the Sunday schools, charity schools, the new monitorial schools, and beyond. With the teacher putting the same questions to each child, and punishing any marked deviation from the ideal answers by lowering the pupil's rank within the class, the catechistic method has the superficial appearance of dialogue, but in reality was an effective means of bludgeoning children into mental submission.

The monitorial (or Madras) system is perhaps the most celebrated (or notorious) educational innovation of the period. This system, which had as much to do with school organisation as with teaching methods, was developed independently by Andrew Bell, at a school for the half-caste children of British soldiers in Madras, and Joseph Lancaster, at a school in Southwark that became one of the 'sights' of London. Essentially, it was a way of teaching large numbers of children at very low cost by using the pupils themselves as teachers ('monitors'): by means of a closely-superintended hierarchy of monitors and assistants, each of whom knew only as much as they needed to know and were generally no more than a few steps ahead of the pupils they taught, it was possible for two hundred pupils to be managed by a single schoolmaster – whose enviable job was, in the words of one admirer of the system, 'to see that others work, rather than work themselves'.[12] The principle of emulation was central to the operation of the system: classes were graded according to ability, the rank-order of pupils in each class was constantly changing, complicated reward schemes (involving not only marks of esteem but also material prizes) were in place, elevation from one class to the next brought rewards for both pupil and monitor, and pupils had the additional incentive of striving to become monitors themselves. Closer examination of the system reveals that all subjects were taught by mechanical methods of rote-learning that make the frequent comparisons with industrial processes and shop-floor discipline perfectly appropriate. Textbooks suitable for young children were, it needs saying, virtually non-existent at this time.

There were positive aspects of the monitorial system. Both Bell and Lancaster, for example, were firmly against corporal punishment and the rule of force, preferring a disciplinary regime based on public esteem and disapprobation. Neither pioneer was the heartless Gradgrind of many hostile caricatures: Lancaster writes of his guiding belief that children are 'rational and intelligent beings, with minds capable of expansion, and talents formed for usefulness', and Bell sets great store by getting children to see him as 'their friend, their benefactor, their guide, and their parent', who has their own interests at heart.[13] And the monitorial system at least showed that popular education on a national scale was economically feasible, at a time when the necessity of state control of, and investment in, education was far from universally accepted. Nevertheless, its serious flaws – most obviously, that badly-taught children were bad teachers, and that bright children had their own progress retarded by acting as monitors all the time – were all too apparent to the first generation of school inspectors in the 1840s, and from a modern standpoint it is ironic that the system solved the problem of schools taking children away from the factories by turning schools into factories themselves.

Secondary education

Secondary education in the Romantic period was very much a class-based commodity. When a substantial proportion of the juvenile population was not receiving any schooling at all, clearly it was only the sons (and perhaps the daughters) of the aristocracy, the gentry, and, increasingly, the professional and commercial middle classes who stood to benefit from any kind of secondary education. As Philippe Ariès says in his classic sociological study of childhood, secondary education is a long-drawn-out affair, and until legislation made it compulsory there was no room in the system 'for those who, on account of their station in life, their parents' profession, or their financial circumstances, could neither follow it through, nor intend to follow it through, to the end'.[14]

At the top of the secondary educational apex in this period were the endowed grammar schools, and, within that group, the smaller number of richly endowed and socially exclusive institutions better known as 'public schools'. Strictly speaking, all these schools existed for the purpose of teaching the classical languages, which dominated the curriculum; in the case of many local grammar schools there was no demand for such a massive concentration on the classics, but a legal ruling in 1805 that the schools' endowments could be put to no other purpose meant that a more modern programme of studies could only be added on a fee-paying basis. Given the unrelenting diet of Latin and Greek, which for many boys was reinforced by their career in higher education, it is not surprising that so much written and oral discourse of the period is peppered with quotations from classical authors, forming an impenetrable barrier to those excluded by class or gender from the top stream. Almost inevitably, considering the general tenor of the times, the grammar school attracted an increasing amount of criticism, especially from Dissenters for whom the endowed schools' close affiliation with the Church of England presented obvious difficulties. One of their most vigorous critics was Sydney Smith, who attacked the 'elegant imbecility' produced by the abuse of classical learning in one of an occasional series of essays on education published in the *Edinburgh Review*. Smith approves of the study of Latin and Greek for whatever residual utility they possess, but is in no doubt that for a boy's education to be confined to these subjects from the age of six or seven to twenty-three or twenty-four is an unmitigated disaster:

> he has scarcely a notion that there is any other kind of excellence; and the great system of facts with which he is the most perfectly acquainted, are the intrigues of

the Heathen Gods: with whom Pan slept? – with whom Jupiter? – whom Apollo ravished? These facts the English youth get by heart the moment they quit the nursery; and are most sedulously and industriously instructed in them till the best and most active part of life is passed away.[15]

Although it might be supposed that the Anglican hegemony in grammar school education would ensure some resistance to the heads of 'English youth' being filled with such pagan nonsense, Smith argues that the system's inertia derives from fear on the part of the clergy that other kinds of mental activity will lead to religious scepticism.

Opposition to the classical monopoly did produce change in some quarters: in many of the less prestigious schools a modern curriculum was introduced in the face of law and tradition. But this was only one way in which the grammar schools were perceived to be straying from their original mission: a major source of concern was the trend away from free education of poor children from the local area (the 'foundationers') towards recruitment of boarders (bringing in extra income) from the wealthier classes from all parts of the country. Criticism was also made of boarding arrangements, disciplinary regimes, and moral standards. Here the major public schools, which were often severely under-staffed, came under particularly severe attack. Such schools were typically governed by force rather than consent, provoking occasional rebellions among the inmates: in 1793, perhaps inspired by news from Jacobin France, pupils occupied College buildings at Winchester for two days, while in 1797 boys at Rugby made their point by blowing off the door of the headmaster's study with gunpowder.[16] In another of his articles, Sydney Smith complained that bullying and 'fagging', along with the harsh corporal punishment, meant that every schoolboy was alternately a slave and a tyrant, and that this was no satisfactory preparation for life. As for moral standards, Smith was one of many who feared the consequences of leaving boys to their own devices outside class time: countering the argument that public schools performed a useful service in permitting young men to let off steam before the age at which such tendencies could become harmful, he declares that if the schools 'only prevent men from being corrupted by the world, by corrupting them before their entry into the world, they can then only be looked upon as evils of the greatest magnitude'.[17]

The alternative to a public or grammar school education was a private school, an option favoured by many parents in the professional and commercial classes because the curriculum was more obviously 'useful' or vocational: English grammar and history, mathematics, geography, and a science like chemistry might be supplemented by subjects like navigation, surveying, or bookkeeping, with extras like music, art, dancing, and fencing available. The schools varied widely in size and the age range of their pupils, and the distinction between primary and secondary education breaks down in this area. Most were single-sex, or at the very least segregated, but it was in such establishments that girls, excluded from the endowed schools, were provided with an education if their parents declined the 'domestic' route. The curriculum for girls, inevitably, leaned towards 'accomplishments' and social deportment rather than the work-oriented subjects offered to boys. The quality of private schools varied a lot, but in J.H. Plumb's account competition and the entrepreneurial spirit seem on the whole to have had positive effects: parents had to be attracted to schools, and school advertisements highlighted curricula adapted to future careers or marriageability, along with facilities such as playgrounds, libraries, and musical equipment. In Plumb's view, children 'had become counters in the parents' social aspirations; their son's or daughter's education reflected status',[18] and the dependence of private schools on their reputation for custom must have entailed some attention to standards of care and tuition.

One example of a progressive spirit in the private sector was Hazelwood School, opened in 1819 by Rowland Hill and Matthew Davenport Hill. The school consisted of around a hundred and twenty boys, divided into eight classes each with its own room. The curriculum was modern and broad, with Latin and Greek given no more than an equal allocation of time with subjects like French, geography, and gymnastics. The Hills were keen on promoting a spirit of emulation, and operated a reward system of baffling complexity. Some of the school's customs were bizarre, such as the practice of marching the boys from one class to another to music, but its most radical feature was its highly developed system of pupil self-government, whereby an elected committee of boys was responsible for debating and enacting the laws of the school and managing its budget, and a Jury-Court (modelled on a criminal court) 'tried' fellow-pupils for crimes such as truancy, falsehood, and petty dishonesty. Such practices were highly unorthodox and anomalous in their time, and indeed remain so today, though the Hills' emphasis on active, participative learning has long since become educational cliché.

Higher and adult education

If secondary education was exclusive, this was as nothing compared to the elitism of Oxford and Cambridge, at the beginning of the Romantic period the only two universities in England. The collegiate character of these institutions, whereby each college was a small, self-contained residential unit, with the emphasis on personal interaction between individual students and tutors keenly interested in the formation of character, meant that annual intakes at each university were under five hundred students. Like the grammar schools, the Oxbridge colleges were endowed originally primarily for the benefit of poor students, but in a similar way had evolved to the point where the majority of students were fee-paying sons of respectable families; students of aristocratic birth, moreover, were distinguished from the less well-heeled by embroidered silk gowns and by their exemption from exams. Although Oxford and Cambridge were no longer as exclusively concerned as they once had been with the education of the next generation of clergymen, this was still an important part of their function; in addition, the government of both universities was 'in the hands of a clerical oligarchy',[19] graduation was impossible for those not prepared to take an oath of allegiance to the Church of England, and religion was the underlying principle of all the universities' ancient customs and practices. In light of this, it might seem odd that at Oxford the curriculum was dominated by classics, while at Cambridge theoretical mathematics occupied most of the diligent student's time. Examination arrangements were remote from those of the present day: despite reforms at both universities in the direction of written exams in the last quarter of the eighteenth century, oral examination, in the form of highly artificial disputations (conducted in Latin) between 'respondents' and 'opponents', continued to play an important part well into the next century.

Many of these aspects of Oxbridge came in for serious criticism in the period. Dissenters, who were barred from obtaining degrees that were passports to lucrative offices in Church and State, were prominent in calling for change, and the *Edinburgh Review* extended its attack on the grammar schools to the institutions of higher education. Even a pillar of the system like Samuel Butler, whose Shrewsbury pupils 'swept the board in the scholarship and honours examinations at Oxford and Cambridge',[20] argued vigorously against an outdated system. Butler claimed the mathematics pursued at Cambridge was too speculative, while classics was heavily biased towards pedantically complex prosodic analysis of poets and dramatists. Comparing the talents of Cambridge honours graduates unfavourably with those of a land-surveyor or civil engineer, he asserted that a university should be 'a society of students in all the liberal arts and sciences'.[21] By the time Butler was writing, in 1822, there was a growing feeling that the strengthening of the examination system, which had begun with the introduction of written papers at Cambridge in 1780 and Oxford in 1800, had gone too far, and that 'Students' intellectual interests were being narrowed and only what would "pay" in the examination secured their attention'.[22] For some, however, reform had not gone far enough, with the persistent use of time-consuming and confrontational public viva voce exams a major bone of contention.

The statutes and customs of the universities, widely perceived as either obsolete or inadequately enforced, and the general air of moral depravity surrounding the lives of both staff and students, also caused increasing concern. Compulsory daily attendance at chapel, supposedly a key instrument of college discipline, was rendered ineffectual by the careless and irreverent manner in which the services were conducted. In an open letter to the Chancellor of Oxford in 1789, Vicesimus Knox demanded action to enforce discipline, raise the residency requirement, clamp down on student debt, and, among other things, prohibit the 'keeping of horses and dogs'; a whole raft of measures was needed to restore the 'national lustre' of the University, 'deeply incrusted by the rust of time'.[23] Another revealing document is John Berkenhaut's published *Letters* (1790) to a son at Cambridge. The author warns his son against drinking to excess and making the wrong choice of companions: he should not consort with social superiors with large allowances and a leaning towards 'frivolous and vicious indulgences'. Alluding to the notorious undergraduate fondness for horse racing and gambling, he invites his son to compare the horses at Newmarket to the men – to the detriment of the latter.[24] The general tenor of public and parental concern in the period lends support to the brutal summary of one recent educational historian:

> At the beginning of the nineteenth century, when Humboldt was organizing the University of Berlin under new principles and Napoleon was casting the unitary national university in France, the two (and the only) institutions of higher education in England and Wales were in a deep slumber.[25]

There were, however, alternatives available. To begin with, there were the four ancient Scottish universities: St Andrews, Aberdeen, Glasgow, and Edinburgh. Just as Scotland was far ahead of England and Wales in elementary education, so it was more progressive at the higher level, introducing a cadre of specialised professors, lecture programmes, and a departmental rather than collegiate organisation long before these became features of the English system. For Nonconformist parents who sought a university-level education for their sons, the more obvious route was the Dissenting academies, which existed to remedy the civil disabilities suffered by Dissenters and, specifically, to train young men for the ministry. The academies straddled the worlds of secondary and higher education, with a four-year course said to have comprised the best education available in England. Their curriculum was broad and modern, concentrating on the sciences, humanities, and modern languages, and used English rather than Latin as the medium of instruction; they endorsed freedom of thought and opinion, and provided a range of vocational and academic courses suitable for diverse middle-class destinations in life. Finally, towards the end of the period the landscape of higher education in England was changed with the establishment of the University of London. This began with the opening in 1828 of a college in Gower Street (later to become University College), with a secular constitution, annual fees a fraction of those at Oxford or Cambridge, and a curriculum biased towards modern studies and vocational subjects, notably medicine; in rapid response followed the establishment of King's College in the Strand in 1831, aimed at combining useful knowledge with a solid grounding in Christian theology and ethics (but including also in its syllabus, it is worth mentioning, 'English literature'). Rivalry was eventually smoothed over by the chartering in 1836 of an umbrella institution, the University of London, with degree-awarding powers.

It was under the mantle of the University of London that one of the most notable developments in working-class adult education of the period was eventually to reside, with the establishment of Birkbeck College. This began life in 1823 as the London Mechanics' Institution, which was itself modelled on a similar venture in Glasgow, where George Birkbeck had offered lectures on science to local artisans before moving to London to practise medicine. Birkbeck collaborated with Henry Brougham and others in founding the London Institute, which was soon copied in many other towns and cities. By mid-century, however, the institutes had become more middle-class in composition and orientation, with a programme less geared towards technical and vocational instruction and more towards social recreation. To some extent this reflected tensions present from the beginning: Brougham, in his much-reprinted *Practical Observations upon the Education of the People*, declared that 'the people themselves must be the great agents in accomplishing the work of their own instruction',[26] but this belief in working-class self-determination was tempered by a perceived need for middle-class patrons to exert a strong influence on the initial direction of the institutes. This in turn was one symptom of what Alan Richardson describes as the 'ill-defined but vigorous struggle' in the 1820s and 1830s 'over who should control the provision of education and reading material for the lower classes': the state, the Church, or the workers themselves.[27]

For the demand for improved educational opportunities for adults came from a variety of sources, each with a distinctive agenda: from working people themselves, stimulated by the great political debates of the period to seek greater mental empowerment through cooperative activities like book clubs and mutual improvement societies; from industrialists, who saw that a better-educated workforce would be a more productive one, provided this education did not make its recipients dissatisfied with their station in life; from the Church, its satellite organisations and rival Nonconformist bodies, which pro-moted basic literacy and Bible-reading, in paternalistic ventures like rural night schools and Sunday schools; by politicians, persuaded that social order would be more effectively maintained by managing and directing the new literacy rather than repressing it. This diversity of interests demonstrates the difficulty in treating adult education as an adjunct to another form of provision. It could equally well be handled within a discussion of primary education, since another reason for the decline of the mechanics' institutes was that the workers for whom they were intended had not received the elementary education that would form an adequate foundation for more technical studies. Perhaps what needs emphasising is the way discourse on adult education (as with popular education at all levels) was gradually reshaped during the period, abandoning the heavy stress on Christian duty and social subordination and pressing instead the virtues of self-motivation and rational consent. However, the infantilising approach that was discarded in relation to working-class men continued to be applied to other subordinated groups: to the colonised peoples of the expanding empire, and, nearer to home, to women – a subject that warrants separate discussion.

Female education

Female education is a suitable bridge between an examination of educational opportunities and a discussion of other issues relating to the domestic sphere, because it was precisely in this area that education was most thoroughly domesticated. For parents in the middle and upper classes who had money to spend on their children's education, there was a broad consensus that the 'private' rather than 'public' route was more advisable for daughters: the latter were thought to require the close moral superintendence of their mothers to a greater degree than sons, and were more susceptible to the wrong kinds of influence from social inferiors in boarding schools, while the competitive rivalry of a society of peers, which some put forward as a leading advantage of 'public' education, was considered more likely to breed undesirable feelings of pride and jealousy in girls.

There was no question that girls, wherever educated, were being prepared exclusively for their future roles of wives and mothers. In this regard, the different arrangement of Thomas Gisborne's two popular conduct books for men and women is revealing. *An Enquiry into the Duties of Men* (1795) tackles 'the upper and middle classes of the inhabitants of this country according to the several ranks, professions, and employments into which they are distributed',[28] but *An Enquiry into the Duties of the Female Sex* (1797) starts from the premise that marriage is the one factor that separates women into two 'classes' and determines their respective duties. Allowing for this ineluctable destiny, Gisborne's advice is typical of liberal conservative thinking on the subject of female education, emphasising the inculcation of right principles on a sound religious basis: having nursed her daughters and nipped in the bud 'the first shoots of caprice, obstinacy, and passion', a mother's prime duty is to instruct them in the doctrines of Christianity.[29] However, this is to be done in such a way as to secure independent conviction of their truth and value, since Gisborne supports the ideas of rationalist educators so far as improving the 'reasoning powers' of girls and providing more 'useful and interesting' knowledge are concerned. It is a line of argument shared by, for example, Hannah More, who states bluntly that the 'profession' of women is that of daughters, wives, and mothers, and they should therefore be educated 'with a view to these several conditions, and be furnished with a stock of ideas, and principles, and qualifications, and habits, ready to be applied and appropriated, as occasion may demand, to each of these respective situations'.[30]

One thing on which all writers on female education in the period, radical to conservative, were agreed was the danger of dedicating too much time and attention to fashionable accomplishments. More applies herself at length to the 'Phrenzy of accomplishments' she sees as having spread downwards from the aristocracy to the middle orders of society, even to the daughters of tradesmen and farmers; she deplores this 'revolution' in middle-class manners – a phrase that ironically recalls Mary Wollstonecraft's advocacy of a very different kind of transformation in female education – as having 'altered the character of the age' (pp. 69–70). She derides the whole shallow pursuit of accomplishments as a machinery for overcoming the tediousness of time, and asks how young women will cope with the tediousness of eternity. Insofar as there was a social rationale for this focus on accomplishments, it had to do with improving the exchange value of young women in the contemporary marriage market. In another of its series of essays on education, the *Edinburgh Review* ridicules the current state of affairs on the grounds that accomplishments are useless after the first few years of adult life (spent capturing a husband), and mocks 'hanging the understanding of a woman upon walls, or hearing it vibrate upon strings'. Its progressive position is that rationally educated women will be more equal to the heavy responsibility of educating children in the early years of life, will make better wives once marriage has become 'an intercourse of understanding as well as of affection', and will have other contributions to make to society once half the talent in the universe no longer runs to waste.[31]

While writers across the ideological divide could find common cause in the critique of accomplishments, they parted company on the subject of the female character that it was the business of education to mould and refine, and on the practical and institutional reforms that might be necessary. Here the views of more conservative writers have to be seen not simply as a defence of the status quo but as symptoms of a backlash against new thinking, on matters of gender as on everything else, in the wake of the French Revolution. The traditional view was that women's subjection to men was dictated by nature (inferior strength and the need for protection in childbearing) and confirmed by social arrangements which gave men all the laborious offices of life; hence female education should concentrate on how best to please and serve men at all times. In addition, women's unequal responsibility for the legitimacy of offspring (and thus the secure transmission of property) put a premium on chastity. The ideal female character was therefore one that contrived simultaneously to be sexually pleasing to the opposite sex but also modest, passive, and retiring. In an exceptionally strident conduct book pronouncement, arch-conservative novelist and propagandist Jane West accepts the basis of this sexual character, which governs women's relations to fathers, brothers, husbands, and indeed all men except servants and tradesmen, and puts the alleged widespread desertion of modesty, diligence, and self-denial among middle-class women in a wider context:

> in most of the realms that have been overcome by the arms of France, a notorious dereliction of female principle prevailed; and the state of manners in France itself, as far as related to our sex, had obtained such dreadful publicity, as allows us to ascribe the fall of that country in a great measure to the dissipated indelicate behaviour and loose morals of its women. Thus, though we are not entitled to a place in the senate, we become *legislators* in the most important sense of the word.[32]

This astonishing series of observations can hardly be taken seriously as historical analysis, but its designation of women as moral legislators for society at large underlines the complexity of the development whereby women's confinement to the domestic sphere gave them a new cultural authority, on the one hand, but at the cost of excluding them from other kinds of social participation, on the other. In giving the disciplining of female subjectivity a significance extending far beyond the home, it also suggests strongly that the conduct books were responding to a perceived crisis in sexual behaviour that was associated with larger threats to the social order.

More radical perspectives on female education could, however, be found. With the rising prestige of progressive, rationalist educational thought in the Locke–Rousseau tradition, early feminist thinkers were quick to draw from theories of the environmental determination of character the obvious conclusions regarding the ideal woman projected by conduct-book orthodoxy. Catharine Macaulay argues passionately for giving boys and girls the same education, denouncing the 'false idea of female excellence' that leads to the enfeeblement of girls' bodies (through severe restraints on physical activity) and minds (through the denial of a proper course of rational education):

> and what with the vigilance of those who are appointed to superintend her conduct, and the false bias they have imposed on her mind, every vigorous exertion is suppressed, the mind and body yield to the tyranny of error, and Nature is charged with all those imperfections which we alone owe to the blunders of art.

For Macaulay, educating the sexes alike would break down artificially produced differences in physical and mental aptitudes, and educating them together would accustom them to each other's company and provide for less romantically idealised, more rationally based relationships 'at the age of desire'.[33] Mary Wollstonecraft follows Macaulay in many respects, insisting on the social construction of femininity, on the rational equality of creatures deemed in law and religion accountable for their conduct, and on the indefensibility of keeping women charged with the care and education of children 'in a state of childhood' themselves. However, Wollstonecraft goes further than Macaulay in linking gender oppression to an entire patriarchal social and political order ('The *divine right* of husbands, like the divine right of kings, may, it is to be hoped, in this enlightened age, be contested without danger'); she makes a more comprehensive assault on the ideal of chastity and the sexual double standard; and she is bolder in demanding access for women – at least those of a 'superior cast' – to a wider range of career paths, to give them 'a civil existence in the State'. Because of the interdependency of the whole system of oppression and the power of popular opinion, she sees little hope from reforming the private education of daughters; instead, she proposes a national system of coeducational day schools where boys and girls, rich and poor, would be taught together between the ages of five and nine, after which they would be separated into academic and vocational tracks.[34] As Anne Mellor notes, Wollstonecraft defended female equality, but in arguing that better-educated women would make 'better mothers' and 'more interesting wives' she also made a calculated appeal 'to male self-interest'.[35]

During the long war against Revolutionary and Napoleonic France that began not long after the publication of Wollstonecraft's *Vindication*, the general climate of opinion became reactionary. Elizabeth Hamilton, notably, reasserted the social explanation of women's apparent deficiencies in mental powers, even using the same provocative comparison of British women with those in Eastern harems that Wollstonecraft had deployed: 'Experience shews us daily examples of the fatal consequences of carrying the system of *zenana* education into practice, in a country where women are called to act an important part on the theatre of society [the care of young children].'[36] In the main, though, radical thinking on female education had a rough ride, and the field was shared between extreme conservatives like More and West, and moderate reformers like Gisborne, Erasmus Darwin, John Aikin, and Sydney Smith. The language of rights was largely succeeded by a language of duties and responsibility. Smith contended that the benefits of equalising educational opportunities for women would be felt in more companionable marriages and better childcare, scorning the proposition that the 'perpetual solicitude which a mother feels for her children, depends upon her ignorance of Greek and mathematics; and that she would desert an infant for a quadratic equation'; Darwin advocated an impressively broad curriculum for young women within a framework set by conventional notions of female character; while Aikin, advising his son (in a very male-centred discourse) on the choice of a wife, praised energy of body and mind in potential mates, and supported educating boys and girls to a similarity of character – 'virtue, wisdom, presence of mind, patience, vigour, capacity, and application' – rather than sexual qualities.[37] This subordination of questions of women's natural rights to considerations of reforming marriage in the direction of closer affective relationships is typical of liberal (often Nonconformist or evangelical) discourse on female education in the war years; it links logically to a broader discussion of love and marriage in the period.

Courtship and marriage

The logical destiny for which education prepared young women was marriage and household management. Consequently, within those social strata that produced and consumed the conduct manuals, novels of manners, and other texts in which such issues featured prominently, marriage choice was a topic of lively debate throughout the period. The question of the relative distribution of power between parents and children in spouse selection was important, but less so, in the conduct literature, than the question of what considerations should be paramount in choosing a husband or wife. Lawrence Stone identifies four possible motives of marriage choice in early modern England: the 'economic or social or political consolidation or aggrandizement of the family', personal affection and companionship, physical attraction (often subject to pre-marital experimentation among those of very high or low rank), and 'romantic love as portrayed in fiction and on the stage'.[38] In his view, between 1660 and 1800 the emphasis had shifted from the first to the second of these criteria, along with a shift in the balance of power in decision-making towards children; while towards the very end of the eighteenth century romantic love, the product of learned cultural expectations, also (ominously) became acceptable as a basis for marriage. There is certainly supporting evidence for this analysis in the conduct literature, where there is constant emphasis on the need to think in terms of long-term compatibility, coupled with dire warnings against overvaluing physical attributes and being misled by foolish notions of love derived from circulating library fiction. Thomas Gisborne recommends nearness in age, similarity of disposition, and solid affection for a successful marriage, and cautions women that neglecting the 'moral character' of potential husbands makes an alliance 'a very hazardous experiment'. He expresses alarm that romantic novels create a 'premature warmth of tender emotions' that leads women into inappropriate and unhappy marriages, while the earnestness with which he attacks the priority accorded to 'interest' and 'ambition' in evaluating a 'good match' suggests that the whole issue of spouse selection was confused and contested.[39] John Aikin confirms this, in setting out his views 'On the Choice of a Wife', by observing that advice on this topic usually produces the least effect. He downplays 'personal charms' and identifies a range of qualities – good sense, even temperament, energy of body and mind – that equip the ideal wife for her chief roles of 'companion' and 'helper'. The adversarial nature of Aikin's argument, and his equivocation on considerations of family and fortune ('extraneous' to the real concerns of character, yet still to be treated with 'common prudence'), give the strong impression that this is a live cultural debate.[40] Greater equality of opportunity in education, and a closer, shared upbringing for boys and girls, are seen by some commentators, such as Catharine Macaulay, as vital groundwork for rational marriage choices in later life.

At the same time as debate was raging over conflicting criteria in marriage choice, parents were relinquishing the right they had previously assumed to play the leading role in decision-making, or at least were showing greater respect than formerly for the independent preferences of their children. The pace at which this change in attitudes occurred seems to have varied considerably between different social classes, and no doubt varied considerably between individual families within the same class, but a good rule of thumb, in Michael Anderson's words, is that 'whenever and wherever parents have controlled resources vital to their children's future standard of living they have been able to influence strongly their children's choice of spouses'.[41] In practice this meant that in the upper-middle and landed classes, and in traditional rural communities where small plots of land were still passed from one generation to the next, parents continued to exercise their authority, whereas in the lower-middle and wage-earning classes parental power was withering away. However, in the wealthier classes parents were now more likely to secure the desired outcome through consent rather than enforced obedience, using closer and more affectionate relations with their children to convince the latter that it was their future happiness they were chiefly concerned for. Complete freedom of choice was in any case something of an illusion, since the very structure of social life ensured that young people in the middle and upper classes only came into contact with potential partners from within acceptable social limits. Ultimately, it was only to be expected that most young people would internalise the values of their parents and peer groups and form relationships with social, if not intellectual, equals.

It would be wrong to suppose that the increasing freedom of children to determine their own marital destinies led inevitably to earlier marriages. The mean age of marriage remained high throughout the period, falling only from around twenty-six to twenty-five for men and from around twenty-five to twenty-three for women, though variations between different communities and socioeconomic groups were considerable. This pattern of late marriage, which according to Anderson is unique in world history, may well have served human happiness by ensuring greater emotional maturity among the couples concerned, but seems to have been linked to practical, financial considerations, coupled with the peculiar British custom of setting up house on one's own immediately after marriage. The legal framework for marriage in the period had been set by the Marriage Act of 1753, which terminated the rights of betrothal (the exchange of oral promises before witnesses, considered binding for life) and outlawed clandestine marriages and marriages entered into without parental consent by persons under twenty-one. 'After 1754', John Gillis summarises, 'no vow other than that made in the Church of England, Quaker Meetings, or a Jewish Synagogue had any legal standing as marriage', despite protests that this would consolidate the power of the wealthy, obstruct marriage among the poor, and be detrimental to women by abolishing the binding character of precontracts. The Act was a major step forward in the secularisation of marriage, laying stress on bureaucratic regulation rather than sacramental significance. However, as Gillis also argues, among lower socio-economic groups the clampdown intended by the Marriage Act had less purchase, and young people continued 'making marriages in their own way, regardless of the laws of church and state':[42] thus there was a sharp rise in the number of common-law unions in the late eighteenth and early nineteenth centuries, correlating with equally marked increases in prenuptial concep-tions and illegitimate births. And just as marriage might take different forms depending on one's position in the social scale, so the options for ending an unsatisfactory relationship varied considerably. Divorce was virtually imposs-ible, except by private Act of Parliament for the very wealthiest members of society, but at the bottom end of the scale, desertion, bigamy, or the contro-versial custom of 'wife-sale' were alternative ways out. For the vast majority, marriage had to be regarded as a lifelong commitment.

One social trend that attracted comment in the late eighteenth and early nineteenth centuries was the practice of newlyweds taking a holiday alone together immediately after marriage; previously the couple had had very little privacy, even on the wedding night, which was characterised by boisterous public rituals at both ends of the social spectrum. Thus was invented the modern 'honeymoon', a word first used in this sense around 1800. It is one symptom of a broad shift that was taking place from one type of family and marital relationship to another: in Michael Anderson's version, it was a move away from a 'relatively emotionless, open, undifferentiated and patriarchal family' towards 'increasing differentiation of the conjugal family as a discrete and private social unit and . . . a growing emphasis on individual autonomy and rights'.[43] Whereas in previous centuries the structures of social life had made solitude or intimacy difficult to attain, in the eighteenth century the rearrange-ment of houses in the wealthier classes (including the introduction of corridors to separate off individual rooms, the confinement of beds to bedrooms, and the greater isolation of servants' quarters) were signs of a movement towards greater privacy, as were changes in visiting habits (calling unannounced was no longer acceptable), eating habits (the invention of the dumb waiter meant that families could dine without the intrusive presence of servants), and forms of address (less deference and subordination between husband and wife, and parents and children). By the end of the century, the formation of the modern nuclear family, with its emphasis on emotional ties among family members, was well advanced.

The ascendancy of what Stone calls the 'companionate marriage', which privileged the pursuit of mutual happiness over the maintenance of property and status, and for some commentators entailed a more liberated approach to sex, is well reflected in the literature and advice books of the period. Gisborne again represents a middle-of-the-road position. He asserts that some degree of subordination on the part of the wife is necessary, but lays equal stress on arguments from Scripture teaching the love and tenderness due from husband to wife; indeed, it is by his affectionate inclination 'to study every reasonable and prudent indulgence' of his wife's wishes, and by accustoming himself 'to dwell rather on her merits than on her imperfections', that the husband wins influence over her. In return, it is the role of the wife to make the conjugal home a haven from the rough-and-tumble of the working environment in which she has no place: 'her unaffected mildness, her ingenuous tenderness, place before [her husband's] mind a forcible contrast to the violence, the artifice, the unfeeling selfishness which he witnesses in his commerce with the world.'[44] It is Gisborne's use of the same vocabulary – 'mildness', 'tenderness' – in respect of both male and female behaviour that perfectly captures the sentimental character of the companionate marriage, the growing normalisation of which amounted to a remarkable transformation in sexual relations.

It was, however, a 'revolution' in personal relations and family life that was severely tested by the more public and conspicuous Revolution in France and the wars that followed. As in so many other areas of British life, the Revolution produced a backlash against the liberalising and modernising tendencies in family relationships – encouraging, in Stone's words, 'a strong revival of moral reform, paternal authority and sexual repression' which reached a peak around 1800 and remained powerful for at least half a century.[45] On the evidence of advice books like Jane West's, the Revolutionary era produced a surcharge of anxiety on such matters, West coupling a 'doctrine of insubordination' with middle-class 'habits of luxury' and a sharply declining interest among women in household management as among the worst evils of modern life. Proposed remedies for this state of decline emphasised what Christopher Flint calls 'the supervisory and spectatorial role of the domestic male' as much as the ideologically enhanced role of the wife as moral guardian, creating a paradoxical situation wherein the increasingly privatised family was subject to ever more intense social surveillance.[46]

Parent–child relations

In her *Strictures* on female education, the evangelical conservative Hannah More poses a question that may well be startling to modern readers:

Is it not a fundamental error to consider children as innocent beings, whose little weaknesses may perhaps want some correction, rather than as beings who bring into the world a corrupt nature and evil dispositions, which it should be the great end of education to rectify?[47]

Remote as these views may be from twenty-first-century philosophies of parenting, it is easy enough to find Romantic-period texts informed by the same grim belief in children's essential depravity. Barbara Hofland's *York House*, for example, presents a series of conversations set in a girls' boarding school that are designed to be illustrative of good behaviour and sound morals. A pious and sensible sixteen-year-old, Emma, kicks off a conversation with the vain and flighty Sophie, three years her junior, by trying earnestly to convince her that she is guilty of breaking all ten commandments: she has broken the second commandment (not to make any graven images), for instance, by her devotions to 'the idol *vain-self*' in front of the mirror.[48] Unfortunately, by the time Emma has dealt with the first four commandments Sophie is so convinced of her eternal damnation that the conversation is terminated, so we never find out in what fashion she has broken the commandments regarding murder and adultery. Another less-than-perfect girl dies after a fall occasioned by taking pears from a tree in the garden, and leaves her school friends with the words: 'you see in me the fatal consequences of disobedience and folly' (p. 184). Readers are plainly intended to concur with this judgement.

If these examples, a world away from the popular Blakean image of a laughing child sitting on a cloud, suggest that it is dangerous to generalise about Romantic attitudes to children, it is also the case that the very relevance of the concept of childhood to the period is a matter of ongoing academic dispute. A succession of family historians, including Philippe Ariès, Edward Shorter, and Lawrence Stone, has promoted the idea that in medieval times childhood did not exist as a recognised, distinct phase in human life; instead, 'as soon as the child could live without the constant solicitude of his mother, his nanny or his cradle-rocker, he belonged to adult society', and before that time, in a real sense, 'simply "did not count"' (Ariès quotes Molière).[49] According to this theory, it was in the seventeenth century that the modern conception of childhood began to emerge, at least in the higher social classes, and only in the eighteenth century that the 'new world of children' (to quote J.H. Plumb) was definitively born, with the appearance of a wide range of institutions, practices, and commodities explicable only in relation to childhood as a qualitatively unique phase of life. In particular, childhood was increasingly redefined by changes in education: as the average duration of schooling lengthened, pupils began to be separated into separate classes according to age, new teaching methods were devised in the light of developing notions of child psychology, and the modern idea of a long childhood, divided into several stages, and requiring careful, specialised attention, came into being. Some historians have sought to disprove this evolutionary history of childhood: Linda Pollock, for instance, has called it 'a myth brought about by over-hasty reading, a burning desire to find material to support the thesis and a wilful misinterpretation of evidence'. However, even Pollock concedes that parental attitudes and concerns were significantly different in the eighteenth century, that 'parental interference in a child's development' increased, and that there was much more talk of 'the *abstract* nature of childhood': to the outsider, this looks very much like the appearance of a new cultural formation.[50]

Among the evidence brought forward to substantiate claims for the novelty of childhood as a concept in the period are the rapid creation of a market in toys and games, often but not always of an educational nature, which was well established by 1780 and of commercial significance by 1820;[51] the multiplication of other forms of children's entertainment, including zoos, puppet shows, and circuses; the popularisation of special ranges of children's clothing among the fashion-conscious middle and upper classes; the growing informality of family portraits, suggesting an attitude towards children as beings to be cherished and enjoyed; and documented changes in behaviour such as more affectionate modes of address and the abandonment of customs such as children kneeling or standing in the presence of their parents. Of particular importance was the rapid enlargement and diversification of the market in children's literature, virtually an invention of the second half of the eighteenth century. The range of such books was huge, covering educational titles on all subjects, pitched at different age groups, as well as didactic literature and works geared towards entertainment and amusement. For the first time, stories were being written about children *for* children of different ages, with their language and structure tailored to the capabilities of their target audience – or at least, as Alan Richardson puts it, 'to adult perceptions of children's abilities and needs'. Richardson argues that the opposition traditionally seen in the period's children's literature between didactic literature and imaginative writing such as fairy-tales is to some extent a false one, since didactic writers often borrowed fairy-tale plots and motifs while fairy-tales were subject to extensive editorial cleansing and rewriting. And whereas some Romantic authors' celebration of fairy-tales has been regarded as affirmatively libertarian, within the 'contemporary politics of literacy' it can be viewed as a conservative preference for harmless food for a new mass readership.[52] Instead, the more socially progressive texts were those authored or sponsored by the rationalist school of educators discussed earlier in this chapter. Maria Edgeworth, for instance, who laid down stringent guidelines for children's reading in *Practical Education* and argued against poetry on the grounds that its 'vague expressions' and 'exaggerated description' were unhelpful to the growing mind,[53] herself produced a range of children's books for different developmental stages, including *Early Lessons: Harry and Lucy* (1809) for the under-tens. A highly influential and much reprinted text was Thomas Day's *The History of Sandford and Merton* (1786), which pits the spoilt son of a Jamaican plantation owner against a strong, good-natured farmer's boy. Anecdotally combining moral lessons with more instructional passages conveying useful knowledge, such as the mechanics of levers and the principles of irrigation, the story perfectly illustrates the style of this dominant vein of children's literature. Needless to say, only a culture with a significant material and psychic investment in the concept of childhood would find it worthwhile to produce or consume such literature.

Even accepting that there *was* a strong concept of childhood of fairly recent provenance in the period, this was neither monolithic nor necessarily favourable to the interests of the children themselves. Stone identifies four conceptions of the child that were current at the end of the eighteenth century, all of which can be tracked in Romantic literary texts: the 'traditional Christian view', popular with evangelicals, that the child was tainted by original sin and needed to be subjected to harsh discipline; the 'environmentalist' view that the child was a blank slate at birth to be inscribed on by experience and education; a 'biological' view, astrologically influenced, that a child's character was predetermined at birth; and the Rousseauesque view that the child was innocent and good until corrupted by society.[54] To these four contrasting perspectives Richardson, with the different focus of a literary critic, adds a fifth, which he calls the 'transcendental': the view that the child 'is informed by a divine or quasi-divine nature which renders it superior to adults, and . . . can be figured as a prophet or angel'.[55] This exalted conception of childhood, exemplified by Wordsworth's 'Immortality' ode, became hugely popular in the Victorian age.

The approach to childhood most commonly encountered in Romantic writing, however, is the environmentalist one, which attached supreme importance to upbringing and fuelled a keen interest in changing practices of childrearing. Catharine Macaulay, for instance, advocates talking to infants constantly – and not just 'babytalk' – in a way that would not look out of place in a modern childcare manual.[56] Her condemnation of swaddling (the immobilising of a child by close-wrapped bands of linen for a period of several months after birth) as an evil now removed (in 1790) reflects Stone's judgement that the practice had been largely abandoned by the final quarter of the eighteenth century. The arguable health benefits of this change seem to have been less persuasive than the ideological purpose of liberating the infant and allowing closer physical intimacy between mother and child. These signs of a stronger emotional bond between parent and child were reinforced by a corresponding shift away from wet-nursing – which had prevailed among the wealthy classes partly because contemporary medical science held that sexual intercourse (which husbands often wished to resume) harmed the mother's milk and endangered the baby – towards maternal breastfeeding. Gisborne writes that a woman's prime maternal duty is to be nurse to her own offspring. Next in importance, in his view, is educating the dispositions of the child, thus highlighting another area of changing practice in childrearing – discipline. There is evidence of a growing disinclination, certainly among middle- and upper-class families, to use corporal punishment as either a first or last resort: Stone underlines the 'extraordinary contrast between . . . reiterated warnings in the eighteenth and early nineteenth centuries about excessive maternal influence and domestic affection, and the complaints in the late seventeenth century about excessive parental indifference and severity'.[57] These and other trends noted earlier in this chapter, such as the preference for home-based education for daughters, announce major strides towards the liberal, child-oriented society familiar in Britain and other parts of the West today.

Under this closer, more affectionate and permissive childrearing regime, doubtless explained partly by a reduction in infant mortality and the spread of contraceptive practices, the role of parent, father as well as mother, became one of friend and mentor more than authority-figure. Or so the conduct books lead us to believe. Of course, as Linda Pollock points out, just as modern parents may well pay little attention to what they read in childcare manuals, advice literature in the eighteenth and early nineteenth centuries may be an unreliable guide to actual behaviour. Pollock, as already noted, denies that parents in earlier centuries were distant or indifferent towards their children, and were certainly not routinely 'battering' them. Yet the weight of argument and evidence presented by Stone and other historians in favour of a shift in attitudes and practices taking place over the course of the eighteenth century seems persuasive, at least in respect of the middle and upper classes – the dominant producers and consumers of literature – for whom evidence is more plentiful. And Pollock herself draws certain corroborative conclusions – finding, for instance, that eighteenth-century diaries show many mothers 'devoting every waking moment to the care of their offspring'. Most significantly, she points to the secularisation of parental care in the eighteenth and nineteenth centuries: in this period 'parents became concerned not with forming a child so as to ensure his salvation but with forming a child who would be accepted by society'.[58] It is in this emphasis on moulding the child's character, in its own and society's best interests, that several of the themes raised in this chapter – progressive educational developments, environmentalist conceptions of childhood, affective family relationships – converge.

Notes

1. Andrew Bell, *An Experiment in Education, Made at the Male Asylum of Madras* (London, 1797), p. 8.

2. *Letters on Education* (London, 1790), p. 11.

3. *Some Thoughts Concerning Education*, ed. Ruth W. Grant and Nathan Tarcov (Indianapolis, 1996), pp. 10, 76, 161.

4. *Practical Education*, 2 vols (London, 1798), I, 124–5.

5. *Practical Education*, I, 319, 322.

6. *English Education 1789–1902* (Cambridge, 1930), pp. 26–7.

7. *A New and Appropriate System of Education for the Labouring People* (London, 1806), pp. 67, 12.

8. *A History of English Education from 1760*, 2nd edn (London, 1961), p. 3.

9. Joseph Lancaster, *Improvements in Education, as it Respects the Industrious Classes of the Community* (London, 1803), pp. 11, 16.

10. *A Plan for the Conduct of Female Education in Boarding Schools* (Derby, 1797), p. 10.

11. Colquhoun, *New and Appropriate System*, pp. 49–50.

12. Colquhoun, *New and Appropriate System*, p. 16.

13. Lancaster, *Improvements*, p. 15; Bell, *An Experiment*, p. 28.

14. *Centuries of Childhood: A Social History of Family Life*, trans. Robert Baldick (New York, 1962), p. 335.

15. *Edinburgh Review*, 15 (October 1809), 45–6.

16. Barnard, *History*, p. 18.

17. *Edinburgh Review*, 16 (August 1810), 333.

18. 'The New World of Children in Eighteenth-Century England', *Past and Present*, 67 (1975), 64–93 (p. 80).

19. Adamson, *English Education*, p. 70.

20. Barnard, *History*, p. 73.

21. *Thoughts on the Present System of Academic Education in the University of Cambridge* (London, 1822), p. 12.

22. Adamson, *English Education*, p. 80.

23. *A Letter to the Right Hon. Lord North, Chancellor of the University of Oxford* (London, 1789), pp. vi–vii.

24. *A Volume of Letters from Dr. Berkenhaut to his Son at the University* (Cambridge, 1790), pp. 147, 149.

25. Burton R. Clark, *Places of Inquiry* (Berkeley and Los Angeles, 1995), p. 58.

26. *Practical Observations upon the Education of the People* (London, 1825), p. 1.

27. *Literature, Education, and Romanticism: Reading as Social Practice, 1780–1832* (Cambridge, 1994), p. 215.

28. *An Enquiry into the Duties of Men in the Higher and Middle Classes of Society in Great Britain, Resulting from their Respective Stations, Professions, and Employments*, 2nd edn, 2 vols (London, 1795), I, 3.

29. *An Enquiry into the Duties of the Female Sex* (London, 1797), p. 365.

30. *Strictures on the Modern System of Female Education*, 3rd edn (London, 1799), p. 107.

31. *Edinburgh Review*, 15 (February 1810), 309, 314.

32. *Letters to a Young Lady, in which the Duties and Character of Women are Considered*, 3 vols (London, 1806), I, 58.

33. *Letters on Education*, pp. 47, 50.

34. *Vindication of the Rights of Woman*, ed. Miriam Brody (Harmondsworth, 1975), pp. 101, 127, 259, 262.

35. *Romanticism and Gender* (London, 1993), pp. 33–4.

36. *Letters on the Elementary Principles of Education*, 2nd edn, 2 vols (Bath, 1801–2), II, 25.

37. *Edinburgh Review*, 15 (February 1810), 302; Darwin, *Plan for the Conduct of Female Education*, passim; Aikin, *Letters from a Father to his Son* (London, 1793), p. 341.

38. *The Family, Sex and Marriage in England 1500–1800*, revised edn (London, 1979), pp. 182–3.

39. *Duties of the Female Sex*, pp. 237, 217.

40. *Letters from a Father*, pp. 332, 343.

41. *Approaches to the History of the Western Family 1500–1914* (Basingstoke, 1980), p. 51.

42. *For Better, For Worse: British Marriages, 1600 to the Present* (Oxford, 1985), pp. 141, 110.

43. *Approaches*, p. 44.

44. *Duties of Men*, II, 428; *Duties of the Female Sex*, p. 331.

45. *Family, Sex and Marriage*, p. 422.

46. *Family Fictions: Narrative and Domestic Relations in Britain, 1688–1798* (Stanford, 1998), p. 75.

47. *Strictures*, p. 64.

48. *York House, or, Conversations in a Ladies' School*, 2nd edn (London, 1820), p. 43.

49. *Centuries*, p. 128.

50. *Forgotten Children: Parent–Child Relations from 1500 to 1900* (Cambridge, 1983), pp. 271, 123, 269.

51. Plumb, 'New World', 90.

52. *Literature, Education, and Romanticism*, pp. 131, 122.

53. *Practical Education*, I, 367.

54. *Family, Sex and Marriage*, pp. 254–6.

55. *Literature, Education, and Romanticism*, p. 11.

56. *Letters on Education*, p. 34.

57. *Family, Sex and Marriage*, p. 278.

58. *Forgotten Children*, pp. 120, 123.

Chapter Five

Science

The brilliant German explorer and scientist Alexander von Humboldt (1769–1859) includes a fascinating short allegorical tale, first published in 1795, in his popular *Views of Nature* (1808). He describes a portico in ancient Syracuse adorned with pictures of gods and heroes, among which there is one, said to come from Rhodes, which attracts particular attention and baffles interpretation. It depicts a group of youths and maidens, manifestly 'creatures of the earth', with arms 'extended towards each other with impassioned longing', but with their gaze fixed upon a haloed 'Genius' in their midst. The Genius has a butterfly on one shoulder and holds a flaming torch in his right hand; he regards the youths and maidens 'imperiously'.[1] None of the many explanations of this painting offered by citizens is conclusive. Eventually the arrival of a ship from Rhodes discloses a picture immediately recognised as a companion-piece to the 'Rhodian Genius': in it, the Genius has lost the butterfly and his torch is 'extinguished and reversed', while the youths and maidens frolic in mutual embrace, with looks expressing 'a wild emancipation from restraint, and the gratification of long-nourished passion' (p. 382). A venerable local philosopher is called upon to pronounce definitive judgement on the pair of paintings. He interprets the 'Rhodian Genius' as a symbol of the 'vital force' which produces and sustains organic bodies in defiance of the normal physical and chemical properties of earthly matter, uniting substances 'which in inanimate nature ever flee from each other', and separating those which are 'incessantly striving to unite'; in the second painting, a 'picture of death', the vital force has been extinguished and earthly matter (as represented by the youths and maidens) is free to behave according to primary qualities of 'affinity and antagonism' (p. 384). The story ends with the aged philosopher sensing the decline of his own vital force and the resurgent activity of brute matter. In a note written several years after the tale itself, Humboldt asserts that he no longer has the same faith in 'peculiar vital forces', and that the same effects 'may possibly be produced only by the combined action of the separate already long known substances and their material forces' (p. 387). He remains impressed by the complex internal organisation of organic bodies, and their apparently self-determining nature, but is less certain how to account scientifically for these 'vital phenomena' in the absence of a 'formative impulse' or spiritual principle (p. 388).

In this brief allegory and Humboldt's later annotation are illustrated several key features of Romantic-period science and its cultural transmission: the competing claims of vitalist and materialist biological theories to provide an explanation of life; preoccupation with what distinguishes the organic and inorganic realms, as well as fresh insight into what they have in common; a controlling vision of the unity-in-diversity of all nature; high intellectual respect for the scientist or 'natural philosopher', coupled with a sense (not evident in my synopsis) of science's democratising potential; and the rhetorical strategy of embodying 'a physiological idea in a semi-mythical garb' (p. 386). This kind of literary packaging of science was attractive to Romantic readers, and was something for which Humboldt had a wonderful facility. His *Personal Narrative* of his travels in Central and South America, translated into English by Helen Maria Williams between 1814 and 1829, achieves a similar feat by blending scientific observations in such fields as geography, geology, and botany with aesthetic descriptions and a rich vein of interiority. A more complex example would be Goethe's novel, *Elective Affinities* (1809), which systematic-ally applies contemporary theories of chemical affinity to the erotic interactions of its four main characters.

As for the science itself, rather than its presentation, the notion that signific-ant transformations in the theory and practice of science took place around the turn of the eighteenth century has wide acceptance. Raymond Williams points out that the very term 'science' only took on its now familiar meaning at around this time: once denoting knowledge in general, and from the mid-seventeenth century onwards opposed to 'art' in the limited sense of dis-tinguishing theoretical from practical knowledge, it then developed its more specialised application to the 'natural sciences, primarily physics, chemistry and biology', characterised by the 'hard *objective* character' of their material and method.[2] Andrew Cunningham and Nicholas Jardine go so far as to speak of *two* 'Scientific Revolutions': the first, and better known, spanning the lives of Copernicus (1473–1543) and Newton (1642–1727) and marking the final destruction of traditional Christianised Greek cosmology and the advent of modern experimental science; the second occurring alongside the many other revolutions, notably political and industrial, associated with the Romantic period, and signalling the establishment of modern scientific disciplines, greater institutional support for science, and the beginnings of professionalisation.[3] The first Revolution entailed, among other things, the rise of the new astronomy in which the earth was no longer the centre of the universe and humanity no longer enjoyed a special position in creation; the substitution of reason for theological doctrine as the chief guide to understanding the world and one's place within it; the preference given to the rational formulation of natural laws of a kind susceptible of mathematical demonstration; the evolution of the mechanical philosophy in which matter and motion were seen as the essential realities and mechanistic explanations were increasingly applied to controversial areas like mental life and social behaviour; and the progressive subjection of a newly objectified nature to the rigours of observation and experiment.

The second Revolution, with which I am more concerned in this chapter, built upon the first in many ways, but in some respects appears as a reaction against it. To explain this contradiction I shall look below at selected develop-ments in the period, with a bias towards the British dimension, in what we would now think of as the physical sciences and the life sciences. But to begin with, it is worth taking stock of a movement in German scientific thinking that had an impact in Britain, and that brought together empirical science and Romantic ideas and ideals in deep and detailed ways.

Naturphilosophie

In literary criticism of the Romantic period it is commonplace to speak of certain times and places when circumstances and personalities conspired to produce remarkable creativity: Somerset in 1797–8 for the Wordsworth circle, Geneva in the summer of 1816 for the Shelleys and Byron. In addressing the scientific dimensions of German Romanticism, the University of Jena in the very early 1800s appears a configuration of matching importance: here and then were brought together the philosopher F.W.J. Schelling, the physicist Johann Wilhelm Ritter, the biologist Lorenz Oken, and more briefly the Danish physicist and chemist Hans Christian Oersted, not to mention Goethe a stone's throw away in Weimar. These are all key names in any account of *Naturphilosophie*. These men shared an interest in the metaphysical foundations of scientific thought, and a belief that the most fundamental truths are those that can be known a priori – that is, truths that are independent of experience, and are both necessary and universal. They worked in the tradition of Kantian idealism, the latest version of the venerable philosophical doctrine that ideas rather than matter or 'things' are the ultimate reality. It was Kant who licensed the transcendental approach to science favoured by the *Naturphilosophen*, their method (in the absence of a proof of God's existence) of investigating phenomena *as though* they were the products of a divine plan, and their teleological bias – their belief in the systematic unity and *purpose* of the universe. Schelling, the presiding spirit of the movement, found in Kant the grounds for a new dynamical understanding of nature to set against the mechanical philosophy espoused by Enlightenment thinkers, but one constructed entirely through enquiry into the human mind, using a faculty called 'intellectual intuition'. For Schelling and his followers, empirical investigation was not required to establish 'facts' about the world, or to furnish the basis of scientific laws, though it might be expected to confirm or illustrate what the mind had been able to determine for itself through the operations of pure reason.

Schelling's philosophy, couched as it is in a language of almost impenetrable abstraction, is extraordinarily difficult to follow even for the philosophically trained. But one thing that emerges clearly in his *Ideas for a Philosophy of Nature* (1797) is a passionate need to overcome the separation of mind and nature: a separation that is to some degree the inevitable result of the growth of mental self-reflection, but which mechanistic habits of thought have led the spiritually enslaved majority to see as a permanent state of affairs. What is needed, Schelling suggests, is a redemptive passage past this regrettable but necessary Fall in which the self will recognise its absolute freedom and by the same token achieve its longed-for reintegration with the natural order. This is

101

possible because, for Schelling, mind and nature are essentially one; nature, in fact, is the product of mind. He views the self as the centre of an originally unconfined activity; it is only the limitation of this activity by an opposed activity that circumscribes the self (prevents it from expanding to infinity) and produces our sense of matter or reality. Self-consciousness and consciousness of the external world are thus reciprocally determined: conviction of the reality of one strengthens conviction of the reality of the other. This confrontation of two free and unconfined activities precedes all thinking and representation, all mental processing of data furnished by the senses; moreover, the 'opposed' activity, which is none other than the material world, must itself consist in a polarity of forces, because 'the mind can oppose *to itself* only what is analogous to itself'.[4] In an almost mythological rendering of this intuitive process, Schelling says that

> in the *mental being* there is an *original* conflict of opposed activities, and from this conflict there first proceeds – (a creation out of nothing) – a real world. . . . No objective existence is possible without a mind to know it, and conversely, no mind is possible without a world existing for it. (p. 177)

Schelling implies, oddly, that some people, perhaps the majority, never inhabit a real world, because they have never felt their mind's potential freedom, and therefore never endured and overcame this fundamental conflict of self-consciousness. Furthermore, the idea of a divinity inherent in external nature makes sense only if this divine mind is so analogous to the human mind as to make no difference: 'For only in a mind able to create can concept and actuality, ideal and real, so interpenetrate and unite that no separation is possible between them.' (p. 35) Put more crudely, nature and the human mind are built upon the same principles, and it is this which gives us our assurance that our ideas coincide perfectly with reality, and which makes science possible: 'Nature should be Mind made visible, Mind the invisible Nature.' (p. 42)

The nature whose inner properties Schelling claims to have transcendentally deduced is thus essentially dynamic and holistic: that is, it is constituted by the variable play of opposing forces, and it is seen as both infinite and yet one – its ruling metaphor is that of the cosmic organism, rather than the cosmic clock which so often serves to caricature the mechanical world-view. He opposes the mechanists' view of matter as composed of hard, impenetrable atoms brought into motion by external forces, and argues instead that matter must be conceived as a state of equilibrium between polar forces of attraction and repulsion; indeed, 'matter is itself nothing but the product of original, reciprocally self-limiting forces' (p. 166). Different qualities of matter are explained as the result of differing degrees of intensity of these forces, or disturbances one way or the other of the basic equilibrium; thus greater mass results from a predominance of the attractive force. This fundamentally dynamical philosophy of nature consistently motivates Schelling's more technical discussions of heat, combustion, light, air, electricity, and magnetism, on all of which he has novel things to say yet all of which he brings within the framework of a single universal law. Barry Gower highlights the importance of the concept of polarity to a dynamical theory like Schelling's that sought to encompass all known phenomena:

> all types of physical action – gravitational, optical, magnetic, electrical, chemical – were regarded as the effect of polarization of forces. This polarization could be brought about, to a greater or lesser extent, in many different ways; friction, for example, could produce electrical polarization, and a prism could effect optical polarization.[5]

Seeing polarity in everything, it was not too big a step to a biocentric vision that would flatten the hierarchies of the Great Chain of Being and assuage the self-conscious isolation that beset humanity at the top of the ladder. Walter D. Wetzels draws this conclusion:

> Magnetic and electric polarity is but one manifestation of a universal *Urpolarität* which is the principle of life throughout nature from crystals to man. The omnipresence of this principle renders the formerly sharp distinctions between inorganic and organic nature, between man and the rest of creation, as mere gradual differentiations.[6]

Despite Schelling's insistence on legitimising his scientific thinking through a priori reasoning, his work, no less than that of the other *Naturphilosophen*, shows a keen interest in all branches of contemporary empirical research; but, as Wetzels indicates, the latest discoveries and results are programmatically interpreted to give further proof of a unified, animated nature.

It is worth looking briefly at the work of some of those writers within the circle of *Naturphilosophie* who belong more to the camp of experimental scientists, to demonstrate some of the 'applications' of this philosophical trend. Ritter (1776–1810) is one of the most important of these. Popular with major German Romantic writers like Novalis, the Schlegel brothers, and Goethe, his career is a good illustration of 'how the scientific spirit is directed by that central force of the Romantics, the imagination'.[7] The clearest evidence of this is his readiness to deploy grand metaphors for the perceived unity of inorganic and organic matter – referring, for example, to the 'cosmic-animal'.[8] The grounds of this unity are electricity or 'galvanism', the so-called 'animal electricity' thought by Luigi Galvani to be generated within nerves and muscles. Through a series of experiments, Ritter attempted to show that organic bodies naturally and constantly met the conditions for galvanic action theorised by Alessandro Volta (inventor of the silver-zinc battery), and was elated at the thought that he had found the principle of life itself. Using the new Voltaic pile, he pioneered the science of electrophysiology, discovering polar qualities in each of the senses and arguing that the latter could all be construed as manifestations of a primary electrical sense: for instance, with the amazing sang-froid typical of Romantic scientists he stuck electrodes in his own eyes and discovered that the positive pole made the eye see red, while the negative pole made it see blue. It was experiments like these that led him to believe that 'the entire animal organism represented one huge voltaic pile; and its "vitality" depended on its voltage, which in turn was directly related to the chemical composition of its various galvanic cells'; this anticipated the modern view that 'organic cells are electrical elements'.[9] Ritter was also the virtual founder of the science of electrochemistry. He became convinced that there was no sharp distinction between electrical and chemical action, seeing both as modifications of a process he called 'fusion' (which inevitably had its complementary process, 'fission'); in a manner reminiscent of Schelling, he conceived substances as the dynamic product of two fundamental forces interacting in various ways, and fusion involved the restoration of equilibrium between these forces when two substances were brought into contact. The significance of the experiments that he carried out in this area was, as Wetzels puts it, that 'the traditional demarcation lines between organic and inorganic nature vanished', and – though Ritter's conclusions ran ahead of his evidence – that galvanism emerged as 'the organizing principle of all matter' and 'the unifying force in nature'.[10] One other aspect of his work that deserves mention is his discovery of ultraviolet light. This seems to have been a direct result of his Romantic obsession with unity and polarity in nature: symmetry demanded a counterpart at the opposite end of the spectrum to the infra-red rays recently identified by Herschel, and experiment then produced the phenomenon to order.

Hans Christian Oersted (1777–1851) was another *Naturphilosoph* whose scientific accomplishments outlived the metaphysical credo that inspired them. Oersted studied at the University of Copenhagen and wrote his doctoral dissertation on Kant's natural philosophy; it was his grounding in Kant that convinced him of the need for an a priori basis for science and predisposed him to the speculative approach of *Naturphilosophie*. In the early 1800s he undertook a kind of scientific Grand Tour and made contact with many of the leading physicists and chemists in western Europe; his own work thereafter showed the competing influences of German metaphysics and French empiricism. In particular, he formed a close friendship with Ritter, and was stimulated by the latter's belief that electricity and magnetism were closely related.

From the outset, Oersted held that all natural phenomena – including light, heat, electricity, and magnetism – would be found to be manifestations of the same principle, and his major achievement, the discovery of electromagnetism, was, as H.A.M. Snelders says, 'a direct consequence of this metaphysical belief in the unity of all natural forces'.[11] Before this sensational breakthrough, Oersted, responding to a contemporary feeling that chemistry still awaited its Newton, had worked to establish his own dynamical chemistry that would reduce all chemical reactions to certain primary laws. Key to this was his proposed classification of elements according to their combustibility, and a typically polar theory of chemical behaviour as depending upon conflict between a force of combustibility and a force of supporting combustion; he linked these forces to positive and negative electricity, confirming his desire to determine the link between chemical phenomena and electricity. Then, in 1820, he published a short Latin pamphlet that was quickly translated into the major European languages, and ensured his celebrity. In deceptively plain language he describes the results of an experiment in which a current-carrying wire was brought into proximity with a magnetic needle:

Let the straight part of this wire be placed horizontally above the magnetic needle, properly suspended, and parallel to it. If necessary, the uniting wire is bent so as to assume a proper position for the experiment. Things being in this state, the needle will be moved, and the end of it next the negative side of the battery will go westward.[12]

By the time Oersted published his findings, proof of a connection between electricity and magnetism was not especially surprising to scientists, but the fact that the needle was deflected at right angles to the wire carrying the current was. The experiment demonstrated that electric currents produce magnetic fields, and that these radiate from the conductor in circular lines of force: in Oersted's words, the 'conflict performs circles' (p. 276). His language here shows his continuing commitment to the polar principle, for he sees the presence of electricity in a wire not as a current but as the 'continuous disturbance and restoration of an equilibrium'.[13] Barry Gower's judgement seems apt, that 'Oersted's belief that the various kinds of physical action could be understood in terms of a few fundamental physical concepts like force and polarity, and that they could be explained by means of laws involving these concepts, remained unshaken though his enthusiasm for *Naturphilosophie* gradually waned'.[14]

As a final example of 'applied' *Naturphilosophie*, there is the biologist Lorenz Oken (1779–1851). Oken studied at the University of Freiburg, and went to work at the University of Jena in 1807, recommended by Goethe. His troubled career was played out against a backdrop of foreign invasion – the previous year, Jena had been the site of one of Napoleon's most crushing victories over Prussia – and political turmoil, and Oken's own active nationalism was ultimately responsible for his professional downfall. His twin aims have been described as 'the realization of a strong German natural scientific tradition founded upon *Naturphilosophie* and the establishment of a unified German state founded upon enlightened political ideals',[15] and he believed the intellectual reform represented by the former was crucial to the success of the latter. His first work, published while he was still a student, related the five classes of animals to human sense organs: for example, invertebrates were seen as skin animals, fishes were tongue animals (because in them the tongue made its first appearance), while amphibians were nose animals because in them the brain was sufficiently developed to allow a sense of smell. This rather peculiar-looking system demonstrates Oken's concern to account for the diversity of individual species while confirming an underlying unity in nature. In his next book, *Generation* (1805), he extended his studies in embryology and produced what has come to be seen as prototypical cell theory. At Jena he became a committed and important contributor to the idealist science of transcendental anatomy, central to which was the quest to uncover 'unity of plan' in the animal and plant kingdoms – the single ideal plan or archetype from which every species was somehow derived. His *Compendium of the System of Nature Philosophy* (1809–11) was the pinnacle of his achievement in this genre. It is divided into three parts, the first providing what is essentially a scientific creation myth, the second dealing with matters of geology. The third part addresses the creation of life, which Oken attributes to galvanism, heat, and light. His understanding of organic life was dynamic rather than static, imagining all organisms, including man, to be constantly striving through reproduction to approach their archetype, and all archetypes as really parts of a single archetype. In Pierce Mullen's summary:

> Phenomenological man is but an imperfect and ever improving approximation of the archetype. It was as if nature were extruding living matter through this archetype, each extrusion representing a species or a population and each representing one or more of the salient features of the archetype. Man was nearest the limit.[16]

As this makes clear, it was taken for granted within Oken's system, as it was in *Naturphilosophie* generally, that man had the highest place in the scheme of things. In this respect the *Naturphilosophen* remained in thrall to the ancient idea of the Great Chain of Being, although the temporalisation of this concept in Romantic science marked a distinctive new development, and one that anticipated in some ways Darwinian evolutionism.

The fact that Coleridge owned and annotated copies of Oken's works is one indication of the latter's broad appeal to Romantic thinkers, and of the international cultural impact of *Naturphilosophie*. In a longer historical perspective, Barry Gower's judgement on this philosophical enterprise is cautious but persuasive: acknowledging the 'temptation to sacrifice empirical detail for the sake of theoretical generality', he values Schelling's focus upon the philosophical foundations of scientific thought, and specifically his effort to find a priori principles that would regulate the construction of theories favouring the 'systematic and purposive unity of nature'; conversely, he respects experimental scientists like Ritter and Oersted for their attempt 'to endow scientific thought with a sensitivity not only to philosophical criticism but also to the general intellectual reformation created by the Romantics'.[17]

The physical sciences

Precisely because many scientists, notably the German *Naturphilosophen* discussed in the previous section, sought to overcome the boundary between the organic and inorganic realms, the distinction between physical sciences and life sciences is blurred in the period. Nevertheless, for ease of treatment there is some merit in organising a survey along modern disciplinary lines.

One area of physics where there was a sharp opposition between Romantic science and the reigning Newtonian orthodoxy was optics. Newton's famous experiments in his camera obscura, whereby he observed light enter a darkened room through a prism placed before a small hole and separate into its component colours, had seemingly established that colour was the product of differential refrangibility; this was linked to his corpuscular theory of light, which held that light consisted of a stream of minute particles. In a celebrated controversy, Goethe challenged Newton's insistence that light and colour could be accounted for by mechanical laws. His own experiment involved looking through a prism at a white wall, and observing how 'light that was blocked by the narrow bar in the window appeared to radiate in bands of violet and blue on one side, red and yellow on the other side; he deduced that color arose on the surface or boundary because of the interaction or tension between light and darkness'; he further speculated that the red/yellow end of the spectrum 'participated more in the brightness, vitality, and warmth of light', while the blue/violet end 'shared more of the shade, infirmity, and cold of darkness'.[18] This idea that colour resulted from a conflict of opposed forces – light and darkness – reflects, of course, the mentality of *Naturphilosophie*, with which Goethe had intellectual sympathies; but Newton's prestige was such that his argument was tantamount at the time to challenging the authority of science itself. However, historians of science have been willing to reappraise Goethe's contribution more favourably, valuing his attention to both subjective and objective colour phenomena, as opposed to Newton who was concerned purely with the physical nature of light. Goethe's distinction between physiological, physical, and chemical colours (those due to the normal workings of the eye; those produced by a process of mediation such as refraction or diffraction; and those fixed in bodies) is relevant in this context; even chemical colours were not seen as completely objective because they could alter by, for example, a movement of the eye. His *Theory of Colours* (1810) also discusses the psychological, moral, and aesthetic dimensions of colour, and in the latter domain formulated a 'law of totality' to account for the powerful forces of complementation and reconciliation experienced in colour perception. His argument that the eye seeks harmony in colour, that it cannot remain satisfied with a single hue but will always seek to supplement it with another to round out the chromatic scale, was of obvious interest to artists, notably Turner. His ultimate aim was to discover the laws governing colour phenomena at the most fundamental level, and for a time he believed he had made a break-through in his study of the sunset, where changes observed in the colour of the setting sun and the colour of the sky were interpreted in typically polar fashion as a darkening of light and a lightening of darkness, respectively.

The major developments of the period in electrical science have already been outlined: first, the unification of electricity and chemistry, and second, the discovery of electromagnetism. Alessandro Volta's invention of the electric battery in 1800, which made available a steady electric current in place of the static electricity generators devised by eighteenth-century scientists, was of huge significance, though the large-scale technological applications of electricity, first in communications systems and then in lighting, transport, and engineering, were to arrive only in the later nineteenth century. In general terms, electricity was exciting to the Romantic mind because it offered an alternative to the mechanical world-view, a way into understanding the internal structure or principle of things that was not accessible to the senses. In 1829, Sir Humphry Davy, in his last book, writes of electrical science and chemistry as dealing with 'the intimate nature of bodies' and explaining those changes 'which do not merely depend upon the motion or division of masses of matter'.[19] By that time, Galvani and Volta had succeeded in making electricity central to chemistry, indeed to public awareness of science, and Davy himself had taken up electrical research to become the 'Newton' who would explain chemical relations in terms of forces. Davy's contribution to a 'dynamical chemistry' will be discussed below, but it was the experiments with galvanism that caught the imagination of the general public. It is not hard to see why on looking at a popular book like the *Account of the Late Improvements in Galvanism* by Giovanni Aldini, nephew and stout defender of Galvani. The experiments recorded in this book are alleged to prove the existence of an electric fluid that is conducted through the nervous system of animals and is responsible for muscular activity. Aldini reports the contractions produced in frogs when connected to the tissues of recently slaughtered animals (in a typical example, he holds a prepared frog in one hand while sticking a moistened finger into the ear of an ox). He makes use of the Voltaic pile to distribute the 'energetic fluid' and 'command the vital powers' – an ambitious phrase which suggests that galvanic action may be close to, or even identical with, the source of life itself.[20] The most macabre of the experiments involve the corpses of recently executed criminals, an entire appendix being devoted to experiments performed on the body of a 'malefactor' hanged at Newgate:

> One arc being applied to the mouth, and another to the ear, wetted with a solution of muriate of soda (common salt), Galvanism was communicated by means of three troughs combined together, each of which contained forty plates of zinc, and as many of copper. On the first application of the arcs the jaw began to quiver, the adjoining muscles were horribly contorted, and the left eye actually opened. (p. 193)

Aldini tries to emphasise the possible medical benefits of galvanism in helping to restore to health the victims of asphyxia, drowning, 'suspended animation', and other accidents, but it is obvious how appealing it might be to elide an agency capable of *exciting* the 'vital powers' with the vital force itself.

The less spectacular, but more durable contribution of electricity to scientific progress in the period, in the field of electrochemistry, can be assessed by reviewing the work of Davy (1778–1829) – virtually the first professional scientist in Britain, and one of the most famous men in the country. His work can be compared with that of another man credited with causing a 'chemical revolution', the Frenchman Antoine Lavoisier (1743–94). Lavoisier launched his revolution with his *Elements of Chemistry*, published appropriately in 1789, but fell victim to the Terror a few years later. He is credited with introducing the modern table of simple substances or elements (and conceiving these as bearing individual properties), with establishing a more rational and systematic chemical language, and with putting chemistry on a sound quantitative basis through the development and use of highly accurate scientific instruments. More particularly, his work on gases led him finally to demolish the theory that combustion was due to a substance or principle called 'phlogiston' contained within inflammable bodies and liberated in the process of combustion. Lavoisier's use of the precision balance demonstrated that combustion entailed a weight gain rather than a loss, and helped him understand the crucial role of oxygen (recently discovered by Joseph Priestley) in the process.

Davy studied Lavoisier as a young man and his work is testimony to the success of the latter's 'revolution', but Davy was temperamentally and ideologically a very different kind of chemical philosopher. He had a Romantic yearning for unity in nature, and always believed that chemical research would eventually show that 'arrangements of a very simple nature will explain those phenomena which are now referred to complicated and diversified agents';[21] he practised, moreover, a 'dynamical chemistry' which held that 'powers rather than matter' were 'the fundamental agency of order and change'.[22] Thus when he disproved Lavoisier's theory that oxygen was the principle of acidity, he did so without formulating an alternative theory of his own: he preferred not to see such a state as the property of a particular element, but rather as the outcome of a mysterious concatenation of forces. The question of what these forces were was part of a wider concern with the forces responsible for chemical reactions or 'affinities', which it was widely agreed at the time must be different from the universal forces of attraction and repulsion posited by Newton. Responding to what he called Volta's 'alarm-bell', Davy carried out a series of experiments at the Royal Institution (his employer) to test his hypothesis that electricity was the cause of such phenomena. He demonstrated that water could be electrolytically decomposed into hydrogen and oxygen only, with no by-products, and on the basis of this and other experiments theorised that chemical combination took place between substances of opposite electrical charge. He went on to use electrolysis successfully to separate potassium and sodium from the compounds, potash and soda, proving that the alkalis were light metals in combination with oxygen (Lavoisier's acidity principle); and shortly afterwards isolated calcium, barium, strontium, and magnesium. It was this electrochemical research that encouraged the *Edinburgh Review* to compare Davy to Newton, and from the point of view of a modern historian of science it still appears

> a great milestone on the way to the postulation of conservation of energy and that understanding of electricity and matter which forms the basis of twentieth-century physics. Electricity had seemed something to do with thunderstorms and parlour tricks; Davy made it central to our understanding of the processes of nature, a force as important as gravity. We are all Davyans now.[23]

Such was Davy's fame that he had no trouble in persuading the sponsors of the Royal Institution to fund the construction of a much more powerful Voltaic battery – in Davy's hands, as David Knight notes, chemistry 'was becoming a "big science" needing expensive toys'[24] – and it was with this new apparatus that he conducted important research on the greenish-yellow gas that he was to rename chlorine, the first of a new family of elements that would also include iodine, bromine, and fluorine (the halogens).

Much of Davy's work at the Royal Institution took the form of applied research: in addition to the miner's safety-lamp that bears his name, he made a contribution to the theory and practice of tanning, produced a treatise on agricultural chemistry (fertilisers, insecticides, and so on) which remained the standard work for half a century, and did research on artists' pigments that forms the basis of the modern science of picture restoration. These facts help explain the multi-faceted rhetoric of a famous lecture on chemistry that Davy gave in 1802, celebrating both the self-sufficient quest for scientific under-standing and the powerful utility of new knowledge: man, he declares, is not simply 'a scholar, passive and seeking only to understand [nature's] operations, but rather . . . a master, active with his own instruments'; not content 'with what is found upon the surface of the earth', he has 'penetrated into her bosom . . . for the purpose of allaying the restlessness of his desires, or of extending and increasing his power'.[25]

One area where Davy, because of his commitment to a 'dynamical chemistry', was out of step with developments that would transform scientific under-standing, was atomic theory. Here, he had a mutually respectful but sometimes uneasy relationship with John Dalton (1766–1844), a Quaker teacher who became professor of mathematics at the New College in Manchester, and later secretary, then president, of the Manchester Literary and Philosophical Society. A man with an impressive range of scientific interests, including meteorology and colour blindness, Dalton's important early researches on gases, which held that gases consisted of globular particles that mixed mechanically (rather than combining chemically) with other gases, led directly to the atomic theory for which he is best remembered. Although Dalton correctly saw this theory as continuous with the corpuscular beliefs about matter that held sway at the time, and indeed with a much longer tradition of philosophical atomism, his claim that the atoms of each element were irredu-cibly different and combined with atoms of other elements in definite simple and multiple proportions was a significant departure: it made possible the computation of atomic weights and laid the basis for a quantitative chemistry. Partly due to the inaccuracy of the instruments he was using, Dalton's own table of atomic weights proved ultimately to be some way off the mark, but this does not lessen his achievement in the eyes of modern historians of science. Davy saw the value of Dalton's laws of combination but was opposed to his atomic theory, since it ascribed the properties of matter to the characteristics of different atoms rather than to the forces at work within it. As David Knight puts it, 'one had either to choose with Dalton a world composed of a large number of elements, whose arrangements in compounds were relatively simple; or to believe in very few elements of which the atoms were extremely simple in properties, but were arranged in complex and various ways to produce all the richness and variety we encounter in the world'.[26] There were developments in Davy's lifetime – such as isomerism, in which the same atoms, differently combined, yield compounds with different properties, and allotropy, in which the same element exists in two or more physical forms – that seemed to vindicate his belief in greater simplicity in the design of nature; but in this respect the future lay with Dalton. It was ironic, though, that general acceptance of the atomic theory by the late nineteenth century was swiftly followed by the discovery of sub-atomic particles, thereby demolishing Dalton's assumption that atoms were the solid, indivisible foundation of matter.

Any picture of developments in the physical sciences in the period would be incomplete without reference to the new science of geology. A subject of mixed intellectual origins, this was distinguished from cosmogony through its preoccupation with the earth's crust and with the observable relations between physical objects and structures; and from natural history through its concern with causal explanations rather than description and classification. In Britain, development took place via an uneven and class-ridden coalition of interests: on the one hand, there were men like miners and surveyors with a professional interest in rock stratigraphy, who were in a position to demonstrate the economic utility of scientific knowledge in a country dependent on mineral resources for its accelerating industrialisation; on the other, there were better-educated gentlemen of leisure, often though not always of a Dissenting or radical cast of mind, who formed a kind of geological intelligentsia and whose amateur scientific enthusiasm found appropriate outlets in the newly-created Geological Society of London and Royal Society of Edinburgh. Both in Britain and on the Continent, geology was one science among others which had to tread carefully in the wake of the French Revolution: what had once been of little interest to the Church and the guardians of morality now risked seeming a source of atheistical speculation and dangerous novelty, so it responded, according to Roy Porter, by 'drawing its public intellectual boundaries very narrowly'.[27]

Geology was constituted as a science around the turn of the eighteenth century, despite these problems of cultural politics, because the evidence for massive and multiple changes in the face of the earth, for the extinction of species, and for a planetary time-scale far longer than the few thousand years indicated by the Bible, had become too overwhelming to ignore. In particular, modern palaeontological research, in which the Continent was far ahead of Britain, proved beyond doubt that the land and the sea had repeatedly changed places over unimaginably long periods of time. The German palaeontologist Johann Blumenbach (1752–1840) posited three periods of earth history, the earliest terminated by a major global upheaval, following which the life-force repopulated the earth with creatures suited to the new environment. In France, Georges Cuvier (1769–1832) was driven by his own extensive fossil studies, especially of terrestrial quadrupeds, to posit successive 'revolutions' in the history of the globe, and to conjure a vista of 'thousands of ages' preceding humanity and 'thousands of animals that never were contemporaneous with his species'.[28] The brilliant Scot, James Hutton, whose geological theory was to outlast those of his Continental rivals, felt it necessary to imagine three distinct 'worlds' or periods of existence, each of indefinite duration, and memorably saw 'no vestige of a beginning – no prospect of an end' to geological time.[29]

Three related questions summarise the vigorous debates characterising this nascent discipline: How had rocks been formed? Were those natural processes observable in the present sufficient to account for the earth's topography? And were the answers to these questions reconcilable with religious teaching? The first question was the focus of a lively debate between so-called 'Neptunists',

'Vulcanists', and 'Plutonists': the Neptunists, headed by Abraham Werner (1749–1817), lecturer at the Mining Academy in Freiburg, held that sedimentary rocks (as they are now called) had been formed by chemical precipitation out of the waters of a universal ocean, perhaps the biblical flood; Vulcanists believed in an igneous origin for at least some of the rocks that the Neptunists classed as precipitates; while the Plutonists, led by Hutton, agreed that sedimentary rocks had been formed from eroded material deposited in the ocean, but argued that pressure and heat were responsible for solidifying this material and for elevating it into new land forms. The second question marks a sharp difference between Hutton and Cuvier. Cuvier could not convince himself that mechanisms currently at work on the surface of the planet explained the making of the landscape, and was therefore forced to invoke a series of 'catastrophes' that had wiped out entire species of animals and redistributed others across land masses that were 'instantaneously elevated'.[30] By contrast, Hutton had no problem with contemplating an endless cycle of denudation of the land through erosion and its regeneration by the 'internal fire' of the earth; articulating the principle of uniformitarianism which still underpins modern geology, he looked around him and saw 'the actual existence of those productive causes, which are now laying the foundation of land in the unfathomable regions of the sea, and which will, in time, give birth to future continents'.[31] On the third question, Cuvier goes into contortions in trying to forestall accusations that his argument points to either successive creations or to gradual evolution, either of which was theologically unacceptable, and concludes with the ingenious proposition that the most recent and devastating revolution of the globe (the few human survivors of which effectively began human history) was quite recent – no more than six thousand years ago, in fact, conveniently in line with Noah's flood. Hutton gives less ground to biblical cosmology: he sees the 'beautiful oeconomy' of the forces of decay and restoration, admirably suited to the ends of humanity, as evidence of beneficent design, but, in positing a perfect, self-regulating, proto-ecological cycle with no conceivable beginning and no imaginable end, seems to leave little significant place for God.

It is not hard to see the appeal of geology to the intellectually curious in this period. As Roy Porter suggests, the Romantic mind 'wished to take the Earth as it was in Nature, not in the laboratory', and geology, with its grand narrative of 'the struggle of titanic Earth forces', so much more spectacular and imaginative than anything mineralogy or natural history had to offer, was precisely the kind of knowledge it craved.[32] It is also the case, however, as Nicholas Rupke argues, that Hutton's steady state theory was not especially congenial to Romantic philosophies that favoured the idea of historical progress, or which, in characteristically idealising manner, saw human history as 'a recapitulation of the whole history of the earth and life'.[33] But to point to these areas of disagreement, where matters of organic succession are so important, is to tread on the territory of the life sciences, to which I now turn.

The life sciences

The rapid popularisation of the new term 'biology' around the turn of the eighteenth century marks the wide support for a new synthetic science of life, one which would bring together investigations into the fundamental laws of organic phenomena and which would, in contrast to the static classificatory approach of natural history, be characterised by a historical, causal, or genetic methodology. Among the fields of study embraced by the new discipline were physiology, medicine, comparative anatomy, and the early theory of evolution, aspects of which I shall consider in this section.

Galvanism, as described in the previous section, excited such scientific and popular interest because it seemed to promise the discovery of the principle of life. But galvanism was only one part of a much broader debate on the nature and properties of living things in the late eighteenth and early nineteenth centuries, a complex debate which had moral, religious, and political dimensions. Broadly speaking, the most important conflict of belief was that between materialism and vitalism – that is, between those who held that life was explicable in terms of physical and chemical processes unique to organised matter, and those who believed in a separate life essence, principle, force, or ethereal substance. That this was not such a sharp opposition in practice is indicated by different interpretations of the work of the French anatomist Xavier Bichat (1771–1802): cited in support by those who were indisputably on the materialist side, Bichat is nonetheless described as a form of vitalist by modern historians of science, and perhaps most carefully defined, by E. Benton, as a 'phenomenalist vitalist'.[34] It was Bichat who put forward the period's most striking definition of life: 'Life consists in the sum of the functions, by which death is resisted.'[35] This proposition, which at first sight seems eerily to prefigure Freud's myth of competing life and death instincts in *Beyond the Pleasure Principle*, significantly declines to derive life from any single source: just as his anatomical research had classified the body into systems, organs, and ultimately tissues, each of which had its own vital properties and none of which therefore constituted a basic material of life, Bichat divides life into organic life (shared by plants and animals) and animal life, considers the different functions belonging to each (for example, nutrition and excretion, on the one hand, sensibility and volition, on the other) and the nature of the organs and tissues that make these possible, but is sceptical as to underlying 'first causes'.

The more extreme and uglier shape that the vitalism/materialism debate could assume is illustrated by a public dispute in Britain between two surgeons, William Lawrence (1783–1865) and John Abernethy (1764–1831), his former teacher. In 1814 Abernethy delivered a series of lectures at the Royal College of Surgeons which drew distinctions between body, life, and mind; within his scheme, life was a separate principle based on some 'subtle substance' similar to electricity. Two years later, at the same institution, Lawrence turned against his mentor, ostentatiously rejecting any separate life-principle and identifying life instead with the functional interdependence of organised bodies (in contemporary discourse, 'organisation' referred to the system characteristic of living things, in which 'a part existed by means of the others and for others as well as for the whole').[36] Abernethy responded in 1817, trying to paint Lawrence into a materialist corner, a position that in his eyes would have moral as well as philosophical consequences. Lawrence retaliated immediately, reasserting his physiological beliefs – which entailed the view that mind was a property of the nervous tissue comprising the brain – and defending freedom of thought with reference to the future supremacy of America. Among his supporters was the liberal Francophile physician Thomas Charles Morgan (1783–1843), who held not only that mental operations were explicable in terms of organic processes, but that 'presentiments of human mentality' could be found 'in the lower reaches of the biological scale' and even in inanimate nature[37] – a vision of nature as one intellectually akin to German *Naturphilosophie*. Lawrence, Morgan, and their supporters came under increasingly harsh attack, culminating in a court case in 1822 in which Lawrence, attempting to defend his copyright, failed because his work was deemed irreligious and hence outside the protection of the law. This perceived defeat for the forces of conservatism was short-lived, since Friedrich Wöhler's artificial synthesis of urea in 1828 proved conclusively that vital functions were not dependent on an immaterial life-principle.

It is important to grasp that the vitalist and materialist positions had moral and political implications that help account for the rancorous nature of this debate. For the vitalist, the doctrine of a separate life-principle was blurred with the question of the existence of an immortal soul; it supported the view that the universe was upheld by divine power and provided for the kind of external (supernatural) sanction for moral injunctions that many thought indispensable for civilised society. Materialists, on the other hand, espoused the utilitarian-sounding creed that 'the criteria of right and wrong must arise from man's organic needs and aptitudes', and that ethics should seek 'to define these and to show how a maximum of satisfaction could be obtained'. Materialism was politically controversial because it was perceived that on this basis 'men could regard themselves as free agents, overthrow existing regimes, and institute whatever government they chose', whereas vitalism supported the idea of a natural order and hierarchy to which libertarian and democratic creeds posed an illegitimate challenge.[38] Conservative politics was at the root of much of the opposition to Lawrence and Morgan, with biological materialism aligned in its antagonists' eyes with the enduring threat of Jacobinism, an association of ideas which Morgan at least actively encouraged. For the materialist, it was natural to argue that, if organised matter was capable in itself of sustaining the living body and its healthy interactions with its environment, there was no need for any interference 'from above' in the organisation of society; for the vitalist, it was equally imperative to argue that, just as an immaterial life-principle implied an active participation by God in the management of nature, so there would always be a need for the exercise of a higher power – the monarchy or a traditional ruling class – in the control and direction of social life.

This interlinking of scientific and political discourses in the physiological arena is somewhat ironic, given that medical practice was one area of culture that did not undergo a revolution in the period. This was not the case in Germany, where the feudal structure of the medical profession was broken and new vitalistic principles brought to bear on treatment, nor in France, where medical institutions were overhauled and the scientific study of disease began in earnest. In Britain, however, the old medical hierarchy of physicians, surgeons, and apothecaries was slow to change, and the inequalities and abuses of a 'system' run largely for private profit were compounded by the growing numbers of unlicensed druggists and itinerant quacks who promoted a still more cynical trade in sickness. With notable exceptions, such as Jenner's development of the smallpox vaccine in 1796, there were few major advances in medical science in the period, and killer diseases such as typhoid, dysentery, and influenza continued to ravage the population, with infants especially at risk; industrialisation and the attendant urban squalor actually increased the threat of diseases like tuberculosis. There were, however, significant moves towards the more humane treatment of mental disorders, with the emphasis shifting towards rest, solitude, and moral and emotional therapy.

For several centuries medical treatment had been based on a principle – that diseases were caused by impurities in bodily fluids – that represented little advance on the medieval theory of the four 'humours'; the 'antigastric' method predicated on this belief essentially comprised a range of techniques for ridding the body of these impurities – laxatives, vomitives, enemas, purgatives, and the notorious blood-leech. In the last quarter of the eighteenth century this method was challenged by an Edinburgh physician, John Brown (1735–88), who put forward a new theory that health and disease were attributable to the level of excitability in the human body; treatment therefore took the form of supporting the body's self-regulating mechanism, either by stimulation (through drugs, diet, or mental stimulation) or (less commonly) calming. Brunonianism played a big part in the medical reforms in Germany, but in general was poorly received in Britain. One exception to this was the radical Bristol physician Thomas Beddoes (1760–1808), whose famous Pneumatic Institution lured the young Humphry Davy away from a medical career to pursue research into gases. It was Beddoes's belief that some of the newly discovered gases could play a role in the treatment of disease by helping to restore the correct proportion of excitability in the system. Largely through self-experimentation, his accounts of which are classic Romantic descriptions of altered states of mind, Davy proved that nitrous oxide was not, as had been claimed elsewhere, a source of contagion, but a powerful and unpredictable stimulant. Brunonian theory suggested that if nitrous oxide was beneficial as a stimulant, then carbon monoxide would be equally effective when the opposite effect was required. Fortunately, Davy saw the weaknesses in Brown's theory and did not take self-administration of the latter gas to the point of finding just how lethally calming it could be. Ultimately, the Pneumatic Institution's research project was a failure: Davy did not share his employer's stubborn confidence that nitrous oxide might cure tuberculosis, and soon moved on to higher things, while even Beddoes himself focused more on his long-standing interest in preventive medicine in the last decade of his life.

One movement in biological science that was Romantic to the core, and which had a far-reaching influence, was transcendental anatomy (more or less synonymous with 'transcendental morphology'). This was of German parentage, though it was taken up in France and was being assimilated in Britain before the end of the period. In Germany the key players were Goethe and Lorenz Oken, whose contribution to the field has been sketched earlier in this chapter. Philip Rehbock has helpfully summarised the key features of transcendental anatomy as follows: belief in an ideal Plan or archetype underlying the multitude of different species to be found in the natural world (or perhaps separate Plans for the animal and plant kingdoms); a presupposition that it was this Plan that dictated structure, rather than the functional demands imposed by environmental factors; acceptance that the Plan had an ideal rather than material existence, so that it suggested a way of interpreting evidence rather than being a product of the latter; and a search for secondary laws that would help explain what might seem to be deviations from the key principle of unity of plan.[39] Goethe, whose interest in comparative anatomy stemmed back to the 1780s, applied these transcendental principles to it: the outcome, in H.B. Nisbet's words,

> was his theory of the archetypal plant or 'Urpflanze', according to which the flowering plants (or possibly all plants) are constructed on a single model, and his equivalent anatomical theory of the archetypal animal, the 'Typus' or 'Urtier', of which all vertebrate species (or possibly all animal species) are the endlessly varied manifestations.[40]

In an extension of this theory, Goethe put forward the idea that there was a single basic unit of design in what seemed to be complex structures: thus the different parts of a plant were taken to be modifications of a primal leaf, and the vertebra was dubbed the ur-unit of the higher animals. An intricate parallelism therefore existed between the parts of an organism, the organism itself, and the total living universe. In France, the key proponent of transcendental anatomy was Geoffroy Saint-Hilaire (1772–1844), whose advocacy of this idealist creed caused a rift with his great colleague at the Muséum d'Histoire Naturelle, Cuvier, who held to a functionalist view of animal design. Geoffroy further refined the concept of unity of plan by his pursuit of homology (the identification, for each organ of a particular species, of counterpart organs in other species, the crucial invariant being the organ's interrelationships with surrounding parts), and introduced a 'principle of compensation' (overdevelopment of one organ at the expense of another) to help account for the sheer diversity of the living forms. Interestingly, Geoffroy did not believe, as did Goethe and Oken, that man represented the closest approximation to the ideal archetype.

In Britain, Richard Owen (1804–92) became the best-known conduit of transcendental anatomy, but his work lies outside the period. He was, however, anticipated in this project of scientific translation by Robert Knox

(1793–1863). Knox learned comparative anatomy from John Barclay (1758–1826) at the medical school at Edinburgh University, but also benefited from a year's sabbatical in Paris with Geoffroy, Cuvier, and Henri de Blainville (1777–1850), who mediated *Naturphilosophie* for him. Knox lectured on human anatomy from 1825 to 1842, expounding the principles of unity of plan and the law of compensation gleaned first-hand in Paris. Unfortunately, the pressing need for corpses for dissection led Knox to resort to body-snatchers, and he became a major client of the notorious mass-murderers, Burke and Hare.

One of Knox's more personal contributions was a conservative form of evolutionism in which genera were seen as the permanent result of a single act of Creation, whereas different species were produced through time by actualising certain possibilities in the generic embryo and not others. This links to another important aspect of this branch of idealist science: just as comparative anatomy provided an important source of experimental support, so did embryology, a form of study made possible by improved microscope technology. Here again the pace was set in Germany. The dominant eighteenth-century embryological theory had been preformationism, which held that the adult organism was already represented in miniature in the male sperm or female ovum, so that growth was no more than a progressive unfolding of what already existed. By the 1790s, however, beginning with the work of C.F. Woolf (1734–94) and progressed by men like Blumenbach, the rival theory of epigenesis had taken hold, according to which plants and animals emerged in stages until the end product bore no resemblance to the original seed. The distinctive quality of this theory was that it represented a 'historical' understanding of life as a process in which everything that happens has its appointed place – a process in which, under the impulse of some internal principle or genetic force, structures develop as and when necessary to fulfil the needs of the individual organism. Ontogeny could therefore be interpreted, in idealist fashion, as the gradual realisation of an idea, and it was then an easy step for the Romantic biologist to apply the same model to the successive appearance of different yet related species in course of time: in this light, as Owsei Temkin puts it, the Great Chain of Being 'would be but one process of ontogeny', and the entire history of nature could be seen as the progressive materialisation of a single cosmic blueprint.[41] One piece of evidence apparently in support of this theory was the embryological observation that many species temporarily generated structures in the early stages of life that resembled the adult forms of 'lower' organisms; this phenomenon of 'embryological recapitulation', as it was called, became a favourite law of transcendental anatomy. It is also worth mentioning here the deep congruence between epigenesis or 'historical' physiology and other forms of historical thinking that came into vogue at this time, and which are the subject of Chapter 7.

It needs emphasising that, despite making room in their theories for the successive emergence of new species in course of time, the transcendental anatomists did not for the most part favour an evolutionary perspective or subscribe to the principle of 'descent' as Charles Darwin was later to theorise it. However, the theory of evolution was not a virgin birth, and its mixed beginnings can be traced to some other notable writers and thinkers of the Romantic period. Its controversial emergence was a challenge to two powerful eighteenth-century traditions of thought. First, the Neoplatonic concept of the Great Chain of Being, by which all created species (and higher spiritual beings) were imagined in a single linear hierarchical succession, becoming progressively less transcendent and more corporeal as one moved by minute gradations down the chain, still held currency in the second half of the eighteenth century. Secondly, the systematic taxonomies of the natural world pioneered by the Swede, Carolus Linnaeus (1707–78) were static classifications based largely on a study of external characteristics, and as far as the animal kingdom was concerned rested on the assumption that the members of each species bred only with each other and could not mutate into other species. The major conceptual shift that took place in the Romantic period was towards the temporalisation of nature: transcendental anatomy accommodated time in its own peculiar way, but the more radical and enduring move towards a *history* of nature came with evolutionism.

Among the important pre-Darwinian spokesmen for evolution were Jean-Baptiste Lamarck (1744–1829) and Georges Cuvier. Lamarck, one of the first to use the new term 'biology', held a hierarchical view of creation similar to the Great Chain, but saw it more as an escalator up which organisms could move slowly in the course of time. His *Philosophie Zoologique* of 1809 first formulated the laws (later refined) of the 'progressive' form of evolutionism with which his name came to be synonymous: essentially, these state that animal organs are strengthened and developed, or weakened and ultimately lost completely, according to the demands placed upon them by the environment in which the animal lives, and that all such modifications are passed on by reproductive pairs to their offspring. Lamarck's theory allowed for the appearance of new species without conceding the possibility of extinction: it held that new, simple organisms were constantly produced at the bottom of the Chain by spontaneous generation, but that life generally was 'a continuous process of complexification'.[42] The evidence of increasing diversity and complexity furnished by the fossil record was of interest to Cuvier too, but his catastrophism (discussed in the previous section) was a way of reconciling this evidence with the non-evolutionary biology, and the static taxonomies, that he favoured. The fact that his classifications were based on the functional adaptation of anatomical design to different conditions of existence meant, however, that his work could be painlessly co-opted by later theorists of evolution.

In Britain, the fate of evolution as a concept is closely intertwined with the intellectual backlash provoked by the French Revolution. In a newly conservative climate, its only acceptable face was the doctrine of 'progressionism', described by Evelleen Richards as 'evolution without physical continuity', where the continuity 'exists only in the mind of God who has created a succession of new and higher life forms after the extinction of all their predecessors'.[43] Not evolution in the post-Darwinian sense, then, but a philosophy of nature that had much in common with German Romanticism and the embryological laws proclaimed by transcendental anatomy. William Lawrence, whose controversial statements of biological materialism have already been discussed, was one of those who adopted a more radical position. His *Lectures on Physiology, Zoology, and the Natural History of Man* (1819) uncompromisingly consider man as part of the animal kingdom and provocatively debate whether there is one or several species of humanity: 'how many Adams must we admit?' His conclusion, that the human species is single and that the striking dissimilarities between separate peoples are to be accounted different varieties of that species, is based on a theory of development whereby congenital variations are transmitted by hereditary succession, with a state of culture – as with the domestication of animals – productive of a greater degree of variation. This theory includes much of what would later become Darwinian orthodoxy, though the Eurocentric and racist manner in which Lawrence asserts the superiority of the Caucasian variety over all others is an uncomfortable foretaste of some of the socially divisive uses to which Darwinism would be put.

Another significant precursor of evolutionism, and one of the most colourful characters of the period, was Erasmus Darwin, grandfather of Charles. Darwin was a practising doctor, spare-time inventor, and poet, whose friends and acquaintances comprise a roll call of the literary and scientific liberal intelligentsia of the late eighteenth century. An important figure in the Lunar Society of Birmingham, one of the leading provincial scientific societies, and intimate with Midlands manufacturers such as Matthew Boulton and James Watt, his inventions ran the gamut from a rocket motor to a canal lift to a machine for moving chessmen. His interest in evolution stemmed from the discovery of fossils during the construction of the Grand Trunk Canal, a project that he supported. In his remarkable exercises in versified science, *The Loves of the Plants* (1789) and *The Economy of Vegetation* (1792), and in his medical treatise, *Zoonamia* (1794), he elaborated an understanding of evolution occurring over hundreds of millions of years, with lust, hunger, and security the engines of change, to produce from the simplest original forms the diversity of the present-day natural world:

> Would it be too bold to imagine, that all warm-blooded animals have arisen from one living filament, which THE GREAT FIRST CAUSE endued with animality, with the power of acquiring new parts, attended with new propensities, directed by irritations, sensations, volitions, and associations; and thus possessing the faculty of continuing to improve by its own inherent activity, and of delivering down those improvements by generation to its posterity, world without end![44]

As this passage makes clear, Darwin was attracted to the Lamarckian belief in the heritability of characteristics acquired by the individual during its lifetime as a result of its own efforts; but the importance he attached to 'lust', by which he comprehended the drive for the strongest animal to propagate the species, showed him mindful too of the role of sexual selection which his grandson would highlight. Natural selection as *The Origin of Species* would theorise it also encompasses the competition for life between species and between males and females of the same species, and Erasmus Darwin's final publication, the posthumous *Temple of Nature* (1803), shows him aware of these factors too – describing, for example, the competitive advantages afforded man over other species by his hand (with its opposable thumb) and brain, and presenting multifarious images of the general struggle for existence in nature:

> – Air, earth, and ocean, to astonish'd day
> One scene of blood, one mighty tomb display!
> From Hunger's arm the shafts of Death are hurl'd,
> And one great Slaughter-house the warring world![45]

The Temple of Nature, with its comprehensive view of the history of life on earth, justifies James Harrison's view that 'Erasmus Darwin had in his grasp all, or almost all, the constituent parts of the full theory of evolution by natural selection . . . without ever piecing them together in the way his grandson was able to'.[46]

Darwin's early works, despite their progressive scientific theorising, were well received in both Whig and Tory journals, reflecting the generally comfortable relationship between science and religion in the later eighteenth century and, indeed, growing scepticism among many prominent Anglicans who were themselves seeking a more rational Christianity. However, the intellectual backlash provoked by the French Revolution meant that by the mid-1790s scientific opinions were no longer ideologically neutral: against the background of the French experience the ruling classes did not want their own scepticism reproduced among the lower orders, and urged their countrymen to prevent revolution by protecting their religious institutions and values. Darwin's reputation was a casualty of this turnaround. His earlier work was reassessed and subjected to hostile caricature and parody, previously supportive periodicals reversed their positions, and *The Temple of Nature* was effectively stillborn on publication.

The nature of science

The fate of Erasmus Darwin's reputation exemplifies the close link between science and politics in the period: when Darwin's friend, James Watt, wrote to him in 1790 that he was 'becoming all French both in chemistry and politics', he nicely encapsulated the relationship plainly seen by its opponents between the 'second scientific revolution', on the one hand, and the grand social experiment that had begun across the Channel, on the other. During the long years of the war against France, these radical scientific tendencies were held in check, and the conservative Royal Society, under the vigorous presidency of Sir Joseph Banks, reinforced its centrality to the country's scientific culture and strengthened its bond with the establishment. In the second half of the eighteenth century provincial towns and cities had emerged as important sites of scientific activity, facilitated by the formation of societies such as the Lunar Society and the Manchester Literary and Philosophical Society. One effect of the patriotic backlash against France was to stifle the heady mix of scientific enthusiasm and political radicalism that the provincial societies, in which rational Dissenters found a natural home, had fostered, as well as to further concentrate cultural power in London (rivalled in some fields by Edinburgh).

What the provincial societies shared with the Royal Society was a gentlemanly ambience, an amateur breadth of interests, and a focus upon the practical applications of science to social improvement and wealth-creation. These facets of Romantic-period science are all pilloried in Charles Babbage's *Reflections on the Decline of Science in England* (1830), a work that neatly marks the transition to a more recognisably modern ordering of disciplines and the growth of professional disinterestedness. Babbage asserts that in international terms Britain is behind in 'pure' science despite its pre-eminence in 'mechanical and manufacturing ingenuity'. He highlights the anomaly whereby the pursuit of science 'does not, in England, constitute a distinct profession, as it does in many other countries', laments the fact that government support for science is based short-sightedly on principles of commercial utility, and concludes that 'scarcely any man can be expected to pursue abstract science unless he possess a private fortune, and unless he can resolve to give up all intention of improving it'.[47] In Babbage's eyes, professionalism is good because it inspires emulation and *esprit de corps*, suppresses anti-social conduct, and establishes systems of peer esteem that provide reliable indicators for the public. The campaign which he led to reform the scientific establishment and create a viable career structure for British scientists began to bear fruit in the period, with the formation of specialised societies like the Astronomical Society of London (1820) and the Zoological Society of London (1826), of which Banks disapproved, and the foundation of the British Association for the Advancement of Science in 1831. The development of science within a higher education environment still lay in the future; indeed, Babbage cites disapprovingly the negative effects of having a scientist of the calibre of John Dalton 'employed in the drudgery of elementary instruction'.

Notes

1. 'Vital Force, or the Rhodian Genius', in *Views of Nature: Or Contemplations on the Sublime Phenomena of Creation*, trans. E.C. Otté and Henry G. Bohn (London, 1850), pp. 380–5 (p. 381).

2. *Keywords: A Vocabulary of Culture and Society*, revised edn (London, 1983), pp. 276–80.

3. 'Introduction: The Age of Reflexion', in *Romanticism and the Sciences*, ed. Andrew Cunningham and Nicholas Jardine (Cambridge, 1990), pp. 1–9 (p. 1).

4. *Ideas for a Philosophy of Nature*, trans. Errol E. Harris and Peter Heath (Cambridge, 1988), p. 175.

5. 'Speculation in Physics: The History and Practice of *Naturphilosophie*', *Studies in History and Philosophy of Science*, 3 (1973), 301–56 (p. 325).

6. 'Aspects of Natural Science in German Romanticism', *Studies in Romanticism*, 10 (1971), 44–59 (p. 45).

7. Noel Deeney, 'The Romantic Science of J.W. Ritter', *The Maynooth Review*, 8 (1983), 43–59 (p. 47).

8. Cited in Walter D. Wetzels, 'Johann Wilhelm Ritter: Romantic Physics in Germany', in *Romanticism and the Sciences*, pp. 199–212 (p. 203).

9. Wetzels, 'Aspects', 54.

10. 'Johann Wilhelm Ritter', pp. 204–5.

11. 'Romanticism and Naturphilosophie and the Inorganic Natural Sciences 1797–1840: An Introductory Survey', *Studies in Romanticism*, 9 (1970), 193–215 (p. 202).

12. 'Experiments on the Effect of a Current of Electricity on the Magnetic Needle', *Annals of Philosophy*, 16 (1820), 273–6 (p. 274).

13. H.A.M. Snelders, 'Oersted's Discovery of Electromagnetism', in *Romanticism and the Sciences*, pp. 228–40 (p. 235).

14. 'Speculation in Physics', 348–9.

15. Philip F. Rehbock, 'Transcendental Anatomy', in *Romanticism and the Sciences*, pp. 144–60 (p. 147).

16. Pierce C. Mullen, 'The Romantic as Scientist: Lorenz Oken', *Studies in Romanticism*, 16 (1977), 381–99 (p. 389).

17. 'Speculation in Physics', 354–5.

18. Frederick Burwick, *The Damnation of Newton: Goethe's Color Theory and Romantic Perception* (Berlin and New York, 1986), pp. 11, 19.

19. *Consolations in Travel; Or, the Last Days of a Philosopher*, in *The Collected Works of Sir Humphry Davy*, ed. John Davy, 9 vols (London, 1839–40), IX, 207–388 (p. 363).

20. *An Account of the Late Improvements in Galvanism, with a Series of Curious and Interesting Experiments* (London, 1803), p. 53.

21. Royal Institution of Great Britain, MS 4 (December 1809), cited in Trevor Levere, 'The Rich Economy of Nature: Chemistry in the Nineteenth Century', in *Nature and the Victorian Imagination*, ed. U.C. Knoepflmacher and G.B. Tennyson (Berkeley, 1977), pp. 189–200 (p. 197).

22. Christopher Lawrence, 'The Power and the Glory: Humphry Davy and Romanticism', in *Romanticism and the Sciences*, pp. 213–27 (p. 222).

23. David Knight, *Humphry Davy: Science and Power* (Cambridge, 1992), p. 72.

24. *Humphry Davy*, p. 85.

25. 'A Discourse Introductory to a Course of Lectures on Chemistry, Delivered in the Theatre of the Royal Institution, on the 21st January, 1802', in *Collected Works*, II, 311–26 (pp. 318–19).

26. *Atoms and Elements: A Study of Theories of Matter in the Nineteenth Century* (London, 1967), pp. 28–9.

27. *The Making of Geology: Earth Science in Britain 1660–1815* (Cambridge, 1977), pp. 205–6.

28. *Essay on the Theory of the Earth*, trans. Robert Kerr (Edinburgh, 1813), p. 181.

29. *Theory of the Earth, with Proofs and Illustrations*, 2 vols (Edinburgh, 1795), I, 200.

30. *Essay*, pp. 15–17.

31. *Theory*, pp. 181–2.

32. *Making*, p. 142.

33. 'Caves, Fossils and the History of the Earth', in *Romanticism and the Sciences*, pp. 241–59 (p. 256).

34. 'Vitalism in Nineteenth-Century Scientific Thought: A Typology and Reassessment', *Studies in History and Philosophy of Science*, 5 (1974), 17–48 (pp. 25–9).

35. *Physiological Researches on Life and Death*, trans. F. Gold (London, 1815), p. 21.

36. Owsei Temkin, 'Basic Science, Medicine, and the Romantic Era', *Bulletin of the History of Medicine*, 37 (1963), 97–129 (pp. 98, 118).

37. L.S. Jacyna, 'Immanence or Transcendence: Theories of Life and Organization in Britain, 1790–1835', *Isis*, 74 (1983), 311–29 (pp. 314–15).

38. Jacyna, 'Immanence', 320, 354.

39. 'Transcendental Anatomy', in *Romanticism and the Sciences*, pp. 144–60 (pp. 144–5). See also Rehbock's *The Philosophical Naturalists: Themes in Early Nineteenth-Century British Biology* (Madison, 1983), pp. 15–30.

40. *Goethe and the Scientific Tradition* (London, 1972), pp. 17–18.

41. 'German Concepts of Ontogeny and History Around 1800', *Bulletin of the History of Medicine*, 24 (1950), 227–46 (p. 242).

42. D.R. Oldroyd, *Darwinian Impacts: An Introduction to the Darwinian Revolution* (Milton Keynes, 1980), p. 32.

43. '"Metaphorical Mystifications": The Romantic Gestation of Nature in British Biology', in *Romanticism and the Sciences*, pp. 130–43 (p. 136).

44. *Zoonamia; Or, The Laws of Organic Life*, 2 vols (London, 1794), I, 505.

45. *The Temple of Nature; Or, The Origin of Society*, facsimile edn (Menston, 1973), p. 134, IV.63–6.

46. 'Erasmus Darwin's View of Evolution', *Journal of the History of Ideas*, 32 (1971), 247–64 (pp. 260–1).

47. *Reflections on the Decline of Science in England* (London, 1830), pp. 1, 10–11, 38.

Chapter Six

Religion and Ethics

'The generation overshadowed by the French Revolution was', it has been said, 'the most important generation in the modern history not only of English religion, but of most of the Christian world.'[1] Important for the history of religion, then, but how important is this for *literary* history? The answer is that religion in this period mattered politically, was central to the cultural and intellectual life of the nation, and was part of the fabric of ordinary lives, to an extent barely imaginable today; it helped shape everything from family life to foreign and imperial policy, and therefore *has* to matter to any study of the literature of that period.

Roy Porter observes that many Georgians 'rarely went through a church porch between their christening and burial', yet 'practically everyone, in his own fashion, had faith'.[2] There were many such 'fashions', but Britain was essentially a Christian country, and in broad sectarian terms was overwhelmingly Protestant. Linda Colley has argued that a shared Protestantism was a major factor in the invention of the modern nation following the Union of England and Scotland in 1707 (and hence a major source of strife following the Union of Britain with Catholic Ireland in 1800), and that it 'lay at the core of British national identity'.[3] Equally, religious divides, not only between Protestants and Catholics but also between Anglicans and Protestant Nonconformists, and between different groups among the latter, ran deep; while part of the ideological case for an Established Church was that religion provided the cement of an ordered and harmonious society, it just as readily acted as the motor of social and political disunity. The identities, beliefs, and aspirations of Romantic-period writers were formed during an age in which the religious, spiritual, and moral state of the nation was permanently in question. In this chapter I aim to orientate the reader in this often perplexing area by sketching the religious map of Britain at the end of the eighteenth century; analysing the complex and contentious religious politics of the period; opening up some of the key areas of intellectual debate; and giving a brief account of major developments in moral philosophy.

The religious spectrum

One crude way of picturing the spread of Christian denominations in the period is as a scale of relative orthodoxy and heterodoxy stretching from Roman Catholicism at one extreme to outright unbelief at the other. With Anglicanism (representing English, if not British) national orthodoxy at one important remove from Catholicism, one passes through the various forms of Protestant Nonconformity, encompassing both 'Old Dissent' and the new evangelical phenomenon of Methodism, to the important non-Trinitarian grouping of Unitarians or rational Dissenters, before arriving at the non-institutional 'natural religion' of deism and, finally, the unadulterated atheism with which it was often elided. Clearly, there are problems with such a linear scale: Catholicism is obviously misrepresented, in a British context, as the benchmark of orthodoxy, and lack of parallelism between doctrinal orthodoxy, on the one hand, and social or political orthodoxy, on the other, is completely overlooked. Nevertheless, the scale is helpful insofar as it captures something of the variety and vitality of religious belief.

At the far from still centre of the turning religious world was, of course, the Church of England. Following the sixteenth-century Reformation and the constitutional changes attending the Glorious Revolution of 1688–9, the Church had enjoyed a privileged status as one half of an alliance of civil and ecclesiastical power that was deemed mutually beneficial:

> The Church upheld the 'natural' hierarchy of mutual obligations which were thought to provide social cohesion; the State, for its part, protected the legal Establishment of Christianity as the appropriate agent for the diffusion of benevolence and public morality.[4]

The Church was the nation's wealthiest institution, although this wealth was very unevenly distributed: while a bishop could earn in excess of £10,000 per annum, the meanest livings were worth less than £50. The notorious problems of pluralism (the holding of more than one living) and non-residence (which in 1810 affected more than half of all benefices) were partly ways of relieving clerical poverty. The price of establishment was political control of the selection of bishops and archbishops, while the appointment of lower clergy was locked into a complex system of patronage: roughly half of all livings were in the gift of great landowning families, with the remainder disposed of by the Crown, cathedral chapters, Oxbridge colleges, and public schools. In other ways, too, there was a close interweaving of the clergy with the social and political order: the parish, for example, was the basic unit of local government, and ministers were appointed as magistrates in increasing numbers.

After the fury of the religious wars of the seventeenth century, Anglicanism (as the belief system of the Church of England came to be called) evolved in the eighteenth century as a tolerant and inclusive creed, with the emphasis more on ethics than on the finer points of doctrine. Its disinclination for theological dispute was not seriously challenged until the turmoil of the 1790s revived old battles and opened new wounds. At the level of popular culture, it provided a comforting and undemanding element of ritual and tradition in lives organised around the customary calendar: David Hempton says that for many people it was 'a delicate mixture of social utility, rural entertainment and moral consensus in which the parish church and all its associated values was closely enmeshed'.[5] This 'delicate mixture' came under strain in the period, as the struggle for religious liberty on the part of those outside the Established

Church was yoked to the powerful new discourse of natural rights, and the rapid rise of evangelical Nonconformity asked searching new questions of the individual conscience.

Aside from interdenominational warfare, and the running sores of pluralism and non-residence, the main problems faced by the state Church in the period were mass abstention from worship, and the weaknesses of its parochial structure in the context of seismic demographic change. Essentially, the Church was losing ground because it was too slow to adapt to the pace and pattern of urbanisation and too slow to respond to the challenge of a new industrial working class. Richard Yates's clarion call, *The Church in Danger* (1815), points out that the Church's parochial organisation relates to a bygone age, and makes no provision for a hugely increased population or the rapid growth of London and the northern industrial towns. Whereas in some counties with stable populations, he says, there are an average 640 persons per parish or per minister, in the London suburbs there are 1,162,300 inhabitants in ninety-three parishes, meaning (on the assumption that each parish church accommodates at most two thousand people) that there are 946,000 persons with no access to a church, minister, religious instruction, or pastoral care. 'The mind shrinks', Yates says, 'from the contemplation of such a concentrated mass of Exclusion, Separation, and necessary Disaffection to the Established Church.'[6] His appeal did not fall on deaf ears: in 1818 Parliament established a Church Building Commission and gave it a million pounds to spend, a 'substantial first measure of ecclesiastical collectivism' that inspired churchmen with a vision of new social cohesion – until evidence emerged that the new churches were just as poorly attended as the old ones.[7]

The Church of England's sluggish response to change opened up fertile ground for the Nonconformists. Lord Harrowby said in the House of Lords in 1810 that the day would come when a majority of the population would be Nonconformist, and in terms of practising believers he was right. Nonconformism, or Dissent, is an umbrella term for all those Protestants who disowned some aspect of the doctrine, liturgy, or organisation of the Established Church; typically, they rejected the hierarchical form of Church government as represented by the Anglican episcopacy, and in theological terms held to the strict Calvinist doctrines of justification by faith (that is, salvation comes not through living a good life but through faith in the sacrifice that Christ made on one's behalf at the Crucifixion) and predestination (that is, the number of those so 'justified' is a small fraction of the total number of all living souls, pre-selected by God with no possibility of appeal). In the eighteenth century the main Dissenting groups were – roughly in order of wealth and social status – Presbyterians, Congregationalists, Baptists, and Quakers. Members of these Churches (collectively referred to as 'Old Dissent') were legally entitled to practise their religion, but suffered a number of key civil disabilities, including disqualification from posts in local and central government and exclusion from the universities of Oxford and Cambridge. Although the impact of these restrictions was moderated by a classically British fudge known as 'occasional conformity', official second-class status still rankled, and gave Dissent a political edge that was liable to be sharpened given the right circumstances. It was the administration of oaths required to enforce this religious discrimination, undertaken more or less scrupulously at different times in different parts of the country, that made Britain what historians call a 'confessional state'.

Recruitment to the Dissenting Churches was stagnant for much of the eighteenth century, but increased sharply through the Romantic period, with all the main sects bar the Quakers significantly expanding their numbers. The growth was particularly impressive in Wales, where chapel building proceeded at the rate of one chapel a week in the early decades of the nineteenth century, and where Dissenters outnumbered Anglicans by a ratio of 4:1 by the time of the 1851 census. Here, Nonconformism, liberal politics, and Welsh identity seemed to blend in a strangely powerful brew.[8] In Scotland the position was very different, because the Presbyterian Established Church was guaranteed by the Act of Union, creating an unusual situation wherein the king defended different faiths north and south of the border. Anglicans were an embattled minority in Scotland, where the intellectually combative General Assembly of the Church of Scotland more than compensated for the lack of a parliament. In Ireland, where the majority of the population was Catholic, the Protestant Church of Ireland (merged with the Church of England under the Act of Union) ministered to a small number of Anglo-Irish residents, while in the northern counties the majority Presbyterians, descendants of seventeenth-century Scottish immigrants, maintained their own defiant subculture in a context of steadily deepening ethnic tension. In England, meanwhile, Dissenters, after a century of official 'toleration', were prospering in many towns and cities like Birmingham, Bristol, and Norwich, exhibiting 'a sturdy and self-reliant culture built on the chapel foundations of pulpit oratory, fervent prayer and well-loved hymns, and schooled for civic service by years of petty exclusion and disciplined organisation'.[9]

Worldly success had somewhat blunted the rigour and purity of Old Dissent, overwhelmingly associated with the respectable middle classes. Most Nonconformists had become more liberal and rationalistic in their beliefs, a development reflected in, and reinforced by, the vitality of their excellent Dissenting academies. Many Presbyterians, in particular, were tending by the late eighteenth century to disavow the Trinity in favour of either Arianism (the belief that Christ was of a lesser order of divinity than God) or Socinianism (the belief that Christ was fully human, a position that entails rejection of the doctrine of Christ's sacrificial atonement for a fallen humanity); eventually these 'rational Dissenters' separated off into the new denomination of Unitarianism. Such anti-Trinitarian views were excluded from the provisions of the Toleration Act until a law passed in 1813, but legal discrimination and Establishment vilification did not prevent Unitarians achieving considerable cultural influence, and they provided the intellectual leadership for Dissenters' political campaigning throughout the period.

One factor impeding the growth of Old Dissent was an inward-looking tendency that resulted from earlier persecution: the more strictly Calvinist the theology, the more likely the elect (those predestined to enjoy eternal life) were to rest on their laurels, convinced they had no right or reason to try to convert their fellow human beings. This stance was transformed by the evangelical revival beginning in the first half of the eighteenth century, which reversed the drift towards a rational Christianity with a highly intuitive, emotional, gospel-based religion. With more or less simultaneous beginnings in America, Germany, Wales, and England, in the latter it was associated most with the names of George Whitefield, an inspirational preacher, and John Wesley, also an excellent orator but with organisational and managerial skills that Whitefield lacked. The evangelical movement pioneered by these founder 'Methodists' (originally a term of abuse) started as a pressure group within the Established Church, but by the end of the century friction with the Church, and pressure from within its own ranks, were such that a breakaway into formal Dissent had become inevitable. The characteristics of the fundamentalist Christian revival pursued by Whitefield, Wesley, and their followers are neatly summarised by D.W. Bebbington:

> *conversionism*, the belief that lives need to be changed; *activism*, the expression of the gospel in effort; *biblicism*, a particular regard for the Bible; and what may be called *crucicentrism*, a stress on the sacrifice of Christ on the cross. Together they form a quadrilateral of priorities that is the basis of Evangelicalism.

Whitefield's purer Calvinism gave Methodism in Wales its distinctive cast, but, owing to his autocratic control of the movement, it was Wesley's moderate 'Arminianism' (the belief that salvation was available to all) that became the dominant creed of English Methodism. For all evangelicals, however, conversion (a sudden, powerfully emotional experience by which one became assured of one's personal salvation) was paramount, and the 'line between those who had undergone the experience and those who had not was the sharpest in the world'.[10] It was this that fuelled the Methodists' commitment to itinerant preaching, and galvanised their travels on a regional, national, and, eventually, an international basis, to spread the gospel and find new souls to convert.

The growth of Methodism was the big religious success story of the Romantic period. Membership increased from around 38,000 in 1781 to around 305,000 in 1831, with the majority of converts coming from the poorer social classes. However, this generalised picture of expansion conceals a history of continual self-division, as successive Methodist fractions broke away from the Wesleyan parent body in protest against its strong, centralised Church government or its suppression of forms of evangelistic activity of which it disapproved. Neither was evangelicalism synonymous with Methodism: the movement exerted influence on other Nonconformist sects, especially the Congregationalists and Baptists, propelling the resurgent growth of 'Old Dissent' referred to above. The nature of its impact was to dilute the Calvinism of Nonconformist theology, promoting the message that the way to Jesus was open to all, and to encourage an interest in converting the world rather than separating from it. As a result, the social catchment of these denominations was enlarged on the pattern provided by Methodist congregations: an analysis of Nonconformist baptismal registers has shown that 'the massive expansion of Nonconformity in the first half of the nineteenth century took place predominantly among people who were poor, ill-educated, unsophisticated, and superstitious'.[11] While it improved the health of the old sects (Unitarianism and Quakerism aside) and forced the Methodists, ultimately, to secede from the Church of England, the evangelical awakening also affected Anglicanism itself. Of particular importance were a Cambridge group led by Isaac Milner and Charles Simeon, which acted as a nursery for young evangelical clergy, and the so-called 'Clapham sect' led by William Wilberforce, described by Elie Halévy as 'a group of laymen who linked the Evangelical clergy with the world of politics and business to which they themselves belonged', and who were prepared to work with anyone who had 'a sincere and practical zeal for the reformation of abuses, and the crusade against ignorance and vice'.[12] The abuses and vices against which they campaigned were partly internal to the Church, and partly rife in society at large. The Society for the Suppression of Vice, founded in 1802, was an evangelical initiative, and a vehicle for campaigning on a raft of favourite issues, including the elimination of duelling, blood sports, obscene publications, and prostitution. In their quest to reform national morality, evangelicals also supported causes like child protection and prison reform, and were a driving force in the abolition of the slave trade. In parallel with this tide of evangelical activity at home, the consolidation and expansion of the British empire in the period was accompanied by an unprecedented surge in Protestant evangelism on the global stage: new bishoprics were created in territories in Canada, Africa, and India, numerous missionary societies were founded, and the competition between Anglicanism and Nonconformism for the conversion of souls was exported to the colonies.

To complete the religious map of Britain, one needs first to acknowledge the presence of a significant Catholic minority population. In mainland Britain, this numbered around 130,000 in 1800, but in the same year the Act of Union incorporated over three million Irish Roman Catholics within the British State. In all parts of the country, Catholics laboured under the most extreme official discrimination: while the Catholic Relief Acts of 1778 and 1791 legalised Catholic worship, Catholics were disenfranchised and excluded from participation in civic life. The long, bitter, and politically vexed campaign for Catholic emancipation – all the more explosive in that it involved 'the Irish question' – will be dealt with in the next section. A much smaller, though growing, minority – perhaps around 25,000, mostly living in the East End of London – was constituted by British Jews, the victims more of private than public prejudice and discrimination. While most Jews lived in poverty, a small number, such as the novelist Isaac D'Israeli and the economist David Ricardo, established themselves among the intellectual elite, while others, such as the moneylender Jacob Rey, contributed to radical artisan culture.

For much of the eighteenth century, the religious creed known as 'deism' was perfectly respectable – congenial to some rational Dissenters and only faintly distinguishable from the views of some liberal-minded ('Latitudinarian') Anglicans. A form of Christian minimalism, deism was alternatively referred to as 'natural religion', since its fundamental tenet was that it was only possible to deduce the existence of a (benign) God from the evidence of nature, and it rejected revelation, miracles, mystery, and anything else deemed incompatible with reason. In the wake of the French Revolution, deism was increasingly lumped together with atheism as 'infidelity' (literally, 'non-belief', though its meaning is now confusingly restricted to sexual betrayal), and regarded as suspect not only theologically but also politically, by association with the godless menace of Jacobinism. Viewed objectively as a more radically heterodox position than deism, atheism, the outright denial of the existence of God, was the professed creed of a statistically insignificant but intellectually heavyweight elite in the period, the members of which ran the constant risk of prosecution under the still-operative Blasphemy Act of 1697. It should not, of course, be confused with mere religious indifference, which the religious census of 1851 ultimately confirmed as the most popular spiritual attitude of all.

Religion, politics, revolution

In today's society religion and politics are widely assumed to inhabit separate spheres, and leading bishops are sometimes ridiculed or patronised when they offer commentary on foreign affairs or even social policy. In the Romantic period, the reverse was the case: the peculiar nature of the alliance between Church and State meant that religion and politics were tightly interwoven, and much of the pressure for change stemmed from religious rather than narrowly political motives. Lord Eldon, the Lord Chancellor from 1807 to 1827, was fond of stating that the Established Church existed 'not for the purpose of making the Church political, but for the purpose of making the State religious',[13] but in fact both propositions were true: the Church of England was inherently a political entity, and the operations of the state were overseen by the watchful eye of the national religion.

The controversial work of Jonathan Clark has done much to stimulate debate on these matters. There is a much-quoted passage in his *English Society 1688–1832* that nicely captures how religion permeated social life, and how its official, institutionalised outworkings were a more likely target for the malcontent than any political apparatus:

> The agency of the State which confronted him in his everyday life was not Parliament, reaching out as a machinery of representative democracy: elections were infrequent, contests less frequent still, the franchise restricted, and access to MPs minimal for most electors. The ubiquitous agency of the State was the Church, quartering the land not into a few hundred constituencies but into ten thousand parishes, impinging on the daily concerns of the great majority, supporting its black-coated army of a clerical intelligentsia, bidding for a monopoly of education, piety and political acceptability.[14]

There is a compelling, intuitive logic to this description of a fundamentally religious society. However, Clark's main thesis is altogether bolder than this: he contends that the social and political order that came into question in the

Revolutionary and Napoleonic era had an essentially theological basis – namely, Anglican Protestantism – and that the assault on this British 'ancien régime' was motivated chiefly by religious heterodoxy, and directed to obtaining religious liberties rather than the political rights that historians have typically focused on. Moreover, of the three great legislative changes that mark the end of the period – that is, repeal of the Test and Corporation Acts (1828), Catholic emancipation (1829), and the 1832 Reform Act – parliamentary reform played, according to Clark, a subordinate role, being an accidental by-product of the other two rather than the inevitable consequence of the march of democratic opinion. The correctness or otherwise of the historical arguments involved here is beyond both the scope of this book and the competence of its author, but Clark's interpretation of the way in which the events of the period effected the dissolution of a social order provides, at the very least, a useful whetstone:

> The radicals were fighting old battles, not anticipating modern values; and the radical critique had its origins in theology, not economics. Beside partisanship, there is a large element of truth in a Dissenter's claim that Unitarians 'have been leaders in most of those changes which have transformed the England of the eighteenth century into the England of the present day' [i.e. 1938]. But they did so by destroying 'the past', not by anticipating 'the future'.[15]

Critics of Romanticism are no less prone to identifying with their subject than any other scholars: they would much rather see the period, and its literature, as a beginning, not an end, but exploring the religious cultures and controversies of the time provides a way of testing the validity of that perspective.

The religious politics of the period is best approached in two main phases: the impact of the French Revolution in the 1790s, and the resurgence of radicalism in the post-war period leading up to the flurry of reforms in 1828–32. In looking at aspects of these developments from the standpoint of religion I shall try to avoid repeating material covered in Chapter 1.

It is a truism that the early response to the Revolution in Britain was broadly favourable, and that Dissenters were prominent in welcoming the new dawn across the Channel. In his famous sermon of 4 November 1789 that aroused the wrath of Edmund Burke, the Presbyterian minister, Richard Price, greeted the Revolution as the triumph of thirty million people 'demanding liberty with an irresistible voice'. It is worth noting, however, that Price's enthusiasm for developments in France is as much for the abolition of 'priestcraft' as for the dismantling of absolute monarchy, and his concern in the main body of the sermon, addressed to the British situation, is as much with religious liberty as with civil rights. In commemorating the Glorious Revolution of 1688–9, Price highlights two major imperfections in the constitutional settlement it brought about: the inequality of Parliamentary representation, and the absence of complete religious toleration. 'The TEST LAWS,' he says, are 'still in force; and deprive of eligibility to civil and military offices, all who cannot conform to the established worship', a 'public iniquity' he compares to the French declaration of 'an indefeasible right of all citizens to be equally eligible to public offices'.[16] Price is optimistic that this wrong will soon be righted. The following year, a bill for the repeal of the Test and Corporation Acts, the third in four years, was heavily defeated, and as alarm mounted at the course of the Revolution this proved to be the last chance for a generation to meet this fundamental demand of all Nonconformists.

Among a very mixed community of believers, Revolutionary euphoria produced an upsurge of 'millenarianism' – that is, belief in an (imminent) apocalypse followed by a thousand-year period in which Christ will rule a regenerated earth before the final destruction of the world and Last Judgement, as foretold in the Book of Revelation. Enthusiasts and visionaries rushed to interpret contemporary events in the light of Old and New Testament prophecies of the last things. Perhaps surprisingly, rational Dissenters were caught up in this eschatological frenzy. Richard Price, already inspired by the American Revolution, saw in 1787 'the world outgrowing its evils, superstition giving way, antichrist falling, and the *Millennium* hastening', while in the same sermon quoted above he writes apocalyptically of the light that set America free being reflected to France, 'and there kindled into a blaze that lays despotism in ashes, and warms and illuminates EUROPE'.[17] The controversial Unitarian preacher, Joseph Priestley, identified the French Revolution with the violent earthquake prophesied in Revelation 11, noting biblical evidence that the kingdom of heaven would not be established 'without the greatest convulsions, and the violent overthrow of other kingdoms'; in the wake of the Terror, he wrote in 1795 that he was even more 'persuaded that the calamitous times foretold in the Scriptures are at hand'.[18] On the fringe of organised religion, the Church of the New Jerusalem founded in 1789 by followers of the Swedish mystic Emanuel Swedenborg provided a home for assorted millenarian radicals. At a still less 'respectable' level of popular culture, self-appointed prophets like Richard Brothers ('Nephew of the Almighty') and Joanna Southcott ('bride of Christ') claimed the direct inspiration of God for their visions of national calamity, and achieved large followings in the 1790s.

As described in Chapter 1, British responses to the Revolution altered rapidly as perceptions of violent misrule became the norm. Although the anti-war movement that continued through the 1790s 'was predominantly a Dissenting affair', this retrenchment, encouraged by state prosecution and loyalist persecution of those who stood up against government policy, engulfed Nonconformists along with the rest. The Baptist Robert Hall 'typified the change that came over the political outlook of many Dissenters in the 1790s': having published *Christianity consistent with a Love of Freedom* in 1791, by 1800 he was equating the French Revolution with *Modern Infidelity*.[19] One factor in this trend was undoubtedly the fate of the Church in France itself. Given the long tradition of regarding the Catholic Church as a force of darkness, its disestablishment in France was unlikely from one point of view to cause much anguish in Britain. Nevertheless, once Revolutionary France was seen as a threat, the Church could assume retrospective validity as a stabilising influence, and even those who sought disestablishment in Britain could take no comfort from an apparent tide of irreligion in France. For the pace of change across the Channel was hectic. Under the Civil Constitution of the Clergy of July 1790 ecclesiastical property was nationalised and priests became elected civil servants. Rising anticlericalism during the early years of the Revolution led to a more fundamental breakdown of the new relationship between Church and State, and an officially approved nationwide de-Christianisation campaign in 1793–4, which featured direct action against priests and churches, produced also various experiments in civic religion: the deistic Festival of Reason on 10 November 1793 and the spectacular Festival of the Supreme Being on 8 June 1794 are the landmarks. The inauguration of a new decimal calendar in November 1793 confirmed, as John McManners puts it, that the government 'regarded revolutionary France as a post-Christian country', while popular de-Christianisation was embraced by disparate citizens for whom sacrilegious behaviour was 'a symbol of the determination to destroy the old world'.[20]

The violent course of the Revolution vindicated, for many, Burke's argument that without religion society would descend into anarchy or despotism. Further confirmation of this thesis appeared to arrive, in the context of the invasion scare of 1797–8, in the form of books by the Abbé Barruel and John Robison alleging a carefully plotted conspiracy, on the part of both rationalist philosophers and German 'illuminati' (similar to freemasons), to overthrow the government of France by first demolishing its religious foundations. Brief, popular summaries of these voluminous works gave wide currency to the conspiracy theory, which remained active for years. One such potted account traces the steady progress of the philosophers' campaign over sixty years prior to the Revolution, their insidious deployment of ridicule and sophistry against Christianity preparing the ground for the final triumph of mob rule:

> Though the restraints of Religion had been got the better of, and morality had lost its influence, still an attachment to the laws to which they had been subject, was not entirely subdued. But it was necessary to obtain that victory before a complete revolution could be brought about. To accomplish this grand object became now the principal aim of the conspirators: by preaching up liberty and equality, they excited all nations to destroy the throne of their kings, as they had formerly done to overturn the altars of their Gods.

Religion, in the conspirators' eyes, covered kings with an 'impenetrable shield', and was therefore the 'first victim to be immolated' in their 'war of *extermination*'. Addressing the situation of Britain, the author warns that 'French Atheists', having become 'French Anarchists', now seek to complete their metamorphosis into 'French Invaders'.[21]

In such a volatile atmosphere, it is hardly surprising that religious authorities undertook a fundamental reappraisal of their position vis-à-vis political and social questions. Robert Hole has given a detailed account of the sea change that took place in Christian argument in the 1790s, with political theory increasingly giving way to social theory. For much of the eighteenth century, that is, religious arguments had featured prominently in political discourse about how governments derive and maintain their legitimacy: the same passages of Scripture were repeatedly invoked to draw a clear distinction between 'a divine obligation to submit to government in general, and the freedom of a society to determine for itself what form that government should take';[22] this basic formula was accepted by Anglicans and non-Anglicans alike, despite considerable disagreement on what the preferred or ideal form of government was, and lively dispute over the exact circumstances in which rebellion was permissible. In the years after the French Revolution, this rather abstract philosophising faded from view. In place of such arguments, religious discourse increasingly focused on the need to maintain social order and the role of Christianity in exercising such restraint. The justification of inequality became a favourite theme, with Burke leading the way in portraying the social and economic hierarchy as part of a subtle, harmonious, God-given order that should not be rashly swept aside. The poor were now seen as a major social problem, 'either to be pitied and reformed for their own eternal welfare, or to be feared and controlled for the good of society', and this was where the Church had a function to perform.[23] If this new discursive orientation had a theological component, it was to emphasise the unregenerate, fallen nature of man – a belief that dictated a very different view of government from the alternative belief, still held by beleaguered Unitarians and deists, that humanity was essentially good and capable of progressive improvement.

One other aspect of the religious politics of the 1790s deserves mention. One group that became the particular object of Establishment suspicion and hostility was the Methodists, their itinerant preaching and evangelistic fervour carrying dangerous connotations of demagoguery and disorder. The rumour began to circulate that radicals whose activities had been curbed by the Two Acts of 1795 had cunningly reinvented themselves as Dissenting preachers, that every Methodist minister was a Jacobin in sheep's clothing. Ironically, in the twentieth century historians came to regard Methodists as having prevented, rather than fomented, revolution in the period. The so-called 'Halévy thesis' maintained that, in a country ripe for revolution in many ways, 'the *élite* of the working class, the hard-working and capable bourgeois, had been imbued by the evangelical movement with a spirit from which the established order had nothing to fear'.[24] This thesis has been vigorously contested, with some writers choosing to emphasise the libertarian dimension of the Methodists' Arminian theology and the undoubted tensions between rank and file Methodists and their loyalist leaders. Nevertheless, Michael Watts shows that Halévy's position is still defensible: Methodism, in line with evangelical Nonconformity as a whole, recruited from the poor and uneducated, and while some were inevitably 'driven by economic hardship . . . to challenge the political system under which they lived', for most 'the brevity of life, the certainty of death, and the sense of helplessness in a frightening world, all which had predisposed them to accept the Evangelical message in the first place, militated against either political involvement or revolutionary action'.[25]

In the later years of the war with France and the troubled post-war period, many of the developments already noted remained in force. In the context of economic distress, popular disturbances, and renewed agitation for parliamentary reform, the Church continued to focus on matters of social discipline and hierarchy; to this end, it deepened its interest in religious education, especially the education of the poor, an issue on which Anglicans and Nonconformists could agree in principle but were frequently rivals in practice. The conspiracy theory of the French Revolution refused to die a death. Dissenters rediscovered their political instincts to become actively engaged in the parliamentary reform and anti-slavery movements. The Wesleyan Methodists, as ever, were anxious to dissociate themselves from any social disorder, urging their members to give the Society their undivided loyalty. One new factor in the post-war period was the rise of overt atheism as a political force. As Robert Hole says, views 'which before, if not exactly secret, had been kept private were now proclaimed openly', and there emerged a highly controversial alliance of radicalism and infidelity. Jeremy Bentham, who made the intellectual case for replacing the confessional state with a welfare state, and Richard Carlile, imprisoned repeatedly for publishing blasphemous libel, were two utterly contrasting figures belonging to this tendency who will feature later in this chapter. Overall, the expansion of evangelical Nonconformity, militant atheism, and the self-inflicted wound of Anglicanism's failure to adjust speedily enough to a changing society, conspired towards a progressive weakening of the constitution in Church and State.

It was in this context that the triple hammer blow of Repeal, Emancipation, and Reform was delivered to demolish 'ancien régime' England. After Fox's failed bill of 1790, repeal of the Test and Corporation Acts was a buried cause for the whole of the Revolutionary and Napoleonic period, but was revived in the more liberal atmosphere of the 1820s and eventually won Parliamentary approval in 1828. This campaign had a fraught relationship with the parallel campaign for Catholic emancipation, with many Dissenters opposing the Catholic claims, but the election of the nationalist leader of the Catholic Association in Ireland, Daniel O'Connell, as an MP in July 1828 – O'Connell was, of course, ineligible to take up his seat – finally convinced the government, if not public opinion, that emancipation was necessary. The sheer popular energy of the Catholic Association made civil war in Ireland a serious possibility, and it was political expediency rather than religious toleration that led to the Protestant constitution being breached by a 'democratic movement on the Celtic fringe of the British State'.[26] Emancipation was approved in April 1829. George IV complained that 'every thing was tending to revolution', while the MP John Wilson Croker more accurately predicted 'a revolution gradually accomplished *by due form of law*'. After much electoral chaos and social disorder, during which a conservative rump of bishops in the House of Lords succeeded in casting the Church in a very unfavourable light, Reform was passed at the third attempt in 1832. Destruction of the Anglican monopoly of state power was thus followed by the beginning of a broadening of the franchise; the confessional state, which had come to seem 'a justification of only a part of society, dominating the rest by the mechanics of patronage and corruption', was consigned to history.[27]

Ideas and debates

It is now time to look more closely at some of the key areas of religious debate in the period. In terms of sheer impact, there can be little doubt that the single most important, if not the most intellectually weighty, publication was Thomas Paine's *The Age of Reason* (1794–5), as explosive a contribution to religion as *Rights of Man* was to politics. Written to expose the fraudulent claims of Christianity and to defend deism, the book was regarded as indistinguishable from atheism by many of its readers. Although much of what Paine said had been anticipated in the work of the Scottish Enlightenment philosopher David Hume (1711–76), or more recently in Volney's *Ruins* (see Chapter 2), the cheap price (Part 1 sold for 1*s*. 6*d*.) and its author's unique rhetorical gifts made *The Age of Reason* a powerful intervention in the volatile atmosphere of the mid-1790s.

The opening two pages of Paine's 'individual profession of faith' eloquently announce his creed, setting it (in the lines preceding those quoted) in the context of disestablishment and de-Christianisation in France:

> I believe in one God, and no more; and I hope for happiness beyond this life.
> I believe in the equality of man; and I believe that religious duties consist in doing justice, loving mercy, and endeavouring to make our fellow-creatures happy. . . .
> I do not believe in the creed possessed by the Jewish church, by the Roman church, by the Greek church, by the Turkish church, by the Protestant church, nor by any church that I know of. My own mind is my own church.[28]

The first paragraph's almost throwaway reference to 'one God, and no more' anticipates his later explicit rejection of the divinity of Christ and indeed of orthodox Trinitarian Christianity, while the belief in immortality is slightly undercut by the conditional form of expression. The second paragraph affirms what could just as easily be a secular morality, and says nothing about the religious 'duty' of subordination that was central to the contemporary Christian defence of inequality. The third paragraph explicitly disowns any form of organised religion, its final sentence a magnificent assertion of mental and spiritual self-determination.

From these electrifying beginnings, Part 1 of *The Age of Reason* goes on to heap scorn on the whole edifice of revealed religion (revelation, Paine insists, is only revelation to the first person God speaks to!), on fundamental Christian doctrines like the Resurrection and Atonement (redemption, he says, implies pecuniary, not moral, justice), and on the Bible as a vehicle of morality (the Old Testament is so filled with cruelty and debauchery as to be more 'the word of a demon, than the word of God' (p. 20)). Paine does, however, praise Jesus as a 'virtuous reformer and revolutionist' (p. 14), though he rubbishes the idea that he was 'celestially begotten' (p. 11). His deism tells him that the natural creation is God's universal language, and that science is the grammarian of that language, progressively unveiling principles inherent in the structure of the universe. In a lengthy excursus on the subject of astronomy, Paine finds in the scientific knowledge (and its mechanical applications) gained from a study of planetary motions the real justification for the existence of a plurality of worlds. He has particular fun with the idea that all the planets in our solar system and beyond are inhabited:

> From whence, then, could arise the solitary and strange conceit that the Almighty, who had millions of worlds equally dependent on his protection, should quit the care of all the rest, and come to die in our world, because, they say, one man and one woman had eaten an apple? And, on the other hand, are we to suppose that every world in the boundless creation had an Eve, a serpent, and a redeemer? In this case, the person who is irreverently called the Son of God . . . would have nothing else to do than to travel from world to world, in an endless succession of deaths, with scarcely a momentary interval of life. (pp. 59–60)

With this degree of flippancy, it is no surprise that Paine's rational religion was mistaken as atheism in some quarters. Nor did Part 2 of *The Age of Reason*, a more prolonged assault on the divine authority of the Bible, do anything to repair his reputation. He first exposes the Old Testament books as anonymous compilations of fable, historical anecdote, and fortune-telling; then, switching to the New Testament, he argues, by highlighting their illogicalities, omissions, and internal contradictions, that the four Gospels were 'the production of some unconnected individuals, many years after the things they pretend to relate' (p. 150), and were only later gathered together and advertised as the direct testimony of the apostles.

Paine's book attracted more than forty outraged replies, prominent among them Richard Watson's *Apology for the Bible* (1796), which sought to counter the 'rank weed' of infidelity that threatened to 'overspread the land'.[29] Watson's detailed argument with Paine is essentially a rhetorical one, since there is no shared ground on which they might meet: Watson is predisposed to believe the Bible to be true and to see the historical and miraculous parts as inseparable, the one validating the other, whereas Paine is interested only in taking an axe (his own image) to the fraudulent untruths of the sacred text. Perhaps Watson is most effective when confronting Paine with problems of the existence of evil that have led others from deism to atheism. Paine would not have wished to take this step, but it could be a short one. Indeed, Watson's book itself excited a reply that is said to be the 'second published British declaration of atheism'.[30] Its author, Samuel Francis, happily agrees with Watson that Paine's critique of revealed religion puts pressure on his deistic world-view: defending many of Paine's points, he draws also on evidence from comparative mythology, especially the newly available knowledge of eastern civilizations, to argue that 'in all religious systems men are the type of their gods'.[31]

As an atheist, Francis believed that the causes of the universe were perfectly indifferent to human concerns, whereas Paine was still prepared to believe that the natural world gave witness to the power, wisdom, and munificence of its unknowable first cause, God. The most influential statement of this 'argument from design' in the period came from the Anglican cleric, William Paley, who was certainly no deist. His *View of the Evidences of Christianity* (1794) defends the revealed basis of religion, his main proposition being that the story for which Jesus, his apostles, and the early Church martyrs acted and suffered must be true, for no one would bring upon themselves 'enmity and hatred, danger and death' for the sake of what they knew to be an imposture.[32] At the time of its first appearance, the *Evidences* appeared to be a counterblast to Paine, though in fact it was directed at Hume; Paley complemented it in 1802 with his *Natural Theology*, a more popular work of Christian apologetics that went through multiple editions in the period.

Although its central metaphor is far from original, the opening of *Natural Theology* is undoubtedly a *tour de force*. Paley compares our reactions to finding a stone and a watch on some deserted heath. The stone might have been there forever; the watch, not. But why? The answer is that analysis of the watch indicates that 'its several parts are framed and put together for a purpose', and furthermore that it must have had a maker 'who formed it for the purpose which we find it actually to answer'.[33] Paley next supposes that the watch has the ability to reproduce itself. In such circumstances, it is not the first watch that is the 'cause or author' of the second, but the original watchmaker:

> There cannot be design without a designer; contrivance without a contriver; order without choice; arrangement, without anything capable of arranging; subserviency and relation to a purpose, without that which could intend a purpose; means suitable to an end, and executing their office in accomplishing that end, without the end ever having been contemplated, or the means accommodated to it. Arrangement, disposition of parts, subserviency of means to an end, relation of instruments to an use, imply the presence of intelligence and mind. (p. 12)

The watch, of course, stands for nature, which surpasses such a mechanical contrivance in its complexity, subtlety, and variety; the watchmaker is God. As his leading example of the proof of design, in a wide-ranging summary of research into animal and plant structures, Paley considers the eye, which is subject to innumerable modifications in mammals, birds, and fish. Dissection has revealed how complicated an apparatus the eye is, so why did God not come up with something simpler or give man the faculty of vision 'at once'?

> It is only by the display of contrivance, that the existence, the agency, the wisdom of the Deity, *could* be testified to his rational creatures. This is the scale by which we ascend to all the knowledge of our Creator which we possess, so far as it depends upon the phaenomena, or the works of nature. (p. 42)

The message is that God has set limits to his own power, imposed restrictions on himself, so he can make a more convincing exhibition of his wisdom. Wherever he looks in nature, Paley sees the same ingenious workmanship, finely tuning animal and plant structures to the circumstances in which each species lives. This confidence would eventually become unsustainable under pressure from Darwinian evolutionary theory, but the design argument, with its apparent harmonisation of science and religion, held sway during this period.

Popular as the design argument was, one needs to set against this essentially Latitudinarian tendency the more fundamentalist creed promulgated by the evangelical revival. One of its most influential spokesmen was William Wilberforce, whose *Practical View* (1797) epitomised the religious reaction against both British Jacobinism and 'modernising' trends in Christianity. Paley's religion was objectionable to Wilberforce because Paley seemed to him to have an inadequate sense of sin, his faith ill-adapted 'to the needs of an age in which natural suffering and individual depravity were only too apparent'.[34] Throughout the *Practical View*, Wilberforce draws a severe hierarchical distinction between 'nominal Christians', who are plainly in the ascendant, and 'true' or 'vital' Christians. The former play down the corruption and weakness of human nature to bolster their optimism regarding social improvement, whereas the actual state of humankind is proved by observation not only of 'barbaric' peoples but also of civilised nations, where depravity too often triumphs over the restraints of law, education, and public opinion. Nominal Christians are deficient in their love of Christ – a passion not to be confused with animal attraction but something sincere and deep-seated, excited by 'a strong impression of the worth of its object, and heightened by an abiding sense of great, unmerited, and continually accumulating obligations';[35] they also set too much store by the infinite mercy of God, who is bound by no contract to reward good deeds with eternal life.

Wilberforce is equally unwilling for Christianity to be 'reduced to a mere creed' (p. 144) as he is for it to be limited to a set of 'penal statutes' (p. 180): the practical Christianity he advocates involves an aggressive engagement with the world, a wholehearted waging of war on sin. True Christians are enjoined to devote their bodily and mental faculties to the service of God throughout their daily lives, and not to compartmentalise the claims of religion to certain areas of life or to certain times of the week. While the commercial and professional world hold obvious dangers for the Christian, so too do the otherwise laudable pursuits of art and learning, for 'God requires to set up his throne in the heart, and to reign in it without a rival: if he be kept out of his right, it matters not by what competitor' (pp. 176–7). (It was this tendency to apply the language of 'amatory complaint and bridal sensuality' to the relationship between the soul and God that attracted Leigh Hunt's ridicule in a passionate anti-evangelical essay of 1809.[36]) The correct path is a middle way between 'an inactive and unprofitable life' and the loss of 'spiritual-mindedness' that can accompany immersion in the world (p. 275), and rigorous and constant self-examination is required to satisfy oneself that one has not strayed from this path. Although, therefore, it is Wilberforce's evangelical faith that justification occurs only through faith in the Atonement, his economy of redemption encompasses the Christian's relations with others and his life in the community:

> In short, he is to demean himself, in all the common affairs of life, like an *accountable* creature, who, in correspondence with the Scripture character of Christians, is 'waiting for the coming of the Lord Jesus Christ'. Often therefore he questions himself, 'Am I employing my time, my fortune, my bodily and mental powers, so as to be able to "render up my account with joy, and not with grief"?' (pp. 344–5)

139

Wilberforce's survey of the contemporary state of Christianity suggests that there are few in the higher and middle classes who could answer this question in the affirmative, and he fears the country is heading in the same irreligious direction as France. Nevertheless, with Britain at war, he pins his faith not to the army and navy but to the intercession of those who still 'love and obey the Gospel of Christ' (p. 489), for God will favour the nation to which his trustiest servants belong.

Paine's radical deism, Paley's natural theology, and Wilberforce's evangelicalism together configure much of the religious debate of the period. It remains to glance briefly at a few outcrops of full-blown 'infidelity'. As stated above, aggressively outspoken atheism emerged as a political force in the final third of the period, but it was the professed creed of only a small band of extremists, and self-censorship continued to operate in the literary community at large. The religious opinions of William Godwin are a case in point. Godwin's atheism is certainly inferable from his best-known work, *Political Justice* (1793): in a chapter on 'Political Imposture', for example, he disdains belief in a religious retributive morality:

> all that can be told me of a future world, a world of spirits, or of glorified bodies, where the employments are spiritual . . . or of a scene of retribution, where the mind, doomed to everlasting inactivity, shall be wholly a prey to the upbraidings of remorse, and the sarcasms of devils, is so foreign to everything with which I am acquainted, that my mind in vain endeavours to believe or to understand it.[37]

However, it was not until 1818 that Godwin made fully explicit his 'infidel' position. His essay 'On Religion' declares him 'thoroughly satisfied that no book in existence contains a record and history of the revelation of the will of an invisible being' and describes the autobiographical steps from a strict Presbyterian upbringing to his complete rejection of Christianity. Spurning the false anxieties and terrors of Christian spirituality, he proposes instead contemplation of the wonders of nature and a kind of temple of human creativity celebrating the best of 'human virtue, energy, fortitude, philanthropy, beneficence'.[38] However, it is indicative of Godwin's shrewd survival mentality that this essay, along with the more elaborate *Genius of Christianity Unveiled* (written in 1835), was not published until after his death.

In the post-war years, though, there were other committed atheists prepared to stick their heads above the parapet. The atheist case against Christianity drew ammunition from a number of sources: biblical criticism, comparative mythology, political utility, and materialist science. Iconoclastic as Tom Paine was, his work fitted within a well-established tradition of enquiry into the origins and authenticity of biblical texts, and links to the contemporaneous development of careful linguistic and historical analysis of those texts by Johann Eichhorn and other practitioners of the 'Higher Criticism' in Germany – though this body of work, initially filtered through Unitarian channels in Britain, fell victim like Unitarianism to the anti-Jacobin backlash and was 'virtually ignored' for the next thirty years. Presenting the Bible not as 'divinely inspired', but as 'the record of the myths and aspirations of an ancient and primitive Near Eastern tribe',[39] this textual criticism had much in common with the growth subject of comparative mythology. Volney's *Ruins* and Samuel Francis's *Watson Refuted* have already been noted as early works in this tradition, informed by the intercultural researches of Sir William Jones and his circle of Orientalists. William Drummond's *The Oedipus Judaicus* (1811) and Robert Taylor's *The Diegesis* (1829) continued the project of demystification, demonstrating that the sacred texts of Christianity contained no new revelations but were a composite of earlier mythologies, such as the Egyptian and Indian.[40] Political utility was the chosen weapon of Jeremy Bentham in the assault on religion, focused in three major anti-Christian polemics published between 1818 and 1823. For Bentham, religion would be justified if it could be proved to serve the aims of utility (by which he means the 'temporal happiness of mankind'), but in fact it has the opposite effect, because it discourages that sole reliance on fact and experience which alone makes rational action possible in favour of trust in an illusory supernatural agency. In the long run, his particular brand of atheism was to be more influential than any other, for, as Robert Hole observes, utilitarianism has 'done more than anything else to undermine the centrality of religion and to destroy it as a major intellectual force in modern society'.[41]

The fourth fuel source for militant atheism was the controversial rise of materialist science, aspects of which have already been surveyed in Chapter 5. Here it is worth commenting on one of the leading supporters of such men, and the most important atheist publisher of his time, Richard Carlile. Carlile republished the proscribed works of Paine and fearlessly brought out work by other freethinkers in his periodicals *The Deist* and *The Republican*, his business conducted much of the time from within prison. In his own *Address to Men of Science* (1821), he has no qualms in announcing his commitment to biological materialism:

> Instead of viewing ourselves as the particular and partial objects of the care of a great Deity, or of receiving those dogmas of the priest which teach us that every thing has been made for the convenience and use of man, and that man has been made in the express image of the Deity, we should consider ourselves but as atoms of organized matter, whose pleasure or whose pain, whose existence in a state of organization, or whose non-existence in that state, is a matter of no importance in the laws and operations of Nature. . . .

Carlile's aim is actually to berate, rather than praise, contemporary scientists, who are said to have 'crouched to the established tyrannies of Kingcraft and Priestcraft' out of self-interest and failed to spread to the general public 'those plain truths, which are so clear and so familiar to their own minds'.[42] Scientists should not be an enlightened class apart, but should take upon themselves the eradication of ignorance and superstition that are responsible for so much misery. Writing in his eighteenth month of imprisonment in Dorchester Gaol, Carlile at least had the moral authority to level such accusations.

Directions in ethics

The main premise of this chapter is that religion was the main agent in shaping the morals of the nation in the period, just as it also played a major role in prescribing social duties and responsibilities. Most ordinary people would still have looked to the Church, or to their religious instructors, for guidance on notions of good and evil, or right and wrong, or their own responsibilities within the family or community at large. The rise of evangelical Christianity was of particular importance in this regard, helping to establish the doctrine of separate male and female spheres that became so characteristic a feature of nineteenth-century Britain. Leonore Davidoff and Catherine Hall have shown how evangelical doctrine 'made possible the construction of a new subject – the Christian middle-class man', distinguished by moral earnestness, tender-heartedness, a strong work ethic, and the repudiation of traditional gentry customs and codes. Conversely, the 'new female subject' was a 'godly wife and mother', subordinate yet not inferior, who exercised moral influence within the sanctuary of a 'privatized home'.[43]

Nevertheless, religious injunctions on such matters would only hold weight for as long as the pillars of religious faith remained upright, and this was less certain in an age when the religious scene was becoming more fractious and pluralistic, and when scepticism was spreading, whether in the form of deism and its minimalist belief in a divine creator, or as out-and-out atheism. More-over, in the wake of the French Revolution, as I have explained, all religious bodies became rapidly and deeply politicised, and Christian teaching over-whelmingly focused on matters of social control and the justification of hierarchy and inequality. Clearly, this ran the risk of compromising the integrity of Christianity's approach to fundamental ethical questions. And ethical discussion was not exhausted by a Christian frame of reference: in fact, the period witnessed two seminal developments in theoretical ethics that both attempt to establish what is right independently of religious belief, namely utilitarianism and Kantian deontology, and I shall briefly examine these in this section. To begin with, a few further observations on the Christian ethical tradition are in order.

Theoretical ethics concerns itself with what one ought to do or refrain from doing, and within a Christian framework this is superficially a straightforward matter: an action is right if God commands or allows it, and wrong if he forbids it. However, even accepting that God's commands are to be found in the Bible, there remain huge problems of interpretation with regard to their meaning and application. And even if one is confident of having dealt with these and of knowing how to obey God, there exists, at the level of what is called 'metaethics', the problem of why one should do so. In his succinct treatment of this issue in his *Short History of Ethics*, Alasdair MacIntyre suggests there are three possible answers: one obeys God simply 'because he is God', or because God is good, or because God is powerful. The first answer gives way to the second when one can no longer tolerate the complete self-abasement that it involves. The second answer gives way to the third when one fails to resolves the contradictions it entails: if one obeys God because he is good, then this presupposes independent criteria of goodness that God is following, but if one has access to these criteria, why not cut out the middleman, God? The third answer seems unsatisfactory because it makes doing what is right entirely self-interested – one obeys an all-powerful God to earn one's heavenly reward, or to avoid going to hell – when the purpose of religious morality was supposed to be to combat self-interest. However, this can be a politically useful message in societies where virtuous behaviour does not seem to produce many tangible benefits:

> In a society where disease, famine, hunger, and death at an early age are among the staple components of human life, as they have been for the vast majority of people throughout history, belief in the power of God to make happiness coincide with virtue, at least in another world, if not in this, keeps open the question of the point of moral rules.[44]

There is no doubt that religious leaders in Britain made considerable use of this argument from the 1790s onwards, when defence of the social order came to seem paramount, and when the equality of men and women before God had to be rigorously separated from any notions of political or economic equality. However, the very attempt to present the case for virtue in terms of the kinds of benefits that human beings might reasonably desire, even via some form of deferred gratification, took Christianity into a dangerous fight on the territory of a powerful new ethical discourse, utilitarianism.

Grounded in the mechanical and associationist psychology of John Locke and David Hartley and a native British tradition of moral philosophy that explored the grounds and limits of self-interest, utilitarianism was nonetheless essentially the creation of Jeremy Bentham, under whose leadership it became a major catalyst of legal and social reform. His *Introduction to the Principles of Morals and Legislation* (1789) provides a clear exposition of what philosophers term a 'consequentialist' theory of ethics – that is, one that assesses the rightness or wrongness of an action solely in terms of its likely consequences. Bentham's fundamental psychological assumption is that human beings desire pleasure and seek to avoid pain, and are incapable of acting otherwise. From this he derives his single moral principle, the principle of utility, which states that actions are right insofar as they promote the happiness of the party or parties concerned, or 'prevent the happening of mischief, pain, evil, or unhappiness'.[45] Bentham believes that the amount of happiness or unhappiness produced is susceptible of calculation, and does not restrict his view to the self-interest of the agent: it is crucial to his formulation of utilitarianism that the interest of the wider community should be taken into account, and that no one's happiness is to be rated as more important than anyone else's. By subsequently redefining his core proposition as the 'greatest happiness principle' – that is, right actions are those that promote the greatest happiness of the greatest number – Bentham highlighted its politically controversial nature, and it is this basic democratic aspect of utilitarian ethics that has proved so influential, in the long run, on all those involved in public decision-taking.

143

In the withering second chapter of his *Introduction*, Bentham makes short work of many alternative ethical norms: the principle of asceticism, which, as he observes, has not been 'carried to any considerable length, when applied to the business of government' (p. 19); and various theories of an intuitive moral sense, or common sense, which in his eyes attempt to erect personal approval or disapproval into regulatory principles, and tend wittingly or unwittingly to despotism. He dismisses the idea of the will of God as the basis of personal or political morality, since this raises too many problems of interpretation ('Thou shall not kill', for example, fails to illuminate a whole host of possible situations where killing may be justified), and is usually construed anyway in the light of one of the other principles he rejects.

For Bentham, the main objective is for private self-interest to be channelled into serving the public interest (which was the main focus of his concern), and the only way in which individuals can be made to do something that legislators have deemed desirable is through the enlightened management of pleasure and pain. This in turn requires a full understanding of the different categories of pleasure and pain (Bentham lists fourteen simple pleasures and twelve simple pains), and of the various criteria, such as intensity and duration, according to which these vary, and which need to be factored in to any overall calculation of utility. Once this calculation is made, legislators will consider what sanctions might be used to give 'binding force' to the type of conduct in question: 'political sanctions' are those for which they are directly responsible, but they will also take into account the role of 'moral sanctions' (those brought to bear in an informal way by the community at large) and 'religious sanctions' (those supposed to be brought to bear by a 'superior invisible being'), while all these are ultimately rooted in the 'physical sanctions' that arise through natural causes (pp. 34–5). The reduction of religion to an inferior and unreliable form of sanction is a striking aspect of this theory:

> The pains of piety are the pains that accompany the belief of a man's being obnoxious to the displeasure of the Supreme Being: and in consequence to certain pains to be inflicted by his especial appointment, either in this life or in a life to come. These may also be called . . . the pains of the religious sanction. When the belief is looked upon as well-grounded, these pains are commonly called religious terrors; when looked upon as ill-grounded, superstitious terrors. (p. 48)

Under this ethical system, for example, revolutionary action in France would be judged solely against the standard of utility: traditional religious arguments against rebellion and in favour of hierarchy would be dismissed as 'superstitious terrors', and the new political order would be assessed favourably for as long as it promoted the extension of representative democracy and individual liberty.

The many philosophical problems raised by utilitarianism, and the efforts made to overcome these via modifications or revisions to the theory, are beyond the scope of this discussion. It is sufficient here to underline the radicalism of Bentham's contribution to theoretical ethics in its contemporary cultural context. Equally radical, however, was a rival theory emerging at around the same time in the work of the Prussian philosopher, Immanuel Kant, who 'stands at one of the great dividing points in the history of ethics'.[46] Kant entirely rejects consequences in favour of intentions as the focus of his moral theory, which is much more attuned – in contrast with utilitarianism – to individuals' acts than to collective decision-making. He begins with the proposition that nothing is unconditionally good except a 'good will', and what makes a good will good is not 'what it effects or accomplishes' but its adherence to duty rather than inclination as a motive for action.[47] Acting in accordance with duty entails obedience to a law that is binding on all rational beings; Kant formulates this universal law – a 'categorical imperative' utterly different, as supreme principle, to Bentham's principle of utility – in several ways, two of which have attracted most attention. First, he proposes that you should 'act only on that maxim through which you can at the same time will that it should become a universal law' (p. 88). A maxim being the rule of conduct one is implicitly following in acting as one does, this categorical imperative states that one should only do something if one can, without inconsistency or self-contradiction, commend the rest of the world to do likewise. (One of Kant's examples is a man who borrows money on the strength of a promise to pay it back within a fixed time, knowing he cannot keep this promise; the maxim that condones this action cannot be universalised because universal promise-breaking would illegitimise the very act of promising the man relies on to obtain his money.) One criticism levelled at this theory is that maxims can be formulated in different ways, and that for any self-interested act it is always possible, with a little imagination, to frame a maxim that can be universalised with no inconvenience to oneself. Kant's second version of the categorical imperative seems sounder to many philosophers: namely, that you should 'act in such a way that you always treat humanity, whether in your own person or in the person of any other, never simply as a means, but always at the same time as an end' (p. 96). To treat a person as a mere means is to use them in a way to which they could not consent, typically using deception or coercion; to treat another as an end is to treat him or her as a rational being who exists on the same basis as oneself, with interests and goals that might legitimately be fostered. One way of gauging the strength of this theory is with respect to one of the great moral causes of the period, abolition: Kant's 'Formula of the End in Itself' would immediately outlaw slavery (since it involves coercion), whereas slavery is not so readily debarred, and can even be justified, on utilitarian principles.

As for religion, Kant seems to have had an abstract belief in God and immortality, if only to guarantee that obedience to the moral law would be rewarded with happiness in the next life. But his strong belief in rational autonomy means that he will not countenance God (or any earthly power) as ethical arbiter, insisting instead that each person is his or her own moral authority. His ethical stance is thus well attuned to the individualism of the Revolutionary era, rejecting as it does all external sovereignty over one's moral choices, at the same time as it conspicuously fails to provide much orientation in the world of social needs and purposes – it is better at prohibiting certain kinds of behaviour than recommending how to live a productive, beneficial life.

Kantian ethics has been immensely influential on the Western philosophical tradition. However, owing to problems of translation and transmission, exacerbated by the prolonged war on the Continent, the full impact of his thought postdates the period: despite the best efforts of a number of writers (including Samuel Taylor Coleridge and Thomas De Quincey) to mediate German thought for a domestic audience, his work was the object at best of suspicious interest before 1830, was restricted to a tiny intellectual elite, and had negligible influence on British culture generally. Quite the reverse was the case with Bentham, as I have made clear: his utilitarian ethics was the bedrock of a wide-ranging campaign for reform of Parliament, the law, and educational and other institutions, and the *Westminster Review* became the house journal of the 'philosophical radicals' led by him and his followers (notably James Mill) and an important instrument in their battle for public opinion. The early translation of his works facilitated the spread of his ideas and influence across the world, so that William Hazlitt could observe sardonically in 1825 that Bentham's name was 'little known in England, better in Europe, best of all in the plains of Chile and the mines of Mexico'.[48]

Notes

1. W.R. Ward, *Religion and Society in England 1790–1850* (London, 1972), p. 1.

2. *English Society in the Eighteenth Century*, revised edn (Harmondsworth, 1991), p. 168.

3. Linda Colley, *Britons: Forging the Nation 1707–1837* (London, 1992), p. 388.

4. E.R. Norman, *Church and Society in England 1770–1970* (Oxford, 1976), p. 15.

5. David Hempton, *Religion and Political Culture in Britain and Ireland: From the Glorious Revolution to the Decline of Empire* (Cambridge, 1996), p. 17.

6. Richard Yates, *The Church in Danger: A Statement of the Cause, and of the Probable Means of Averting that Danger Attempted; in a Letter to the Right Honourable Earl of Liverpool* (London, 1815), p. 51.

7. Norman, *Church and Society*, p. 53.

8. See Hempton, *Religion and Political Culture*, pp. 49–63.

9. Hempton, *Religion and Political Culture*, pp. 128–9.

10. D.W. Bebbington, *Evangelicalism in Modern Britain: A History from the 1730s to the 1980s* (London, 1989), pp. 3, 5.

11. Michael R. Watts, *The Dissenters. Vol. II: The Expansion of Evangelical Nonconformity* (Oxford, 1995), pp. 326–7.

12. Elie Halévy, *A History of the English People in the Nineteenth Century, I: England in 1815*, 2nd edn (London, 1949), pp. 435, 438.

13. Quoted in J.C.D. Clark, *English Society 1688–1832: Ideology, Social Structure and Political Practice during the Ancien Regime* (Cambridge, 1985), p. 351.

14. *English Society*, p. 277.

15. *English Society*, p. 347.

16. *A Discourse on the Love of our Country* (London, 1789), pp. 36, 38.

17. *The Evidence for a Future Period of Improvement in the State of Mankind* (London, 1787), p. 2; *Love of our Country*, p. 50.

18. *The Present State of Europe Compared with Ancient Prophecies*, in *The Theological and Miscellaneous Works of Joseph Priestley*, ed. J.T. Rutt, 25 vols (Hackney, 1817–31; repr. New York, 1972), XV, 519–52 (p. 535); letter quoted in Morton D. Paley, *Apocalypse and Millennium in English Romantic Poetry* (Oxford, 1999), p. 111.

19. Watts, *Dissenters II*, pp. 350, 355.

20. *The French Revolution and the Church* (London, 1969), pp. 86, 88.

21. *Jacobinism Displayed; in an Address to the People of England* (Birmingham, 1798), pp. 18–19, 23–4, 31.

22. Robert Hole, *Pulpits, Politics and Public Order in England, 1760–1832* (Cambridge, 1989), p. 15.

23. Hole, *Pulpits*, pp. 131–2.

24. Halévy, *England in 1815*, p. 425.

25. Watts, *Dissenters II*, p. 376.

26. Hempton, *Religion and Political Culture*, p. 81.

27. Clark, *English Society*, pp. 399, 393, 375.

28. *The Age of Reason* (Paris, 1794; repr. New York, 1984), pp. 1–2.

29. *An Apology for the Bible, in a Series of Letters, Addressed to Thomas Paine* (London, 1796), p. 382.

30. Martin Priestman, *Romantic Atheism: Poetry and Freethought, 1780–1830* (Cambridge, 1999), p. 38.

31. *Watson Refuted: Being an Answer to the Apology for the Bible* (1796; repr. London, 1819), p. 15.

32. *A View of the Evidences of Christianity* (1794; repr. London, 1829), p. 181.

33. *Natural Theology: Or, Evidences of the Existence and Attributes of the Deity, Collected from the Appearances of Nature* (London, 1802), pp. 2, 3–4.

34. Boyd Hilton, *The Age of Atonement: The Influence of Evangelicalism on Social and Economic Thought, 1795–1865* (Oxford, 1988), pp. 4–5.

35. *A Practical View of the Prevailing Religious System of Professed Christians, in the Higher and Middle Classes of this Country, Contrasted with Real Christianity* (London, 1797), p. 112.

36. Leigh Hunt, *An Attempt to Shew the Folly and Danger of Methodism* (London, 1809), p. 55.

37. *Enquiry Concerning Political Justice*, ed. Isaac Kramnick (Harmondsworth, 1976), p. 495.

38. 'Of Religion', in *Political and Philosophical Writings of William Godwin*, ed. Mark Philp, 7 vols (London, 1993), VII, 63–73 (pp. 63, 69).

39. Stephen Prickett, 'Romantics and Victorians: From Typology to Symbolism', in *Reading the Text: Biblical Criticism and Literary Theory*, ed. Prickett (Oxford, 1991), pp. 182–224 (pp. 184–5).

40. See Priestman, *Romantic Atheism*, pp. 192–8.

41. *Pulpits*, p. 203.

42. Richard Carlile, *An Address to Men of Science* (London, 1821), pp. 6, 8–9.

43. *Family Fortunes: Men and Women of the English Middle Class 1780–1850*, revised edn (London, 2002), pp. 110, 114–15.

44. Alasdair MacIntyre, *A Short History of Ethics: A History of Moral Philosophy from the Homeric Age to the Twentieth Century*, 2nd edn (London and New York, 1998), p. 110.

45. *An Introduction to the Principles of Morals and Legislation*, ed. J.H. Burns and H.L.A. Hart (London, 1970), p. 12.

46. MacIntyre, *Short History*, p. 183.

47. *The Moral Law: Kant's Groundwork of the Metaphysic of Morals*, trans. H.J. Paton, 3rd edn (London, 1956), p. 62.

48. 'Jeremy Bentham', in *The Spirit of the Age*, in *Complete Works*, XI (1932), 5–16 (p. 5).

Chapter Seven

The Sense of the Past

The title of this book respects the conventional boundaries of literary history and encloses the 'Romantic period' within a span of just over forty years. This particular staking-out of the territory has had a poor press in recent years, with the result that English Romanticism has sometimes been absorbed into either a 'long eighteenth century' or 'long nineteenth century', depending on where the vested interests lie. However, insofar as the term survives in our formal or informal compartmentalising of English literature, as it does on many university syllabuses and in the production of textbooks and anthologies, it demands for its forty-odd years an amount of space and attention equal to, or greater than, that devoted to much longer stretches of time. The only justification for this is its status as a period of 'hot chronology' – that is, a period of unusually dense activity (whether in narrow literary terms or in society and politics at large) in which the 'pressure of history' is felt.[1]

Not only is this perception of high density validated by modern criticism and institutional structures, it also clearly resonates with observations made by writers and commentators in the period itself. Shelley's claim in the preface to *Prometheus Unbound* that the great writers of his own age are 'the companions and forerunners of some unimagined change in our social condition or the opinions which cement it' is just one expression of a widely-shared belief that history was in the making, that the nation was undergoing, or about to undergo, a momentous transformation.[2] What is less easy to appreciate is the way in which this belief took shape in the context of a major shift in historical awareness, one that influenced collective attitudes to the past and the kinds of meanings that could be derived from the study of history. As with so many aspects of Romantic culture treated in this book, the picture is of a state of transition, with many contrasting features and contrary lines of development. On the one hand, for example, it is possible to look back to the early nineteenth century for the origins of modern historical scholarship and historiography; on the other, a cursory acquaintance with Romantic literature is sufficient to show the extent to which writers and their audience were in thrall to a range of imaginary or idealised histories. As Marilyn Gaull puts it, the Romantics may have been the last generation to be without a 'cosmic history', in the sense of a comprehensive scientifically based understanding of the universe and humanity's place in it, but they had a wide variety of illusions.[3]

In this chapter, I shall consider, first, the evidence for a new type of historical consciousness emerging in the Romantic period, then review some of the more popular forms of historical thinking or historical obsession that were current at the time: primitivism and the cult of the 'noble savage'; the reorientation of neoclassicism towards ancient Greece; and the fascination with ancient Britain, the Middle Ages, and the origins of national history. Other important manifestations of the new 'historicism', such as the challenge posed by geology to the traditional Christian account of creation, have been discussed in earlier chapters.

The age of history

In 1831, the utilitarian philosopher John Stuart Mill published a series of articles in the *Political Examiner* on the theme of 'The Spirit of the Age'. This very phrase, which was evidently common currency at the time Mill was writing, is itself indicative of a new historical self-consciousness. Famously used by William Hazlitt as the title for a collection of 'Contemporary Portraits' (biographical and critical essays) in 1825, and by Shelley to celebrate the 'electric life' of contemporary writers in the conclusion to his 'Defence of Poetry' in 1821, it is said by Mill to be no more than fifty years old, making it virtually coterminous with the Romantic period as defined here. The obvious buoyancy and expressiveness of the phrase has led James Chandler, in a book I draw heavily upon in this section, to call the Romantic period 'the age of the spirit of the age'.[4]

For Mill, the leading characteristic of the present age is that it is 'an age of transition', in which people 'have outgrown old institutions and old doctrines, and have not yet acquired new ones'.[5] His particular focus is the decay of the aristocracy as the class of men best equipped to influence public opinion and morality and to exercise worldly power. In a 'natural' state of society, Mill argues, there is uniformity of opinion on important matters of public interest, because power, and fitness for power, are seen as being in alignment. In a 'transitional' state, by contrast – and Mill believes the current age of transition began with the French Revolution, which destroyed the myth of the innate superiority of the aristocracy – there are rival claimants to material and ideological power, and intellectual and moral chaos reigns until some general reconstruction places power once again, to general acceptance, 'in the hands of the most competent' (p. 253). Since he clearly values education, philosophical wisdom, and gentlemanly independence, this presumably means people like Mill himself, especially since, at the age of twenty-four, he fits his own description of the youthful energy and flexibility that in troubled times may be 'the sole hope of society' (p. 295). What is interesting is that Mill distils his idea of the spirit of the age through a series of comparisons of late-Georgian Britain with natural and transitional societies of the past: medieval Christendom, on the one side, for example, Reformation Europe on the other. While transitionality is thus a recurring phenomenon, the intense self-reflexivity of the present is not: 'The idea of comparing one's own age with former ages, or with our notion of those which are yet to come, had occurred to philosophers; but it never before was itself the dominant idea of any age.' (p. 228) One reason it has become the dominant idea is precisely the diffusion of knowledge, and consequent broadening of the base of debate, that have served to weaken the grip of society's 'natural leaders'.

There was thus a remarkably close link in Romantic-period culture between the experience of being in a state of transition and the development of a sense of history. There is wide agreement among scholars working from within different national traditions that such a development was indeed a defining feature of the period. Michel Foucault dates a radical rupture in Western forms of thought to around the end of the eighteenth century, summarising the before and after as a shift from 'Order' (the static definitions and classifications beloved of the Enlightenment) to 'History'. Up to this point, he argues, humanity and everything else on the planet had been thought of as being drawn along in one 'vast historical stream, uniform in each of its points'; afterwards, human beings found themselves dissolved into multiple and discontinuous histories, in which 'things' (both living creatures and inanimate objects) had a timeline proper to themselves and irrelevant to that of humanity. 'Man', Foucault says, 'found himself dispossessed of what constituted the most manifest contents of his history', in that an alienated nature no longer spoke to him 'of the creation or the end of the world, of his dependency or his approaching judgement', but merely of its own imperturbable time. The way in which humankind recovered from the shock of this 'dehistoricisation' was first by imaginatively investing in certain traces of its own past (as with the popular antiquarianism discussed later in this chapter), then, more seriously, by the full-blown invention of the human sciences, which put humanity at the centre of the generation of knowledge. Foucault privileges the disciplines of biology, economics, and philology, but history is crucial too as a subject in its own right and as the foundation of all the others:

> there appears another, more radical, history, that of man himself – a history that now concerns man's very being, since he now realizes that he not only 'has history' all around him, but is himself, in his own historicity, that by means of which a history of human life, a history of economics, and a history of languages are given their form.[6]

Foucault has little directly to say about what this major epistemological shift might mean for the 'history of History', but there is no shortage of thinkers addressing the topic. Friedrich Meinecke's classic study, *Historism: The Rise of a New Historical Outlook*, defines the movement it examines as 'the substitution of a process of *individualising* observation for a *generalising* view of human forces in history', by which is implied the discrediting of a timeless human nature and a wholly new emphasis on 'the profound changes and the variety of forms undergone by the spiritual and intellectual life of individual men and human communities'.[7] Meinecke dates the emergence of this new form of historical thinking to the second half of the eighteenth century, and gives pride of place to the great German thinkers Herder and Goethe for its early flowering. The British philosopher of history, R.G. Collingwood, fixes on the 1780s for the origin of modern 'scientific' history. Writing in 1935, he says:

I do not mean that there were no historians worthy of the name until a century and a half ago; that would be untrue: I do not even mean that since then the bulk of historical knowledge and the output of historical books have enormously increased; that would be true but relatively unimportant. What I mean is that during this time historical thought has worked out a technique of its own, no less definite in its character and certain in its results than its elder sister, the technique of natural science.

Collingwood describes a shift away from what he terms 'scissors-and-paste' history, which involves selecting and combining statements made by various historical actors or witnesses, with more or less attention given to determining their individual reliability, to a method based upon the interpretation of evidence relating to human actions in the past in order to answer questions posed by historians to themselves. He evidently regards this latter method, which resembles the judicial examination of witnesses, as having established itself by 1830, since anyone still practising scissors-and-paste at the time he writes would be 'at least a century out of date'.[8] This agrees broadly with the changes mapped by Thomas Peardon in his survey of English historiography, which identifies a group of 'Romanticist historians', best exemplified by Sharon Turner and Robert Southey, as a vital bridge between the great works of Enlightenment history such as those of Hume and Gibbon, and the equally celebrated accomplishments of nineteenth-century historians like Macaulay and Engels.[9] Between those two bodies of work a wholly new idea of history emerges, marked by the sympathetic reassessment of past cultures once dismissed as barbaric, and the rejection of concepts of human nature as always and everywhere the same that were no longer tenable.

Some of the most striking manifestations of the transitional phenomenon of 'Romanticist history' occurred in Germany, where there was a definite trend for philosophers to produce sweeping speculative analyses of 'world history', which differed widely in particulars but cohered around the idea of purposeful development and the belief that the very meaning of what it was to be human altered significantly from one epoch to another. The premise that human nature was not timeless and invariable was central to the work of Herder (1744–1803). *Yet Another Philosophy of History* (1774) argues that each 'form of human perfection' is 'national and time-bound and, considered most specifically, individual', and in his organic view of culture developments take place as a result of time, climate, circumstance, and accidents of fate, so that mere human potentialities may never be actualised. The very idea of happiness alters from one time and situation to another, so that comparison is pointless. Although he acknowledges that the role of accident in human history means there are no guarantees for the happiness of individuals, Herder has a progressivist belief in each phase of civilisation building on the one before – 'The Egyptian could not have existed without the Oriental, nor the Greek without the Egyptian; the Roman carried on his back the whole world' – and insists that while the 'passage of God over the nations' cannot be grasped as a whole, across the broad sweep of history its footprint is visible. Significantly, he sees the fall of the Roman empire and the rise of the Northern peoples in the

Middle Ages as a period in which the 'whole species underwent a great cure through violent movement'.[10]

Hegel (1770–1831) was another who thought that meaning could be discerned in the total processes of history – a belief foreign to today's dominantly secular world-view but far more conformable to the mentality of Hegel's period. His *Philosophy of History* begins by stating that 'World history is the progress of the consciousness of freedom'.[11] Hegel charts this progress from its beginnings in what he sees as the stationary, despotic civilisations of the East, in which no one but the absolute ruler could be considered as having a will of their own; through the city-states of ancient Greece, where an incomplete freedom flourished on the back of slavery and social morality was so ingrained as to suspend the possibility of free rational choice; the vast Roman empire, which coupled an abstract respect for individual freedom with the repressive machinery of state power; and the radical new belief-system popularised during the Christian era, which proposed a new ideal of spiritual freedom and subordinated the material world to an other-worldly destiny and home; to the last few centuries of development in what Hegel chauvinistically calls the 'Germanic world', in which the Reformation finally liberated the individual conscience from the corrupt authority of the Church and the French Revolution began the process of transforming the real world into an appropriate place for free individuals. This account of world history is not conceived as a series of disconnected events but as a single, dialectical progression, in which each new development builds upon and reconciles tensions in the preceding stage, and the final historical consummation is a logical outcome of the entire process. Almost inevitably, Hegel sees this consummation, a synthesis reconciling the contrary forces of communal unity and free rationality, as having materialised in the Germany of his own time – an ethnocentric bias of which few historians of the period were not guilty.

The lofty speculative histories of Herder, Hegel, and other German Romantic philosophers were unlikely to find much favour in the dour precincts of British common sense, even had they been better known on the other side of the Channel than they actually were. Nevertheless, there are common threads between the German movement and the new historical self-consciousness reshaping British culture. As should be clear by now, this was more a broad intellectual tendency encompassing various modes of discourse – including, of course, literature – than something that affected just history-writing narrowly speaking. One sign of it was the new interest in the second half of the eighteenth century in investigating ancient literature from what Meinecke calls 'a freshly individualising historical standpoint':[12] Robert Lowth's *Sacred Poetry of the Hebrews* (1753) argued for the first time for the need to understand the Bible in the cultural context of 'primitive' peoples far removed from present-day customs and manners, while Robert Wood's essay *On the Original Genius and Writings of Homer* (1775) saw its subject not as a repository of timeless wisdom but as the voice of a remote and very different period (which could nonetheless be appreciated by reference to the geography and culture of modern Ionia since Eastern life was unvarying in many respects). The fallibility of drawing easy parallels between past and present became all the more apparent as the rapidity of change in so many areas of British society gave observers to believe that the here and now were indeed unique and required particular forms of attention. The proliferation of the periodical press described in Chapter 3 signalled a culture getting accustomed to a new mentality of time, according to which significant developments might be measured in days, weeks, months, or at best years, rather than the generations or centuries that might previously have been sufficient. The success of new compendia like *The Annual Register*, a kind of Georgian *Reader's Digest* first published in 1758, which included material resembling the reviews of the year common in today's newspapers around Christmas, is one mark of this general revision of what constituted meaningful human chronology.

As for historiography itself, what was entailed in the emergence of a new historical sense was a move away from the Enlightenment practice of regarding history as a reservoir of examples of private and public virtue and vice for the instruction of readers in any period, towards the study of significant individuals as expressions of the age that moulded them. At the same time, British Romantic historicism was profoundly interested in broader political and cultural histories, especially of the earlier periods of *national* history, which were now (paralleling Herder's researches) treated more positively and even nostalgically. Both tendencies are conspicuous in Sharon Turner's highly influential *History of the Anglo-Saxons* (1807), which discovers in the 'bands of fierce, ignorant, idolatrous, and superstitious pirates' it studies worthy ancestors of a modern nation 'superior to every other in the love and posses- sion of useful liberty',[13] while it couples comprehensive general accounts of the language and customs of the Saxons with several lengthy chapters on the achievements and personal qualities of King Alfred.

One particularly good way of grasping the new idea of history is to see how the importance of the subject was conveyed to young people. Here, Anna Letitia Barbauld, member of a celebrated Dissenting family that produced many fine educational works, offers fascinating evidence in an essay 'On the Uses of History' first published in 1826. Barbauld explains with forceful simplicity how history can open the mind to individual and social difference:

> It gives us, and it only can give us, an extended knowledge of human nature; – not human nature as it exists in one age or climate or particular spot of earth, but human nature under all the various circumstances by which it can be affected. It shows us what is radical and what is adventitious; it shows us that man is still man in Turkey and in Lapland, as a vassal in Russia or a member of a wandering tribe in India, in ancient Athens or modern Rome; yet that his character is susceptible of violent changes, and becomes moulded into infinite diversities by the influence of government, climate, civilization, wealth, and poverty.[14]

There is here no crude division of humanity into 'civilised' and 'savage' nations, but rather a radical acknowledgement that human nature is infinitely malleable. Nor is there a rush to impose some grand providential scheme on the essentially plotless story of the past, though Barbauld believes a 'tendency to amelioration' is discernible from studying the historical record. She under-lines the need to coordinate the study of history and geography, and discusses how to construct a timeline that will provide a universal chronology (centred, arbitrarily, on the birth of Christ) enabling the examination of one country's circumstances relative to others. Chandler argues that what has been grasped here is the emergent concept of 'uneven development' that would later become central to Marxist sociology, whereby societies or nations are seen as moving through a succession of states at different rates of change, and societies in two different periods might exhibit the same state of development (barbarism, for example).[15]

One might add that recognising that a perceived 'barbaric' people are only on a slower course towards higher states of civilisation – a position that depends upon the premise that human nature is an alterable construct – is a way of confirming the possibility of freedom, however circumscribed and conditioned. Without necessarily subscribing to Hegel's view of freedom as the supreme Idea progressively realising itself through time, there are reasons to believe that the emergence of a true historical sense and the development of historical method in the Romantic period were closely linked – Collingwood says logically necessary[16] – to the discovery that human beings are free.

The lure of the past 1: ancient Greece

If the Romantic period was characterised by significant advances in well-grounded historical scholarship, it was also notable, as I began this chapter by observing, for the range and vitality of its imaginative appropriations of the past. Nowhere is this potent cocktail of fact and fantasy more obvious than in the case of ancient Greece, which became the focus of the complex and multi-layered phenomenon known as Romantic Hellenism.

At the start of the period first-hand knowledge of Greece was still in fairly short supply, and scientific study of its antiquities had barely begun. Know-ledge of ancient Greece depended to a large degree on the literary works resurrected during the early modern Renaissance; archaeology in the sense of a strict scholarly discipline based on the collection and interpretation of evidence did not exist. However, the first steps towards a more systematic and forensic investigation of the past had been taken, and, as these efforts continued, a more historically accurate picture of the ancient world, both of Greece and of those other vanished civilisations in the eastern Mediterranean that touched upon it and thus affected the life of the West, started to emerge. A trail had been blazed by excavations of the buried cities of Herculaneum and Pompeii, entombed by a cataclysmic eruption of Vesuvius in AD 79, which began in 1738 and 1748 respectively. The artefacts, sculptures, and wall paintings recovered during these admittedly amateur excavations gave unique insight into domestic life in these Greek-influenced settlements in the first century AD, while the suddenness of the disaster that had overtaken the two cities caught the appalled imagination of contemporaries. In the Near East, Napoleon's invasion of Egypt in 1798, his 38,000 troops supplemented by an army of Orientalist scholars, gave a powerful spur to Western knowledge of a country that had long been difficult to penetrate as part of the Ottoman Empire. Vivant Denon's detailed illustrations of ancient monuments laid the basis for the multi-volume *Description de l'Egypte* (1809–30), a pioneering work of early archaeology that unlocked a strange land of bewildering antiquity:

> When the first Dynasty came into power, about five thousand years ago, so fixing Egyptian history in calendrical time, marvelous cultural forms had already been evolved in the land of the Nile. And when the Twenty-sixth Dynasty died out, still five hundred years separated Egyptian history from our era. The Libyans ruled the land, then the Ethiopians, the Assyrians, the Persians, the Greeks, the Romans – all before the star shone over the stable at Bethlehem.[17]

The most significant of the remains appropriated by the French (and later surrendered to the British as spoils of war) was the Rosetta Stone, a slab of black basalt bearing a parallel text in Greek, Egyptian hieroglyphs, and Egyptian demotic. Brilliantly deciphered by the precocious Jean-François Champollion, who was the first to realise that hieroglyphs had phonetic values (as opposed to being a kind of picture-writing) and began publishing his findings in 1822, the Stone proved the key to unlocking the language and culture of ancient Egypt. In the Middle East, progress towards more scientific research into the remote past was also made in the period. Joseph de Beauchamp undertook a pioneering dig at Babylon in 1786, recovering a number of cuneiform inscriptions – the wedge-shaped symbols used to represent many different languages in ancient Mesopotamia, which were slowly deciphered over the first half of the nineteenth century by a series of European scholars. Beauchamp's lead was followed by Claudius Rich, the East India Company's Resident in Baghdad from 1808 to 1820, who made a precise topographical study of Babylon that prepared the ground for later systematic excavations. In Palestine, Johann Burckhardt made a detailed study of the rose-red Nabataean city of Petra, while Lady Hester Stanhope organised an excavation at Ashkelon, a ruined Philistine city near Gaza.

The researches carried out by these and other European scholars and enthusiasts typically went hand in hand with a colonial mentality that saw no objection to plundering antiquities to fill museums and private collections in the West. Nevertheless, the long-term value of their activities is clear from a twenty-first-century perspective. Just as valuable in the shaping of the primitive discipline of archaeology was the development and application of the stratigraphic principle (deeper layers of sedimentary rock are older than shallower ones) to the study of fossils and human remains. Once the presence of human bones was acknowledged alongside those of extinct animals in the geological record, the days of the biblical account of creation were numbered. This was a massively significant cultural outcome of eighteenth-century and Romantic investigations into the past. It is ironic, as Paul G. Bahn points out, that early explorations and excavations in the Near East were sponsored by Christian fundamentalists, in the hope that evidence would be discovered of places and events described in the Old Testament, since what was actually uncovered, here and in other parts of the world like Australia and North America, eventually proved fatal to their cause: although much of the initial emphasis was on collecting antiquities and prehistoric 'curiosities',

> it would not be long before new questions came to be asked of these relics of the past. Slowly, steadily, increasing numbers of people were querying the validity of Genesis – daring, in other words, to believe that humankind was far more ancient than the Bible said.[18]

As for Greece itself, knowledge of the modern land (still under Turkish rule) steadily improved in the second half of the eighteenth century as a series of travellers produced reliable first-hand accounts, some of them bringing to their writings the interests and expertise of topographers, antiquarians, or collectors of antiquities. By the turn of the century 'it was possible to feel with some confidence that much more was known about Greece than in the time of Milton or of Pope',[19] and this trend continued in the early nineteenth century as the Napoleonic wars disrupted the traditional Grand Tour (see Chapter 2) and made Greece a more attractive destination. By the time Byron visited Greece in the 1810s it was, in his own words, 'infested' with English tourists. Knowledge of ancient Greece was sought and promoted by the Society of Dilettanti, a characterful assembly of scholars, aesthetes, connoisseurs, and *bons vivants*, which between 1734 and 1852 spent an impressive £30,000 on research and publication in the field of classical antiquity. In particular, the Society sponsored the travels of James Stuart and Nicholas Revett, which led to the five sumptuous volumes of *Antiquities of Athens* published between 1762 and 1830, and an expedition to Asia Minor led by Richard Chandler that brought to light *Ionian Antiquities* (1769, with a second edition in 1797). These publications aimed to foster public appreciation of the ruins of ancient Greece, which it was claimed were in danger of falling into oblivion due to the neglect or disrespect of Turkish 'barbarians', and did so by presenting detailed architectural plans and elevations, and exact drawings of the statues and bas-reliefs with which the buildings were decorated, along with technical commentary and pictures of the ruins in their contemporary settings. They represented a unique combination of the scientific eye and aesthetic sensibility. Of particular importance was the second volume of *Antiquities of Athens*, published in 1787, which covered the key monuments of the Acropolis – buildings 'erected while the Athenians were a free people, chiefly during the administration of that great statesman Pericles',[20] but which in more recent times had been ignominiously converted into a Turkish garrison.

The Society of Dilettanti's magnificent enterprise helped to bring about a major refocusing of the well-established artistic movement of neoclassicism, substituting Greek models for the Roman exemplars that had previously held sway. Such a transvaluation is urged explicitly in the *Antiquities* series itself: the first volume of the *Antiquities of Athens* claims that when the Romans subdued Greece, they 'adopted the Grecian style of architecture but failed to reach the same standard of perfection', and that neoclassical architecture has been handicapped by being limited to the remains of Roman times; while the preface to the *Ionian Antiquities* celebrates 'buildings, which surpass in size, strength, and solidity of construction, not only all that the greatest potentates of modern times have been able to accomplish, but all that was ever produced by the unlimited resources and unlimited despotism of the Roman emperors'.[21] Such strong advocacy was a powerful factor in the Greek Revival, as it is now generally known, which was a major aesthetic trend in the period. The Revival found theoretical inspiration in the writings of Johann Winckelmann, a German art historian who worked for a time as Prefect of Papal Antiquities in Rome and visited the excavations at Pompeii and Herculaneum. Although Winckelmann studied mainly Graeco-Roman copies of Greek statues, and was mistaken in his belief that the whiteness of Greek sculpture was an intrinsic property (it was later discovered that the original bright paints had worn off over time), his eloquent praise of what he took to be the Greek cult of ideal beauty was immensely influential. The leading characteristics of this beauty were, he argued, 'a noble simplicity and sedate grandeur', as illustrated by the *Laocoön* (a first-century BC statue of a Trojan prince killed by serpents), in which 'the struggling body and the supporting mind exert themselves with equal strength', and the *Torso Belvedere* (a statue of Hercules), where the source of fascination was the 'elasticity of the muscles . . . admirably balanced between rest and motion'.[22] Under Winckelmann's inspiration, and with the materials furnished by Stuart and Revett, the dignity and majesty of Greek architecture, with its 'appearance of eternal duration' that evoked the sublime (see Chapter 8),[23] had taken hold in Britain by the turn of the century. As J. Mordaunt Crook has shown, the Greek Revival was a form of historicism based on the twin principles of archaeological fidelity and geometrical form, and abhorred any form of unnecessary decoration: 'Primitivism, simplicity, purity – these were now the cardinal virtues, prized far above novelty, variety, flexibility or sophistication.'[24] Grecian became the dominant style for buildings serving legal, administrative, cultural, educational, and religious purposes, and its pervasive influence eventually drew a predictable counter-reaction: by the 1820s the oddity and monotony of churches, post offices, reading rooms, hotels, and so on all resembling Greek temples was being fiercely criticised.

The Greek Revival was perhaps most conspicuous, and has its most enduring legacy, in architecture; but its impact was much wider than this, affecting sculpture, furniture, dress, painting, and poetry (as with the enthusiastic reassessment of Homer already mentioned). The famous *tableaux vivants* performed by Emma Hamilton, who would perform up to two hundred 'attitudes' copied from Graeco-Roman statues and frescoes, put an even more unusual spin on 'Greekomania'. A major boost was given to the Revival by the arrival in London of the Parthenon marbles. Lord Elgin, Ambassador Extraordinary to the Sultan of Turkey, initially had the idea of 'studying' the architecture of ancient Athens by taking drawings and plaster casts, but ended up virtually stripping the Parthenon of the friezes, metopes (square relief panels), and pedimental statues that adorned the famous temple of Athena. Given that the monument was in dire condition, Elgin's own explanation of his motives for removing the sculptures – 'rescuing them from the imminent and unavoidable destruction with which they were threatened, had they been left many years longer the prey of mischievous Turks, who mutilated them for wanton amusement, or for the purpose of selling them piecemeal to occasional travellers'[25] – cannot be discounted. Nevertheless, although there is little doubt that he had the appropriate authorisation from the Turks for their removal (it was a sale, not a theft), the legitimacy of his actions was questioned at the time and the controversy has rumbled on in post-independence Greece to the present day. The Marbles, which came to England in batches between 1803 and 1812 and were on display in several temporary locations before the British Museum purchased them in 1816, caused a sensation: their 'Grecian grandeur' overwhelmed Keats with a sense of mortality and artistic inadequacy, and Hazlitt pronounced 'a revolution in our artists' minds'[26] – confirming that the pendulum of taste had swung from Rome towards Greece.

Hellenism, the intense interest in Greek history and culture that was a hallmark of the period, especially in its latter phase, was, as Herbert J. Muller puts it, a 'romantic' passion, with 'the image of the beloved one' very much 'a creation of the lover'. Undoubtedly, the romanticising of Periclean Athens – where, according to Muller, the modern American businessman would actually have been more at home than the classical scholar – was made possible by the long passage of time, and the Acropolis itself is the perfect illustration of this:

> the Parthenon stands alone in majestic simplicity, in the perfect proportions of its skeletal outlines. And so we forget that these temples were once painted in lively colors and decorated with gold leaf, in something like Oriental luxuriance. We forget the huge statues of the gods that were crowded into them, and about them, in utter disregard of harmony and proportion. We forget the astonishing clutter of slabs, statues, and monuments that filled the Acropolis. . . .[27]

The Romantic image of ancient Greece often had little more than a nodding acquaintance with accurate historical scholarship; nor was it uncontested or homogeneous. The 'beloved one' looked very different in the eyes of different lovers. Politics is a good illustration of this. The very question of accessing Hellenic culture was political, given the social exclusivity (and almost uniquely male prerogative) of a classical education. The unabashed militarism of heroic literature (Roman as well as Greek) was another point of conflict for those who preferred to stress the progress of civilisation or the new doctrine of universal brotherhood. And, as Timothy Webb makes clear, the political biases of interpreters could sanction radically opposed lessons from the past: for some, Greek history was an 'advertisement for the virtues of democracy', for others, it was 'a terrible warning' of the consequences of the same.[28] Those for whom Greece became a potent symbol of freedom were also likely to be philhellenes – that is, committed to the cause of Greek national independence, a guerrilla-led struggle that succeeded with foreign assistance in 1830.

The treatment of Greek mythology is another aspect of Romantic Hellenism that demonstrates the power of the interpreter's eye. Knowledge of mythology improved with the publication of handbooks and encyclopaedias like John Bell's

New Pantheon (1790), in which the longer entries take a distinct anthropo-logical turn, explicating elements of fable in terms of a culture making sense of its own history, and making links between Greek and Roman gods and heroes and other mythological and religious traditions. The subversive potential of this anthropological and comparative approach was given impetus by Richard Payne Knight's *Inquiry into the Symbolical Language of Ancient Art and Mythology* (1818), a revised version of an even more explicit 'Discourse on the Worship of Priapus' circulated to the Society of Dilettanti in 1786. Freely ranging between the 'primitive religions' of Greece, Egypt, and Asia, Knight elucidates the mysteries of the 'Orphic faith' they have in common: essentially, this involves the celebration of Love, or of that 'principle of desire, or mutual attraction, which leads to universal harmony, and mutual co-operation', and its veneration of the powers of production and reproduction implies belief in the 'universal expansion' of a 'creative Spirit', whereby 'not only men, but all animals, and even vegetables' are 'impregnated with some particles of the Divine nature'.[29] It is not hard to see how such a theory might suggest to Romantic writers much more radical functions for myth than the ornamental use of classical deities standard in eighteenth-century verse; in Marilyn Butler's view, the younger Romantics in particular were inspired by Knight and others to cultivate a self-conscious paganism in opposition to 'a resurgent, institutional, politically reactionary Christianity'.[30]

Primitivism

Dissenters from the veneration of ancient Athens could claim heavyweight support. In his *Discourse on the Arts and Sciences*, the prize-winning essay of 1750 that launched his career, Rousseau had argued that the cultivation of the arts and sciences is invariably accompanied by moral degeneration, and that history offers numerous examples of progress in these fields rendering a people liable to conquest and slavery: 'Take Greece', he says, 'once peopled by heroes, who twice vanquished Asia', until devotion to the arts 'produced a dissoluteness of manners, and the imposition of the Macedonian yoke'. In fact, Rousseau draws distinctions between the city-states of ancient Greece, comparing cultivated Athens unfavourably with the 'happy ignorance' and heroic virtue of the Spartans, and aligning with the latter other nations safe from the 'contagion of useless knowledge': the Persians, the Scythians, early Germanic tribes, and in more recent times the Swiss and the American 'savages' eulogised in the essays of Montaigne (1533–92).[31] Here one glimpses the larger conceptual structures underpinning Rousseau's commendation of Socrates' praise of ignorance: the primitivism – belief in the superiority of a pre-civilised state, taken as having existed at some stage in the past, and perhaps as still existing in certain undeveloped parts of the world – with which he is most closely associated, and the related ideal of the 'noble savage'. Primitivism, in all its varied manifestations (some of which are discussed in Chapter 2), was not a new phenomenon but retained enormous power in the period.

H.N. Fairchild, in his exhaustive study of the transmission of the noble savage myth, defines it as 'any free and wild being who draws directly from nature virtues which raise doubts as to the value of civilization',[32] highlighting the way in which a fiction of the past is typically used as a stick to beat the present. He analyses the idea of the noble savage as a compound of explorers' observations, classical and medieval conventions, and philosophical reflections: for, although encounters between European travellers and the inhabitants of the New World from Columbus onwards provided raw material for writers and thinkers to work with, those travellers themselves were predisposed to romanticise what they found by their familiarity with the ancient conception of a Golden Age and the legends of the Hesperides, the Fortunate Isles, the Garden of Eden and other terrestrial paradises. As the idea developed in the eighteenth century in contradiction of complacent views of the progress of civilisation, the essential characteristics of the noble savage emerged: natural beauty and robust good health; instinctive goodness, or an ignorance of evil; a simple way of life, moderate in wants and free from false sophistication and the vanities and cares of modern society; and equality with fellow savages, with whom he coexisted, if at all, in a communistic form of society.

In the late eighteenth century, the literature of American travel and exploration continued to breathe life into the myth concocted by Columbus, Raleigh, and other early explorers, and given intellectual respectability by such as Montaigne and Erasmus. Jonathan Carver's influential *Travels through the Interior Parts of North America* (1778–9), described by Fairchild as 'a compilation from various sources, with perhaps a judicious admixture of pure imagination', romanticises the 'tranquil, contented and indolent' Indians in order to criticise the manners of so-called civilised countries;[33] Crèvecoeur's *Letters from an American Farmer* (1782) praises the Indians as the 'undefiled offspring' of nature and points out that captured Europeans have often subsequently declined to give up the carefree existence they have been enjoying;[34] while William Bartram's authentic *Travels*, as I showed in Chapter 2, is by no means clear of all traces of noble savagery. The growth and popularity of the literature of South Seas exploration in the late eighteenth century (again, as discussed in Chapter 2) opened up a whole new realm in which the primitivist imagination could disport, ably led by John Hawkesworth's cavalier account of Cook's first voyage, *A New Voyage Round the World* (1774). What these and other travel texts blending fact and fantasy help to underline is an important distinction concerning the structure of feeling under discussion: chronological primitivism projected its ideal state into the remote prehistory of man, whereas cultural primitivism recognised its features among the uncivilised nations of the modern world. The concept of 'uneven development' mentioned earlier allowed for some communication between these two varieties of primitivism.

The most important source for Romantic primitivism was, however, Rousseau's second discourse. The *Discourse on the Origin of Inequality* (1755) resonates strongly throughout the period. One of the paradoxes of this foundational text is that the original condition, or 'primitive state' of humanity that is counterposed so forcefully to the physical and mental afflictions of civilised life is acknowledged to have a purely conjectural status: it is a state 'which no longer exists, perhaps never did exist, and probably never will exist'.[35] It is still more paradoxical that Rousseau draws 'evidence' from 'savage' nations described in contemporary travel narratives to ground his description of a state of nature that is said to be no more than a theoretical construct. Nevertheless, he is prepared to live with these paradoxes, concerned as he is to explain what is wrong with the society of his day by uncovering what is most fundamental in human nature and showing how that original nature has been transformed (for the worse) by the subsequent development of social life and social institutions. The recognition that human nature is 'historical' in this sense is one radical aspect of Rousseau's thesis.

In a state of nature, according to Rousseau, man unreflectively follows the promptings of two basic instincts: the desire for self-preservation, and revulsion at the spectacle of pain or suffering in any living thing. At this stage, virtue or vice have little meaning except insofar as they relate to self-preservation; the ruthlessness with which this aim is pursued is moderated by natural compassion, which is the seed of other virtues such as generosity, clemency, and friendship. Spontaneous compassion is strong in a state of nature – 'it is this which . . . supplies the place of laws, morals, and virtues, with the advantage that none are tempted to disobey its gentle voice' (p. 76) – but, in rational man, falls prey to selfish calculation. In a state of nature, in fact, human beings have little to do with each other and therefore no inclination towards vanity, deference, and other artificial feelings, just as they also have no concept of personal property and no abstract notions of justice. The sexual passion is the only thing threatening the tranquillity of this self-regulating order. Here, Rousseau distinguishes between the physical and moral aspects of love, the latter a factitious social feeling cultivated by women for their own self-aggrandisement; for natural man, 'every woman equally answers his purpose' (p. 78), and destructive quarrels over sexual love are unlikely because the laws and social conventions regarding chastity, fidelity, and so forth do not exist.

Rousseau's aim, as the title of his *Discourse* indicates, is to trace the causes of the inequalities that produce so much misery in today's society. He acknowledges the fact of certain innate inequalities between one person and another, but says that these would mean little in a state where humans had minimal contact with each other: 'Where there is no love, of what advantage is beauty? Of what use is wit to those who do not converse, or cunning to those who have no business with others?' (p. 81) When people are self-sufficient and there is no private property, it is difficult to see how the 'bonds of servitude' could come about. However, Rousseau offers a conjectural history of humanity to provide one dazzlingly neat explanation. Beginning in the simple, solitary, unselfconscious existence of a savage, seeking the means of subsistence and blindly propagating the species, this moves through such events as the invention of hunting and the discovery of fire to the recognition of advantages in cooperation with others, the building of huts, and the establishment of family units. With the growth of domesticity comes the sexual division of labour and the gradual conversion of conveniences into necessities. A more settled way of life leads, ominously, to greater ease of comparison with others, producing 'vanity and contempt' and 'shame and envy' (p. 90); feelings of resentment and revenge become more common, although the dread of reprisals acts as a continual restraint. There then follows the 'fatal accident' of the invention of metallurgy and agriculture (p. 91), twin developments that require organised labour and make possible the accumulation of wealth. All the while, new mental powers are being brought into play and new wants are being created, estranging humans from their original nature. The growth of private property increases inequality and crime proliferates, with avarice and ambition stifling the cries of natural compassion. Reflecting on the unstable situation thus created, rich men conclude that institutions of law and justice are needed to protect their position, and manage to convince everyone else that it would be in their interests too: a social contract is made for the first time that fixes 'the law of property and inequality', and, 'for the advantage of a few ambitious individuals', subjects everyone 'to perpetual labour, slavery, and wretchedness' (p. 99). Once the delegation of authority to magistrates, and finally the conversion of legitimate into arbitrary power, have taken place, adding to the division of rich and poor that of master and slave, the destructive process is complete – pending reform or revolution. It is important to note that, in Rousseau's eyes, although it has been made an instrument of oppression by powerful individuals, the social contract must originally have been conceived by the people at large as a way of protecting their liberty and securing the public interest, and it could be made to serve these purposes again. Of course, his eloquent defence of the social contract as an agreement in which citizens have 'concentrated all their wills in one' (p. 106) to make and enforce laws for their mutual benefit helped build his reputation as one of the philosophical parents of the French Revolution, and was one reason for his popularity among British radicals. Equally resonant for Romantic readers, however, was the second *Discourse*'s elegiac appeal to an earlier, more natural way of life: Rousseau has no illusions that this can ever be recovered, and in fact seems to believe that to do so would mean denying the 'voice of heaven' (p. 125) and its call to a higher form of existence, but the idea acts as a check upon the evils and abuses of an irreversibly civilised society.

One thing that perplexes Rousseau as he narrates his descent of man is how to explain the origin of language, there being no obvious need for it among savages living in a pre-social condition. Even given the need for language, the question of how the conventional bonds between articulate sounds and ideas came about – which could only have happened by consent – proves impossibly difficult, leaving him in the impasse that 'speech must needs have existed before its use could be established' (p. 67). Nevertheless, his concern with this problem is symptomatic of a new concern at this time with understanding language from a historical point of view, which did not bear serious fruit until the nineteenth century, when the science of comparative philology established principles for the investigation of how languages change over time and how they relate to each other within an 'evolutionary' schema. At the time Rousseau was writing, there was still support for the notion of a universal grammar – that is, the belief that language was a product of human reason, which was a universal constant, so there had to be a common structure to languages (analysis of which was usually restricted to the parts of speech) even though words and expressions differed from one to another. Since a high level of education was required in order to apprehend the principles of this pure language of mind, of which the classical languages were taken to be the best approximations, there was inevitably a political aspect to this linguistic theory and to the many practical grammars derived from it.

By the end of the eighteenth century universal grammar was a lost cause, as empiricism largely superseded rationalism and a priori reasoning gave way before the high tide of historicism. But in Britain, at any rate, this did not mean that the study of language became any less 'philosophical', or any more restricted to objective facts, and for most of the Romantic period the new historical outlook was characterised by false dawns and wrong turnings. Of these the most idiosyncratic yet influential was J. Horne Tooke's *The Diversions of Purley* (1786–1805), which might be called a work of linguistic primitivism. Building on Locke's principle that ideas originate in sense impressions, Tooke puts forward a theory that essentially reduces the complexity of language to nouns and verbs (that is, these are the only necessary words, from which all others can be etymologically derived) – and, were he able to, Tooke would clearly like to reduce verbs to nouns too. Not only does he drastically simplify the parts of speech, he also takes the bolder step of reducing thought to language:

> The business of the mind, as far as it concerns Language, appears to me to be very simple. It extends no farther than to receive Impressions, that is, to have Sensations or Feelings. What are called its operations, are merely the operations of Language. A consideration of *Ideas*, or of the *Mind*, or of *Things* (relative to the Parts of Speech) will lead us no farther than to *Nouns*: i.e., the signs of those impressions, or names of ideas.[36]

What might appear to be representations in language of more complex mental acts are in reality, according to Tooke, the product of various forms of abbreviation, which have achieved economy of utterance at the expense of some of the concrete simplicity of words. Even abstract nouns are, it seems, merely participles or adjectives that need to be etymologically demystified, as part of a war on metaphysical imposture (for example, 'truth' is derived from 'to trow', meaning 'to think, to believe firmly'). As a theory of language, this is plainly very materialist or 'thing-oriented'; it is also counter-cultural, in that Tooke aims to prove the falsity of explaining English in terms of Latin by tracing everything back to Anglo-Saxon roots, and politically radical, in that the core of a language is seen as communal property that needs to be cleared of 'mountains of learned rubbish'.[37]

Unfortunately, as Hans Aarsleff has shown, the most obvious impact of Tooke's book, in particular his speculative etymologies, was to lead his many imitators into publishing a great deal of pure nonsense.[38] Instead, as Aarsleff also makes plain, the new philology found more fertile soil in Germany, where an interest in the links between language and national character served to broaden the linguistic horizons of scholars in productive ways, and where Herder's organic view of culture incorporated the study of language as simply another branch of natural history. The main British contribution to the discipline of comparative philology came not from Tooke and his admirers but from Sir William Jones's work on the relations between Sanskrit, Greek, and Latin, which led to a detailed genealogy of the Indo-European family of languages. The understandable interest of German scholars in the early Germanic languages meant that these were increasingly put on a par with Latin and Greek, and their researches ultimately revolutionised the study of early English language, literature, and culture: the new philology finally crossed the Channel in 1830 with Benjamin Thorpe's translation of Rasmus Rask's *Grammar of the Anglo-Saxon Tongue*, bringing scientific rigour to a field of learning previously dominated by antiquaries and amateur historians.

The lure of the past 2: ancient Britain and the Middle Ages

Interest in native cultural traditions was keen and growing at the end of the eighteenth century, rivalling the passion for ancient Greece explored above. Interest was distributed across a very broad chronological span, from the hazy prehistory of pre-Roman Britain, to the Anglo-Saxon era lasting from the fifth to the eleventh century AD, to the Late Middle Ages from the Norman Conquest up to around 1500. Whichever period of history or prehistory was the particular focus, reconstructions of the British national past shared with the Greek Revival an irrepressible tendency to romanticise their object of study – almost inevitably, at a time when archaeology had not been invented, 'scientific' history was in its infancy, and the labours of antiquarians lacked a critical methodology and were hampered in some cases by over-reliance on the factual accuracy of the Old Testament and a limited number of classical sources.

Nowhere are these features more pronounced than in the case of pre-Roman Britain and its inhabitants, a remote past of which reliable knowledge was almost non-existent, with the Book of Genesis still taken as an authoritative demographic guide, and where imaginations in search of mysterious or romantic origins, noble or ignoble savages, could run riot. There was no established chronology for the study of prehistory: although the idea of successive Stone, Bronze, and Iron Ages had been around for centuries it had not gained general acceptance, and it was not until the reorganisation of the Danish National Museum in Copenhagen, beginning in 1817, that it finally gained institutional backing. Christian Thomsen's rearrangement of Danish antiquities, grouping objects of all kinds according to whether they had been found with tools of stone, bronze, or iron, brought 'order to chaos' and 'initiated a quiet revolution'.[39] In the absence of such an agreed framework, antiquarian research had made little advance in the understanding of British prehistory for over a century, uncovering a good deal of new primary evidence but lacking the tools to interpret it correctly; instead, it traded in a version of the past in which Celts (as described by writers like Julius Caesar and Tacitus) erroneously became an all-purpose name for the original inhabitants of Britain, and extravagant fantasies flourished concerning their biblical ancestry, their rites and customs, and, in particular, their druidic leaders. Edward Davies's *Celtic Researches*, published in 1804, presents a summation of this mythicised view of ancient Britons.

The kind of 'conjectural history' of society repeatedly elaborated during the eighteenth century, tracing human progress from savagery to civilisation (beginning with hunting and gathering, then moving through pasturage and agriculture to commerce), could be interpreted both positively and negatively – with Rousseau's second *Discourse* representing the elegiac alternative. Davies chooses to reassert a Christian perspective that denies primal savagery, and sees man as having always been distinct from other animals 'by his erect countenance, and his capacity for sublime contemplation'. Shaping his historical vision is the account in Genesis 6–11 of the Flood, the building of the Tower of Babel, and the distribution of the earth among the descendants of Noah. On somewhat obscure grounds, he believes that the presumptuous Tower-builders were but a majority of Noah's progeny, who, handicapped by the confusion of tongues, degenerated into the savage nations of the earth. A minority, however, kept their primitive language and religion intact, and some of them – to be specific, descendants of Ashkenaz, one of Noah's grandsons – multiplied to become the Celts and, in due course, colonised Britain.

In common with many eighteenth-century antiquarians, Davies is fascinated by the druids, the priestly caste (chosen from the privileged families of the Celts) that by this stage was associated with virtually every prehistoric monument in the country. (It was, for instance, accepted as fact that Stonehenge was a druid temple where human sacrifices were carried out – a mistake that has persisted until the present day.) The druids, he says, retained the patriarchal religion, and jealously preserved primitive doctrines, which they communicated 'by *symbols* and by enigmas, or dark allegories'. They focused their philosophy on 'the changes and revolutions to which nature and man were exposed', beginning in a lower state of existence where good and evil were intermixed, but eventually attaining, after several cycles of metempsychosis, to the 'point of liberty' or entry to the circle of happiness.[40] Davies thus emphasises the druids' role as natural philosophers, teachers, and guardians of tradition; missing in his discussion – though he mentions their responsibility for the administration of justice – are the more gruesome ceremonies described by previous writers (on the authority of Caesar) over which druids were thought to have presided, notably the burning alive of sacrificial victims in giant wicker men. He thus presents druids as a more learned and peace-loving order than the 'heathen idolators worshipping stocks and stones' pictured by some of his less tolerant predecessors,[41] but he keeps their romance and mystery alive.

The 'Celtomania' that Davies fuelled also gave renewed confidence to the suppressed elements of contemporary British nationhood – Welsh, Irish, Scottish – that could claim links with the supposedly aboriginal Celts. In

Wales, new pride was taken in Welsh history, druids were revered as defenders of the Welsh nation, and new heroes like Caractacus (from the revolt against the Roman occupation) and Owen Glendower (from the struggle against English domination) were consecrated. In Prys Morgan's unsparing assessment, 'The Celts reflected the fantasies of the age, and in Wales they provided the constricted, pathetically small nation, which had little to commend it in its present state, with an unimaginably grandiose past, by way of consolation.'[42] In the late eighteenth and early nineteenth centuries there were various efforts to revive Welsh cultural and linguistic traditions perceived to be in decline, a campaign that involved a healthy amount of valuable new scholarship, publication, and consciousness-raising, but also a good helping of what has been termed the 'invention of tradition'. Among other things, the eisteddfod was relaunched on a grander scale in 1789, providing a platform for native literature and music, though its integrity was tainted by its association from 1819 onwards with the neo-druidic Gorsedd of Bards convened by literary forger Edward Williams; the Welsh language was given a boost with the production of new dictionaries and grammars and an increase in Welsh-language publications, but was compromised by language mythologists like William Pughe, who personally coined thousands of new words on 'scientific' principles; and the genuine tradition of simple stanzas being sung by ordinary people to the music of the harp was not only revived, but given a deceptive facelift by the bogus introduction of the triple harp as an ancient national instrument and the creation of countless 'old' tunes to swell the native repertoire. This rich stew of authentic and inauthentic Welshness played an important role in encouraging people to appreciate their 'heritage', but as the nineteenth century progressed the cultural revival assumed a quaintly conservative air and by the 1840s could no longer keep the forces of modernisation at bay.

In Ireland, there was a similarly vigorous and multi-faceted Celtic renaissance, a revival of the indigenous Gaelic language and culture that was nonetheless significant in a way the Welsh revival was not, owing to the unstable political context. Long treated with distaste or hostility by the ruling Anglo-Irish elite, the late eighteenth century saw a new toleration, and even patronage, of expressions of native Irish identity. This mood of reconciliation was destroyed by the upheavals of the 1790s, culminating in the rebellion of 1798 but rumbling on to emancipation in 1829, which tarred Gaelic cultural militancy with the brush of Catholic discontent. An interesting link between Ireland and the third stronghold of Celticism, Scotland, is the former's resentment of James Macpherson's geographical kidnapping of the legendary Irish warrior and bard, Oisin, for his supposed 'translations' from Ossian, allegedly a third-century Scottish poet. These were the most notorious literary forgeries of their generation, astutely catering for a taste in 'Highland mist' and offering a version of the primitive, strong, and simple as a 'vacation' from modern proprieties.[43] According to Hugh Trevor-Roper, however, this was just the most spectacular instance of a much more far-reaching process of stealing a Highland cultural tradition from the Irish. Against the historical reality of Irish emigration to the Western Highlands from the fifth century AD to the mid-eighteenth century, making Celtic Scotland little more than a 'cultural dependency of Ireland', the late eighteenth century saw the start of a remarkable transformation:

> First, there was the cultural revolt against Ireland: the usurpation of Irish culture and the re-writing of early Scottish history, culminating in the insolent claim that Scotland – Celtic Scotland – was the 'mother-nation' and Ireland the cultural dependency. Secondly, there was the artificial creation of new Highland traditions, presented as ancient, original and distinctive. Thirdly, there was the process by which these new traditions were offered to, and adopted by, historic Lowland Scotland: the Eastern Scotland of the Picts, the Saxons and the Normans.

While Macpherson had an important part to play in the first of these stages, the issue Trevor-Roper focuses on, amusingly, in relation to the later stages is that of Highland dress: the supposedly traditional kilt, woven in a clan-specific tartan. What he demonstrates is that the kilt was invented by an English Quaker industrialist as a more convenient garment for his workmen than the genuinely traditional belted plaid; that there was no differentiation of tartans by clan before the late eighteenth century, and that this had more to do with military requirements and commercial opportunism than with historical authenticity; and that securing general adoption of these invented traditions was the work of the London-based Highland Society (the 'Macpherson mafia') and upper- and middle-class enthusiasts for the cult of primitive peoples. The whole process was consecrated during the king's visit to Scotland in 1822, the ceremonies thoroughly 'tartanised' in a collective 'hallucination' by which Celtic tribes and their fake traditions were made the very essence of Scotland.[44]

As an alternative to all this Celtomania, the English could brandish their own primitive forebears: the Anglo-Saxons. I have already mentioned Sharon Turner's *History of the Anglo-Saxons* as representative of a newly sympathetic approach to this phase of history that gained popularity as English culture tried to shake off its obsession with the classical heritage and take pride in its northern roots. After an opening chapter on the Celts, Turner's introductory remarks on the fifth-century Germanic invasion sets out his stall very clearly:

> This revolution, than which history presents to us none more complete, has made the fortunes of the Saxons, during every period, interesting to us. Though other invaders have appeared in the island, yet the effects of the Anglo-Saxon settlements have prevailed beyond every other. Our language, our government, and our laws, display our Gothic ancestors in every part: they live, not merely, in our annals and traditions, but in our civil institutions and perpetual discourse. The parent tree is indeed greatly amplified, by branches engrafted on it from other regions, and by the new shoots, which the accidents of time, and the improvements of society have produced; but it discovers yet its Saxon origin, and retains its Saxon properties, though more than thirteen centuries have rolled over, with all their tempests and vicissitudes.[45]

Written at a time when Britain, with its English-speaking Hanoverian king, was resisting renewed aggression by those 'other invaders', the French, during the 'tempests and vicissitudes' of the Napoleonic Wars, this passage has more than academic significance: it suggests that Turner's zeal for Anglo-Saxon studies and what Peardon calls his 'religious interpretation of history' and 'generalized pride in all things English'[46] are vitally interlinked at a time when national identity and national destiny are in crisis.

Turner's enthusiasm for the Anglo-Saxons seems partly conditional upon their conversion to Christianity. Before conversion, they were 'fearless, active, and successful pirates', attacking whoever and wherever they could; and although Turner discerns in these pagan brigands outlines of the national character of their modern descendants, their 'direful customs' and 'barbarous education' are said to have 'perverted every good propensity'. The cultural legacy of Romanised Britain was helpful in mitigating their barbarity and 'accelerating their civilization', and Christianisation of the country completed their transformation into good citizens. It is partly for his piety in the service of Christianity that Turner lavishes two hundred pages of praise on Alfred, who is lauded as an exemplary philosopher-king, a benign patron of arts and crafts, a wise legislator, and devoted family man – in short, a sovereign who 'considered his life but as a trust to be used for the benefit of his people', the kind of image that George III had tried to cultivate for himself.[47] Although Turner resists facile idealisations of the Anglo-Saxon period as the birthplace of the free-born Englishman, he unashamedly celebrates their contribution to the national story. This was a story that was rapidly being revised, discarding prior assumptions – hardly politically acceptable around 1800 – that English culture began with the Norman Conquest.

Nevertheless, the Late Middle Ages also benefited from the rush of interest in early popular culture that characterised the new Romantic sense of the past. While the full flowering of the medieval revival – which affected art, architecture, religion, politics, and economics, among other things – came in the mid-nineteenth century, it found abundant expression within the period. The collecting and editing of materials relating to the Middle Ages, especially the heritage of popular culture, was a favourite occupation of antiquarians in the second half of the eighteenth century. From a literary point of view, a central reference point is Thomas Percy's *Reliques of Ancient English Poetry*, first published in 1765 and constantly reprinted, which helped popularise the folk ballad and lauded the spirit of chivalry animating medieval poetry. However, Percy provoked the wrath of a fellow antiquarian, Joseph Ritson, with his allegedly cavalier editorial practices, and the 1790s were notable for a series of interventions by Ritson that did battle with Percy (and others) for the soul of medieval culture. Ritson objected in particular to Percy's presentation of the old songs and ballads as the work of courtly minstrels (and therefore a kind of aristocratic entertainment), and his apparent interference with the manuscript originals to produce more polished versions for a sophisticated audience. For Ritson, the ballads were the authentic voice of the common people, and he preferred a rough, unimproved text. His *Select Collection of English Songs* (1783) aims to present the best of the English Muse, 'unadulterated with the sentimental refinements of Italy or France', and an accompanying 'Historical Essay on the Origin and Progress of National Song' ascribes the suppression of Saxon songs to monkish bigotry and laments the current decline of song among the lower classes as damaging to the character of the nation. The introductory essay to another collection of *Ancient Songs* (1792) launches a long, withering attack on Percy's brand of medievalism, repeatedly denying the existence of 'an order of men who united the arts of poetry and music, and sung verses to the harp of their own composing', and who circulated between the court and great country houses. Ritson has a very different vision of disparate individuals 'destitute of education, and probably unable either to write or read', who wandered up and down the country chanting or singing songs to the accompaniment of various humble instruments, for the amusement of their peers. His own editing technique favours 'the genuine remains of the Minstrel Poets, however mutilated or rude', to Percy's 'fluent or refined' emendations. Another interesting volume is Ritson's *Robin Hood* (1795), compiled in a spirit of admiration for a man who, 'in a barbarous age, and under a complicated tyranny, displayed a spirit of freedom and independence, which has endeared him to the common people'.[48] As such comments make clear, the differences between Ritson and Percy were as much political as academic, and the rift between the avid social climber, Percy, who falsely claimed consanguinity with the noble Percies of Northumberland, and the republican Ritson who associated with the radical intelligentsia in London, was unlikely to be healed in the climate of the 1790s.

As this altercation also demonstrates, medievalism was fundamentally open to interpretation, as indeed was the whole of the national past. Under the influence of a work like John Lingard's Catholic *History of England* (1819–30), it was possible to see the medieval Church as the focus of communal unity, bringing everyone together in worship and applying its wealth to the relief of poverty; under the lens of Francis Douce, the same Church could be seen as having comprehensively lost its way, and a fierce anticlericalism shaped a 'dark, negative medievalism' that, as Marilyn Butler says, fed directly into the Gothic novel.[49] While Gothic fiction traded extensively in the medieval period's connotations of feudal tyranny, social restriction, and poisonous superstition, an alternative link between medievalism and naturalism (for instance, the richness and irregularity of Gothic architecture was seen as an imitation of organic form) developed concurrently. The more the medieval revival flourished in the nineteenth century, the more conservative and nostalgic its orientation became. As a social programme, as Alice Chandler argues, it addressed the mounting concern over industrialisation and urbanisation, holding out the memory of a lost world of small units, where 'Farmer and laborer, apprentice, journeyman, and master were . . . linked together . . . by reciprocal ties now shattered by the social atomism of laissez-faire economics'. As a philosophical programme, it sought to reintegrate humanity into a universe drained of divinity:

> Far from being isolated from nature, medieval man was seen as part of it, and his chivalry mirrored its benevolence. In its hostility to a mechanistic metaphysics, medievalism as a philosophical movement thus paralleled its opposition to machinery on economic and social grounds.

170

Embracing medieval culture out of a desire 'to feel at home in an ordered yet organically vital universe' was the essence of Romantic reaction;[50] in deploying a seductive interpretation of historically remote people and places in order to express an attitude towards change in the present it was characteristic of Romantic uses of the past in general.

Notes

1. These phrases belong to Claude Lévi-Strauss, though I am drawing here on the discussion in James Chandler, *England in 1819: The Politics of Literary Culture and the Case of Romantic Historicism* (Chicago and London, 1998), p. 67.

2. *Shelley's Poetry and Prose*, ed. Donald H. Reiman and Sharon B. Powers (New York, 1977), p. 134.

3. Marilyn Gaull, *English Romanticism: The Human Context* (New York and London, 1988), p. 176.

4. *England in 1819*, pp. 105–14.

5. *Collected Works of John Stuart Mill*, ed. John M. Robson and others, 33 vols (Toronto, 1963–91), XXII, ed. Ann P. Robson and John M. Robson (1986), p. 230.

6. *The Order of Things: An Archaeology of the Human Sciences* (London, 1970; repr. Routledge Classics, 2002), pp. 401–3.

7. *Historism: The Rise of a New Historical Outlook*, trans. J.E. Anderson (London, 1972), pp. lv–lvi.

8. *The Idea of History* (Oxford, 1946), pp. 232, 260.

9. See *The Transition in English Historical Writing 1760–1830* (New York, 1933).

10. *J.G. Herder on Social and Political Culture*, trans. and ed. F.M. Barnard (Cambridge, 1969), pp. 184, 188, 217, 193.

11. *Lectures on the Philosophy of History. Introduction: Reason in History*, trans. H.B. Nisbet (Cambridge, 1975), p. 54.

12. *Historism*, p. 204.

13. *The History of the Anglo-Saxons*, 2nd edn, 2 vols (London, 1807), II, 31.

14. 'On the Uses of History', in *A Legacy for Young Ladies* (London, 1826), pp. 121–2.

15. Barbauld, *Legacy*, p. 134; Chandler, *England in 1819*, pp. 127–30.

16. See *Idea of History*, pp. 319–20.

17. C.W. Ceram, *Gods, Graves, and Scholars: The Story of Archaeology*, trans. E.B. Garside (New York, 1951), pp. 79–80.

18. *The Cambridge Illustrated History of Archaeology* (Cambridge, 1996), p. 79.

19. Timothy Webb, 'Romantic Hellenism', in *The Cambridge Companion to British Romanticism*, ed. Stuart Curran (Cambridge, 1993), pp. 148–76 (p. 162).

20. James Stuart and Nicholas Revett, *The Antiquities of Athens*, 4 vols (London, 1762–1830), II (1787), ii.

21. *Antiquities of Athens*, I, iv; Preface to *Ionian Antiquities*, cited in Timothy Webb, *English Romantic Hellenism 1700–1824* (Manchester, 1982), p. 209.

22. Cited in Webb, *English Romantic Hellenism*, pp. 121, 122, 125.

23. *Antiquities of Athens*, III, xiv.

24. *The Greek Revival: Neoclassical Attitudes in British Architecture, 1760–1870*, revised edn (London, 1995), p. 89.

25. Elgin's submission to Select Committee considering state purchase of the marbles, cited in B.F. Cook, *The Elgin Marbles* (London, 1997), p. 84.

26. Hazlitt, 'The Elgin Marbles', in *Complete Works*, ed. P.P. Howe, XVIII (1933), 100–3 (p. 100).

27. Herbert J. Muller, *The Uses of the Past: Profiles of Former Societies* (New York, 1952), pp. 100, 102.

28. *English Romantic Hellenism*, p. 29.

29. *An Inquiry into the Symbolical Language of Ancient Art and Mythology* (London, 1818), pp. 25, 48.

30. *Romantics, Rebels and Reactionaries: English Literature and its Background 1760–1830* (Oxford, 1981), p. 131.

31. *A Discourse on the Arts and Sciences*, in *The Social Contract and Discourses*, trans. G.D.H. Cole, ed. P.D. Jimack (London, 1993), pp. 8–10.

32. *The Noble Savage: A Study in Romantic Naturalism* (New York, 1928), p. 2.

33. *Noble Savage*, p. 98.

34. J. Hector St John de Crèvecoeur, *Letters from an American Farmer*, ed. Susan Manning (Oxford, 1997), pp. 201–3.

35. *Discourses*, p. 44.

36. *The Diversions of Purley*, 2nd edn, 2 vols (London, 1798), I, 51.

37. *Diversions*, I, 10–11.

38. See *The Study of Language in England, 1780–1860* (Minneapolis, 1983), pp. 73–114, for some rich examples.

39. Bahn, *History of Archaeology*, p. 90.

40. *Celtic Researches on the Origin, Traditions and Language, of the Ancient Britons* (London, 1804), pp. 5, 150, 185–6.

41. Stuart Piggott, *Ancient Britons and the Antiquarian Imagination: Ideas from the Renaissance to the Regency* (London, 1989), p. 149.

42. 'From a Death to a View: The Hunt for the Welsh Past in the Romantic Period', in *The Invention of Tradition*, ed. Eric Hobsbawm and Terence Ranger (Cambridge, 1983), pp. 43–100 (p. 69).

43. Peter Murphy, *Poetry as an Occupation and an Art in Britain, 1760–1830* (Cambridge, 1993), pp. 15–16.

44. 'The Invention of Tradition: The Highland Tradition of Scotland', in Hobsbawm and Ranger (eds), *Invention of Tradition*, pp. 15–41 (pp. 16, 26, 31).

45. *History of the Anglo-Saxons*, I, 27–8.

46. *Transition*, pp. 231–2.

47. *History of the Anglo-Saxons*, II, 2, 4–5, 33; I, 310.

48. *A Select Collection of English Songs*, 3 vols (London, 1783), I, ix; *Ancient Songs from the Time of King Henry the Third to the Revolution* (London, 1792), pp. x, xvi, xxvi; *Robin Hood: A Collection of all the Ancient Poems, Songs, and Ballads, now Extant, Relative to that Celebrated English Outlaw*, 2 vols (London, 1795), I, xi.

49. 'Antiquarianism (Popular)', in *An Oxford Companion to the Romantic Age*, ed. Iain McCalman (Oxford, 1999), pp. 328–38 (p. 334).

50. *A Dream of Order: The Medieval Ideal in Nineteenth-Century English Literature* (London, 1971), pp. 3, 7, 1.

Chapter Eight

Aesthetics and the Visual Arts

It might be thought that with so many world-changing events going on in the forty years between 1789 and 1830, educated debate would have little time to concern itself with such abstruse matters as the nature and purpose of art. Nothing could be further from the truth: the period saw major developments in aesthetic theory, most importantly – and in ways that connect directly with trends in literary criticism and theory – in Germany. Perhaps less surprisingly, the period was notable for vigorous and innovative activity across the full range of the visual arts, just as it was in literature. Four areas of artistic production – landscape gardening, architecture, painting, and printmaking – are discussed in this chapter. The latter is an example of how visual art could be made an explicit tool of political propaganda in the uncompromising exchanges of the Revolution debate and the mounting class hostilities of post-Waterloo Britain; but all forms of art were affected by the great events and controversies of the time and were implicated in the accompanying culture wars.

Aesthetic theory

Some of the major concerns of aesthetic discourse in the period were, indeed, closely related to broader social trends discussed in earlier chapters. Just as the growth of the reading public, as a consequence of mechanisation of the press, rising literacy, and the expansion of the middle classes, was a source of alarm to many conservatives, so the enlargement and democratisation of the public for art caused a significant anxiety. The place and function of art in an increasingly commercial and industrial society, and the implications for both artist and audience of having artworks treated as commodities subject to the laws of the market rather than the laws of the imagination, became the unavoidable stuff of debate. With the market for at least some forms of art, as for literature, spreading beyond the aristocratic male circles that had formerly been thought to monopolise the leisure and mental cultivation deemed necessary to appreciate them, there was also a question mark over the disinterested mentality that was still considered a prerequisite of genuine aesthetic experience.

'Disinterested' meant that one's perspective on the world was not limited by the need to work for a living, which would inevitably bias one towards the interests of whatever occupational group one belonged to and prevent one attaining a comprehensive and impartial understanding of things; confining one's experience to a narrow sphere would also make it difficult to see past local and immediate realities and formulate ideas that had a more general or universal validity. Furthermore, 'disinterested' meant that one had, literally, no interest in the possession or indeed the existence of any object one might subject to the aesthetic gaze: thus the beauty of a stand of trees could not be reliably appraised by someone who was employed as a forester. The ability to make artistic judgements that were uncontaminated by private interest, personal prejudice, or partial experience was what aestheticians of the time called 'taste'. The belief that genuine taste was universal was a commonplace of eighteenth-century aesthetics, and was carried over into the Romantic period, though it was coming under pressure from a number of directions: awareness that standards of beauty varied widely from one culture to another had, for example, become only too apparent from the proliferating literature of travel, and itself became a regular talking-point in treatises on art. An equally fundamental principle of eighteenth-century aesthetics was that the highest forms of art strive after ideal beauty – that is, they abstract from the messy and defective particularities of real objects to present forms more perfect, or more repre-sentative, than any discovered in actuality. Naomi Schor has demonstrated that the language typically used to convey this idealist aesthetics is that of male form imposed on raw female matter, a rhetorical tendency underpinned by a long-standing association of women with nature and with the concrete and the particular, on account of their greater involvement in childrearing, domestic routine, and so on.[1] However, this is just one specific expression of a pervasive gender-bias in eighteenth-century and Romantic aesthetics: with its reliance on 'gentlemanly' disinterestedness and a capacity to abstract and generalise instilled by the kind of education to which few women in the period had access, it is clear that the spectator theorised in such writing is always implicitly, and often as an article of belief, male.

One of the major sources for late eighteenth-century aesthetic doctrine, and the focus of Schor's feminist critique, is Sir Joshua Reynolds's *Discourses*, delivered to the Royal Academy (of which he was the first president) between 1769 and 1790. In Reynolds there is a clear statement of the artistic creed of imitation of nature – not merely imitation of external nature, said to please only vulgar minds, but imitation of 'the perfect state of nature, which the Artist calls the Ideal Beauty' and 'is the great leading principle, by which works of genius are conducted'. In his avowal of the importance of 'genius' and imagina-tion, and belief that the arts are addressed to 'the desires of the mind, to that spark of divinity which we have within, impatient of being circumscribed and pent up by the world which is about us',[2] there is a hint of the subversive effect these concepts would have, in full-blown Romantic literary and aesthetic theory, on the neoclassical verities he expounded.

A major challenge to neoclassicism came from a distinctively British school of aesthetics built upon the philosophy of association, which derived ultimately from the empirical psychology of Locke. One of the key exponents of this philosophy in the period was Archibald Alison, who came at the end of a long line of distinguished post-Lockean commentators on art. For Alison, the emo-tions aroused by a beautiful object are not to be credited to intrinsic qualities of that object, but to the powerful trains of thought it arouses, the play of images kindled by the imagination. For example, the beauty of a natural scene in springtime exists largely in the mind of the beholder:

> The soft and gentle green with which the earth is spread, the feeble texture of the plants and flowers, the young of animals just entering into life, and the remains of winter yet lingering among the woods and hills, all conspire to infuse into our minds somewhat of that fearful tenderness with which infancy is usually beheld. With such a sentiment, how innumerable are the ideas which present themselves to our imagination! Ideas . . . by no means confined to the scene before our eyes, or to the possible desolation which may yet await its infant beauty, but which almost involuntarily extend themselves to analogies with the life of man.

Although Alison pays lip service to the idea of a 'comprehensive taste' that would transcend individual prejudices (and would inevitably be restricted to those in the 'higher stations' of life or the 'liberal professions'),[3] almost everything he says underlines the extent of subjective variation in aesthetic experience: personal history may create pleasurable associations that allow one to see a beauty invisible to others; education or professional knowledge can increase one's stock of associations to similar effect; the bias of individual minds and temperaments is an important factor; accidents of time and place can awaken or deaden one's sensibility; and so on. The result is a pronounced movement away from the objective standards of beauty espoused by Reynolds towards aesthetic relativism, an acceptance that our minds have been conditioned in such unique and dissimilar ways that one person may see beauty in an object that is invisible to others. The same conclusion is reached in another influential work of associationist aesthetics published by Richard Payne Knight. For Knight, too, the pleasure derived from beautiful objects is fundamentally an intellectual pleasure arising from the association of ideas, as with a pleasure taken in pastoral scenery that draws on an associated knowledge of landscape painting, and so will be most intense among those 'whose minds are enriched by a variety of kindred and corresponding imagery'.[4] He also lays great stress on the role of 'sympathy' – especially in his theory of the sublime (discussed in the next section), which he interprets as a sympathetic response to an exertion of great power that has the effect of expanding and elevating the mind – and this again prioritises what happens within the observer rather than what belongs properly to the observed object.

In Germany, the development of modern aesthetics took a very different course, largely unbeknown to those leading the field in Britain. Although the 1780s and 1790s saw a voguish enthusiasm in Britain for German literature, the greater cultural isolation brought about by the Revolutionary wars, coupled with the paucity and poor quality of translations from the German, meant that after around 1800 the stock response to German literature and, especially, philosophy was one of ignorant contempt:[5] Coleridge provides a rare and complex example of a well-informed and sympathetic response to German philosophy in the period, and De Quincey was quick to see its potential as a stick to beat utilitarianism with, but otherwise it was only a few lonely enthusiasts like William Taylor and Henry Crabb Robinson who kept the lines of communication open via articles and reviews. The reverse situation was very different: in the eighteenth century British literature and philosophy were rapidly translated into German, and consequently Kant and his followers were the heirs of a European tradition of writing about art.

Kant's *Critique of Judgement* (1790) is widely regarded as one of the most important works of Western aesthetics. His account of aesthetic contemplation as involving a free play of imagination, detached both from sensuous gratification and from any consideration of what is morally good or useful, and furnishing a delight that is deeply personal and subjective but for which we demand universal agreement, lies behind all subsequent theories that try to establish a separate realm for art and to retain some measure of absolute value. Kant's arguments concerning the beautiful and the sublime are discussed below, so here it is worth just noting a few important contributions made by his contemporaries and immediate successors in Germany. Friedrich Schiller's essay *On the Naïve and Sentimental in Literature* has proved a fruitful reference point for discussion of British Romantic literature, focusing as it does on two contrasting attitudes to nature: a spontaneous, unselfconscious attitude that expresses perfect wholeness of being, exemplified by Homer and Shakespeare who give us nature 'at first hand' because their personalities are nowhere to be seen; and a 'sentimental', moralising attitude more characteristic of the modern poet, in whose work 'we never receive the object, only what the reflecting intelligence of the poet has made of the object'.[6] Whereas naive poets can have only a single approach to their subject, since for them things are simply as they are, the discrepancy between the actual and the ideal that torments the sentimental poet creates a broader range of aesthetic possibilities. The difficult question of the relation between aesthetics and ethics is addressed in another major essay of Schiller's, *On the Aesthetic Education of Man*. This again looks back to ancient Greece as a time when sense and intellect were in balance and human beings were whole personalities, and compares this with a present in which human nature has fragmented into partially developed individuals, each one 'nothing more than the imprint of his occupation or of his specialized knowledge'. The escape from this predicament lies in art, which holds in suspension those opposing impulses – the 'sensuous drive' and the 'rational drive' – that otherwise exist in unhealthy imbalance, and liberates the individual into 'a third joyous kingdom of play and of semblance' in which the normal limitations of our physical nature and moral consciousness do not apply. Its imperative being to embody the ideal, Schiller confidently looks to art for the moral and spiritual awakening of society at large: 'Surround them, wherever you meet them, with the great and noble forms of genius, and encompass them about with the symbols of perfection, until Semblance conquer Reality, and Art triumph over Nature.'[7]

The relation between the life of the senses and the life of the spirit is also central to the theory of art put forward in Hegel's *Lectures on Aesthetics*, delivered between 1823 and 1829. Like Kant, Hegel believes that we relate to a work of art without desire (as opposed to the way we 'consume' external objects in the rest of our lives); neither do we approach a work of art in the same rational way we make sense of the world around us, by attaching concepts to a multitude of concrete particularities, since this would generalise the work out of existence:

> From the practical interest of desire, the interest in art is distinguished by the fact that it lets its object persist freely and on its own account, while desire converts it to its own use by destroying it. On the other hand, the reflection on the work of art differs in an opposite way from theoretical consideration by scientific intelligence, since it cherishes an interest in the object in its individual existence. . . .

Autonomy and singularity therefore emerge as leading characteristics of the work of art, which occupies a middle ground between full materiality and complete ideality, neither purely 'thinglike' nor pure thought, to be appraised by the senses of sight or hearing (taste, smell, and touch have no part in aesthetic experience, according to Hegel) operating in a more spiritualised manner. A simpler way of putting this is that in the work of art the sensuous and the spiritual must be perfectly fused, the creative thought indivisible from its embodiment in marble, paint, or whatever. This notion of organic unity is crucial to Hegel's understanding of the ultimate aim of art. He portrays a harsh opposition between the realm of desire and worldly interest and the realm of duty, of freely doing what our reason tells us is good; rather than conducing directly to our betterment through some detachable moral content, it is art's function to reconcile within itself this opposition between the spirit and the flesh, by unveiling 'the *truth* in the form of sensuous artistic configuration'.[8]

Hegel offers a scheme of the historical development of art in its alliance with changing religious world-views, in which the general trend is from a time when the artist was 'in earnest' with his material and was fully representative of his culture, to a more individualistic era in which any subject-matter is available for treatment in a self-conscious, 'contemporary' style. The distinguishing feature of much modern art is therefore a kind of ironic subjectivity. Hegel did not press this observation quite as far as another major German theorist, Friedrich Schlegel, for whom it was inseparable from the very possibility of communication and interpretation. In a dizzying essay 'On Incomprehensibility' Schlegel distinguishes numerous kinds of irony, including one in which 'one can't disentangle oneself from irony anymore'; he also suggests that some of the most conscious artists of earlier times are 'still carrying on ironically, hundreds of years after their deaths', forever revealing hitherto unsuspected intentions.[9] This reserve of ironisable meaning is what he terms incomprehensibility, which he (playfully?) says will be exploded in a new age of understanding. It is uncannily reminiscent of some of the propositions of late twentieth-century literary theory.

The beautiful and the sublime

For the student of British Romanticism, the paired concepts of the beautiful and the sublime are crucial aids to understanding, reverberating as they do through much of the canonical literature. They are the latitude and longitude of eighteenth-century and early nineteenth-century aesthetics, part of the machinery of thought for any well-educated person. They denote, on the one hand, categories of art or of natural objects or scenery; on the other, the feelings or experiences that these objects characteristically evoke. While these aesthetic principles were widely discussed in the eighteenth century, the single most important British source for the Romantics was Burke's *Philosophical Enquiry into the Origin of our Ideas of the Sublime and Beautiful* (1757), which, although published well before the start of the period, remained so influential that it has to be considered here.

Limiting the focus to natural objects (or representations of them in painting), it is possible to summarise Burke's theory quite concisely. Beauty, he argues, is a matter of certain sensuous qualities that arouse in us the passion of love, or something similar: prime among these are (comparative) smallness; smooth-ness, as with a smooth slope or a smooth skin; gradual variation, as opposed to angularity, of line; delicacy of appearance; and mild colours, such as light greens and pink reds, blended as appropriate. Burke provides surprisingly few topographical illustrations of these features, but it is easy to see how an undulating landscape with a winding river or placid lake, seen in the subdued atmospherics of early morning or twilight, would fit the bill.

Whereas love and its correspondent affections appeal to our social instincts, a sublime experience is more likely to be a solitary one, and appeals to our still stronger instinct of self-preservation:

> Whatever is fitted in any sort to excite the ideas of pain, and danger, that is to say, whatever is in any sort terrible, or is conversant about terrible objects, or operates in a manner analogous to terror, is a source of the *sublime*; that is, it is productive of the strongest emotion which the mind is capable of feeling.[10]

It is important that Burke writes of 'ideas' of pain or danger, for he makes clear that the 'delight' that accompanies the sublime is cancelled if one actually feels physically threatened: the distance, however slight, that enables one to be a spectator rather than a participant is crucial. With that proviso, the leading characteristic of the sublime is one of feeling overwhelmed, of having the mind 'so entirely filled with its object' – perhaps a vertiginous landscape or one of John Martin's apocalyptic biblical paintings – that 'it cannot entertain any other' (p. 53), and is rendered incapable of thinking or acting normally. Burke's keyword for the sublime, 'astonishment', with its root meanings of being 'stunned' or 'stupefied', is particularly apt in this light. The qualities most likely to produce this mental effect are great power, where this is outside our control and has a threatening or punitive aspect; vastness of dimension, with depth, height, and length being sublimely impressive in that order; and a sense of infinity, whether naturally occurring or artificially produced (as, for instance, with identical columns in series). Darkness, solitude, and silence can all either enhance, or provide the core of, a sublime experience by communicating the idea of total and terrifying deprivation, while 'obscurity', by rendering the outlines of the sublime object unclear, can also feature in the scenario.

Burke's analysis of the sublime has manifest relevance to the feelings and sensations aroused by certain kinds of natural landscapes and natural phenomena, such as craggy mountains, mighty waterfalls, violent storms, or active volcanoes – the taste for which became conventionalised, via new forms of travel and tourism, in the late eighteenth and early nineteenth centuries. The genre of landscape art, which came into its own in the same period, shadowed this development in its endeavour to find pictorial strategies for accommodating the new landscape aesthetic that Burke popularised. However, this 'natural sublime' merged almost inevitably with a religious sublime where the grandeur of nature was read as the handiwork of a divine creator, and in the context of scriptural convention according to which, as Burke puts it, 'every thing terrible in nature is called up to heighten the awe and solemnity of the divine presence' (pp. 63–4). Of all the traditional attributes of God, Burke insists that power is the foremost, and so the experience of being overwhelmed by nature is for many synonymous with religious awe, in which 'we shrink into the minuteness of our own nature, and are, in a manner, annihilated before him' (p. 63). By analogy with the forms of human government, a political sublime could also be found in the exercise and display of absolute power or tyrannical authority in human affairs, and indeed Burke was later to aestheticise revolutionary terror in just such a manner in his *Reflections* of 1790.

Burke's explanation of why spectators should take pleasure in scenes or images that threaten their emotional security and sense of self-worth – of why the sublime can be termed a 'delightful horror' – brings out the physiological cast of his theory. The experience of pain or danger, he says, causes a state of nervous tension and muscular contraction, and representations of fearful objects induce a similar reaction; this is beneficial to the system because vigorous exercise of the 'finer organs' involved in imaginative activity keeps them in good working order. By contrast, beautiful objects allay tension and relax mind and body, fostering 'an inward sense of melting and languor' (p. 135). This is more obviously pleasurable, but a prolonged state of such relaxation produces a state of weakness and ill-health that requires, in turn, the bracing influence of the sublime. The sublime is therefore the fitness instructor in the aesthetic gym, the beautiful more of a masseuse. Such metaphors do no more than accentuate the highly gendered character of Burke's theory: the treatise is written entirely from a masculine point of view, so that the beautiful is most memorably illustrated by references to the female body (as with his erotic description of the 'deceitful maze' (p. 105) of a woman's neck and breasts, to illustrate the principle of gradual variation), while the sublime is exemplified by stern, patriarchal authority figures that demand our submission rather than lure us into surrender.

Some of Burke's most significant British successors in the field of aesthetic theory, like Archibald Alison and Richard Payne Knight, were concerned, as described in the previous section, to assert the importance of the association of ideas in place of his more purely empiricist psychology. In the same year that Alison published his *Essays*, in Germany Immanuel Kant published the third of his great *Critiques*, the *Critique of Judgement*. While the latter remained largely unknown and unread across the Channel for a generation, Kant himself was well versed in British aesthetics and in particular was intimate with Burke's *Enquiry*, which he respectfully criticised on the grounds that rooting aesthetic experience in the vagaries of sensibility allowed for no appeal to universal assent. Perhaps his most important contribution for present purposes was to produce a theory of the sublime that seems far more attuned, in some respects, via its insights into forms of mental and spiritual self-empowerment, to British Romantic literature than the ideas of Burke and his fellow native theorists.

It is best to begin, though, as Kant himself does, with his analysis of the beautiful. Absurd as it is to try to sum up Kant's formidably complex argument in a few words, it is possible to hint at the direction it takes. Taste in the beautiful is a disinterested delight, having nothing to do either with gratification of the senses or with considerations of what is morally good or useful. And just as a sentiment of beauty is thus indifferent as to whether its object actually exists or not, so it need not be bothered about the nature of that object. For in aesthetic contemplation our minds are not working as they habitually do, organising the flow of sense data into objects of perception and then attaching these to 'concepts' (just as we differentiate a stream of sound into words and then assign meanings to these words and the larger units they make up); instead our cognitive faculties are put into a state of free play, in which we have a pleasurable sense that our mental powers are perfectly attuned to their task of making sense of the outside world, without going so far as to interpret the objects in question as being what they actually are. It is something like the series of pre-ignition checks that take place automatically just before one starts a car. More particularly, what we intuit when faced by certain natural scenes or works of art is a kind of order and harmony – a unity that seems *meant to be* – that convinces us that nature has our best interests at heart. Kant insists that it is only the formal properties of such objects that can produce this delight in its essential purity, because anything that belongs to sensation contaminates our judgement with desire and is subject to variable preference. In fact, the unity we sense in the beautiful object is the work of our own imagination, which we project outwards onto the object in order that the mind can 'feel itself at home in nature':[11] Kant sources the pleasure associated with beauty to the subject, rather than the object, but in his eyes the subject will always prefer the illusion that the world is designed to provide him or her with disinterested delight, and aesthetic experience comfortingly fuels that illusion.

If we misrecognise our own powers in our spontaneous response to the beautiful in order to reap the benefit of 'a thoroughly interconnected whole of experience' (p. 23), no such self-deception occurs in the case of the sublime, which in Kant's account involves a mental movement resulting in an enhanced sense of self-worth, though at the cost of an initial psychic battering. Kant distinguishes between two types of sublime experience. With the 'mathematical sublime', nature presents us with phenomena of awesome magnitude, whether this is a matter of size or number. To begin with we delight in the extension of our imaginations, but we also desire a sense of totality, and when our mental powers prove insufficient to achieve this a point of blockage is reached and the mind recoils in failure. It is, however, a pleasurable recoil, since we realise that our ability even to think the idea of infinity as a whole, even though our minds have no way of 'computing' this, means that our boundaries are not set by the world of sense: we are compelled to acknowledge within ourselves a 'supersensible faculty' (p. 97) responsible for those yearnings after unity. The mind 'feels itself elevated in its own estimate of itself on finding all the might of imagination still unequal to its ideas' (p. 105), and what appeared at first as an 'abyss' of failure becomes instead the threshold of a higher 'vocation'.

When nature is viewed under the aspect of might or power, it is possible to experience the 'dynamical sublime'. Fearful natural objects and forces like overhanging rocks and tempestuous seas do not simply humiliate and subdue us, as Burke supposed, but 'raise the forces of the soul above the height of vulgar commonplace, and discover within us a power of resistance . . . which gives us courage to be able to measure ourselves against the seeming omnipotence of nature' (p. 111). We recognise that we are helpless as physical beings before the might of nature, but by the same token realise that as spiritual beings we are superior to material concerns and therefore need not feel diminished. Although the grand displays of natural power might be read by the superstitious as manifestations of God's wrath, the upright man can regard them equably because he finds in himself a 'sublimity of disposition' (p. 114) in accord with the sublimity of God. In complete contrast with our experience of the beautiful, therefore, it is the role of the sublime to instruct us that we are ultimately *not* at home in nature.

Landscape gardening: the cult of the picturesque

In the final years of the eighteenth century the priority of the sharply opposed aesthetic categories of the sublime and the beautiful was challenged by a third category, the picturesque, which came to occupy an unsettled and unsettling place somewhere between them. With its origins in an Italian word denoting a bold and vigorous technique drawing attention to the medium of representation, the word was increasingly associated in the eighteenth century with a way of looking at nature in terms of rules and standards derived from painting, and with a way of designing gardens as though they resembled a series of pictures. In the words of its earliest and best historian, Christopher Hussey, the picturesque was a movement in which 'poetry, painting, gardening, architecture, and the art of travel' were 'fused into the single "art of landscape" '.[12] The golden age of the picturesque garden was in the second half of the eighteenth century, with the high noon of picturesque theory arriving in the

1790s, and the entire complex of theory and practice left its footprints all over Romantic literature.

The earliest and most enduring influence of painting on the appreciation of landscape came via acquaintance with the work of two seventeenth-century French painters who lived and worked in Rome, Claude Lorrain and Gaspard Dughet (called Poussin), an acquaintance facilitated by the Grand Tour and the artistic connoisseurship and collecting it encouraged. Claude and Poussin studied nature directly in the countryside around Rome, but aimed not at a realistic art but at a kind of 'ideal landscape', which accentuated certain aspects of nature and gave it a unity and generalised perfection it did not possess in actuality. Claude's landscapes, for Helen Langdon, evoke 'a dream of pastoral peace, where mankind and nature are in harmony, and where summer is eternal'; their characteristic structure employs framing trees that help 'lead the eye, through a series of clearly defined horizontal planes, crossed by rivers and bridges, to a distant vista'.[13] For persons of educated taste, the conventions of ideal landscape became so thoroughly internalised that natural scenes were considered beautiful only insofar as they resembled one of Claude's paintings. Another influential figure was the seventeenth-century Italian artist Salvator Rosa, who specialised in rugged mountain landscapes assailed by terrifying storms and containing hints of animal or human savagery. If Claude and Poussin became the shorthand for natural beauty, Rosa became synonymous with the sublime. Eventually, however, it became apparent that there were many scenes and objects that were pleasurable to behold but which could not be assimilated to the beautiful or sublime so understood. The naturalistic English landscapes of Gainsborough, themselves indebted to the Dutch landscape school of Rubens, Ruisdael, and Hobbema, with their greater attention to local particularities of place and more intense focus on individual objects such as gnarled trees and mossy banks, mark the transition. It was this development, which did not take place in an aesthetic vacuum but was bound up with larger historical processes touched on below, that brought picturesque theorising to its peak in the 1790s.

Perhaps the most unlikely protagonist in this debate was William Gilpin, a country vicar and schoolmaster whose annual tours in various parts of Britain in pursuit of 'picturesque beauty' were written up in a series of influential books beginning with *Observations on the River Wye* in 1782. The theoretical content of these accounts, which established a new visual code of landscape appreciation for the leisured middle classes, was distilled in *Three Essays*, published in 1792. Gilpin here sets out to distinguish the picturesque from conventional notions of beauty, proposing roughness as the main quality of the former in direct disagreement with Burke's much-admired analysis. For instance, an elegant garden needs to be artificially distressed to make it suitable for painting:

> Turn the lawn into a piece of broken ground: plant rugged oaks instead of flowering shrubs: break the edges of the walk: give it the rudeness of a road; mark it with wheel-tracks; and scatter around a few stones, and brush-wood; in a word, instead of making the whole *smooth*, make it *rough*; and you make it also *picturesque*.[14]

Roughness is a matter not just of the line and texture of individual objects but of the composition of whole scenes, where it forms the basis of the variety, contrast, and chiaroscuro that delight the spectator. Gilpin's famous remark that 'nature is most defective in composition' (p. 67) shows the extent to which he believed that the picturesque ideal was something to be achieved in the interaction of landscape and observer, with nature's deficiencies freely corrected in the latter's mind or sketchbook.

Gilpin's own perceived deficiencies were corrected in 1794 by Uvedale Price, a Herefordshire landowner whose *Essay on the Picturesque* was the most substantial contribution to the debate. Price endeavours more systematically than Gilpin to establish the picturesque as a category intermediate between the beautiful and the sublime, capable of moderating either extreme: referring to Burke's physiological explanation, he says that the picturesque 'neither relaxes, nor violently stretches the fibres, but by its active agency keeps them to their full tone; and thus, when mixed with either of the other characters, corrects the languor of beauty, or the horror of sublimity'.[15] He supplements Gilpin's roughness with irregularity and 'sudden variation', and together these are said to produce – in a whole range of natural and man-made objects which Price exhaustively analyses – the variety, intricacy, and 'partial concealments' that arouse our curiosity; and it is curiosity, which in Price's illustrations frequently takes on an erotic or voyeuristic dimension, that is the chief mental effect of the picturesque. Whereas Price believed picturesqueness could be defined in terms of objective properties of the natural or built environment, the third major controversialist, Richard Payne Knight (a neighbouring land-owner in Herefordshire), maintained that only combinations of light, shade, and colour could be appraised in this way, as he stated in his verse dissertation on the subject:

> For nought but light and colour can the eye,
> But through the medium of the mind, descry;
> And oft, in filth and tatter'd rags, it views
> Soft varied tints and nicely blended hues.[16]

To derive an abstract visual pleasure from 'filth and tatter'd rags' in this way, ignoring (for example) the bad smell or the perturbations of our moral conscience, we must acquire the 'painter's eye', and indeed Knight contends that all the enjoyment of specifically picturesque beauty stems from our educated familiarity with painting, which for him meant especially the Dutch landscape tradition. Other kinds of aesthetic pleasure are the result of other networks of association.

Whichever version of picturesque theory one favours, there is no doubt that the picturesque had a nostalgic, conservative aspect: given the fact that it romanticised a landscape that was the slow growth of centuries, in which no sign of human habitation was permissible that had not been partly naturalised by time, and ruin and decay were positive embellishments, it could scarcely have been otherwise. As Ann Bermingham notes, in the context of the accelerating enclosure movement and capitalist modernisation, the picturesque 'idealized a nature that was in fact rapidly vanishing', and may be interpreted as having 'sentimentalized the loss' of 'an old order of rural paternalism'.[17] Price himself explicitly compares a 'good landscape', various and irregular in keeping with his theory, in which all the parts 'are necessary to the beauty, energy, effect, and harmony of the whole' to a 'good government' that takes the middle way between anarchy and despotism, thereby aligning the picturesque with native constitutional liberties. In its maturity, despite the appeal to universal principles, the picturesque expressed a jealous affection and regard for a quintessentially English landscape – an increasingly managed landscape that should nevertheless be kept as 'natural' as possible, just as there should be no rash meddling with the constitution. In the 1790s, when the cult of the picturesque peaked, fear of revolution and the threat of invasion provided a fertile context in which nature came to be synonymous with nation.

The theorising of Gilpin, Price, and Knight, and the picturesque land management practised by the latter two on their estates, were the culmination of over half a century of radical experimentation in landscape gardening that popularised a style sometimes referred to simply as 'English' – although it is arguable that Chinese gardening had a major influence on its development. This style was irregular rather than formal and symmetrical; made abundant use of local, natural materials; applied the lessons of landscape painting, adapted to the more mobile perspective of the visitor walking through the grounds; and sought to engage the mind as well as the eye, not least through the playful use of architecture and statuary to create mood and stimulate reflection. William Kent (1685–1748), who in Walpole's famous words 'leaped the fence, and saw that all nature was a garden', was the first to show a marked preference for natural rather than geometrical forms, and for using pictorial principles and associations so that visitors to his gardens had the experience of walking through a succession of pictures. He was followed by Lancelot 'Capability' Brown (1715–83), much criticised by Price and Knight for his drastic remodelling of estates to create extensive views over vast lawns interspersed with clumps of trees, but who played his part in developing the idea of 'a perfected English scenery'.[18] He was succeeded in professional esteem by Humphry Repton (1752–1818), who in his numerous commissions worked in both Brownian parkland and full-blooded picturesque modes, according to the demands of his client and the local topography, but whose practical perspective led him in general to play down the pictorial model of garden design and to recognise that 'utility must often take the lead of beauty'.[19] Price's own attempts to put the picturesque into practice were restricted to his estate at Foxley, where his aesthetic motives were combined with his active management of the farming estate and a 'complicated mixture of ancient woodland, plantations and coppices'.[20] Within that framework, he strove to bring to life his abstract principles of variety and intricacy, providing for the visitor guided round the estate on carefully constructed paths a visual complement to its diverse human population 'going about its different tasks under the authority of a watchful and caring squire'.[21] Knight's estate at Downton was larger and more lucrative than Price's owing to its mineral wealth and associated industrial yield, but like Price he sought to respect local history and geography in managing the countryside as a working environment. His picturesque landscaping was focused on a narrow gorge that carries the River Teme through the estate; here his labours were directed only at enhancing the visitor's experience of the already dramatic topography, in keeping with the message of *The Landscape*:

Your favourite plants, and native haunts protect,
In wild obscurity and rude neglect. (Book II, ll. 190–1)

Inevitably, given the terrain, his picturesque landscaping leant towards the sublime. Hackfall in Yorkshire, Hafod in Cardiganshire, and Piersfield in Monmouthshire were other examples of mature picturesque landscape gardening that displayed a similar bias, but the style was a short-lived phenomenon because the desired appearance of neglect and accident was paradoxically difficult to achieve and maintain. In the wider world, the picturesque tradition from Kent onward influenced garden design across Europe through the eighteenth century and beyond – though the French, as always, resisted too strong an identification with their cultural rivals across the Channel. The Englischer Garten in Munich, begun in 1789, is one example of a major public space created in the 'English' style, while Catherine the Great, who commissioned a Wedgwood table service with twelve hundred views of Britain, applied her Anglophile vision to several of her estates in Russia; here and elsewhere the picturesque displayed remarkable adaptability to regional or local climate, topography, and cultural identity.

Architecture

One aspect of the eighteenth-century landscape garden barely touched on in the previous section was the incorporation of a wide range of structures intended to interact with the natural scene and stimulate associations – providing the 'human interest' that was then considered indispensable, as it was in painting. In effect, it was a mirror-image of what happened in history painting (the highest-ranking genre), where scenes from the Bible, classical mythology, or human history were represented in appropriate landscape settings: instead, the landscape was made to tell a story or suggest a meaning via the presence of buildings, statues, and inscriptions, lending the garden a theatrical as well as pictorial dimension. It is also possible to see in such architectural insertions the sheer exuberant playfulness of the picturesque, especially in the second half of the century when they became truly multicultural in provenance: thus Greek temples, Gothic arches, Chinese bridges, Turkish tents, and Egyptian obelisks sprouted up in the gardens of England. Stourhead in Wiltshire, one of the best-known picturesque gardens (laid out between 1740 and 1780), boasted a classical Pantheon and temples, a mock-medieval castellated tower, and a Chinese pavilion and parasol, along with a genuine fourteenth-century High Cross transplanted from Bristol. Perhaps the most significant development in the latter part of the century was an increased preference for Gothic insertions over classical, because the former connected more readily with the increased interest in national history and character: a plaque on 'Alfred's Tower' at Stourhead, for example, claimed that the summit where it stood was where Alfred 'erected his standard against Danish invaders', and commemorated him as the 'father of his people, the founder of the English monarchy and liberty'. This tendency continued through the Romantic period, when new landscape architecture conformed to the taste for the picturesque and the sublime: Uvedale Price advised that Gothic buildings were more picturesque than Grecian ones, unless the latter were ruined, and also relished hovels, cottages, mills, and barns, especially if they were old and dilapidated.[22] Alpine bridges, artificial tunnels, robbers' caves, and druid temples were other features that found favour at this time for the manufactured thrills they provided.

Although much that happened in the landscape garden in the period can be regarded as pure aesthetic experiment and superficial exoticism, there is no doubt that civic architecture was taken very seriously in its relation to larger cultural and political concerns. A wider European perspective is especially interesting in this connection. In Revolutionary France, as Barry Bergdoll has shown, architecture became one more tool of propaganda, using 'new symbolic and spatial forms' to mould 'notions of nationhood and an engaged citizenry central to the Revolution's bid to "regenerate" humanity'.[23] The Bastille had its connotations rewritten once demolished, as its stones were recycled for souvenir models and – though this remained a proposal only – a triumphal column on the same site. The conversion to new secular and democratic uses of churches, monasteries, and palaces brought into state ownership gave potent visual confirmation of the diminished power and status of the Church and monarchy. One important innovation was the amphitheatre design of the legislative chamber built for the new National Assembly, first at Versailles then at a series of locations in Paris, which created a more egalitarian organisa-tion of space that would later be copied worldwide; another was the con-struction of vast arenas for the new revolutionary festivals, such as the tiered seating, huge grandstand, and triumphal arch built to accommodate the Festival of Federation in the Champ de Mars in July 1790 in front of three hundred thousand spectators – a wholly new form of public ritual in which ordinary people became part of the spectacle. Following the establishment of the Republic, a series of public competitions were held for new public buildings – everything from Revolutionary monuments to slaughterhouses – reflecting the new ethos of democratic participation and the 'active citizen'.

The use of architecture to express rising national self-consciousness and cultural identity was evident elsewhere in Europe too. In contrast to France, which favoured a classical idiom by way of identification with the glories of the Roman Republic, Gothic – the popular term for medieval forms of architecture, especially castles and cathedrals – was the chosen vehicle in Germany, where it was seen as embodying the soul of the nation and hence as a means of unifying the hundreds of tiny states at a cultural level. Cologne Cathedral, which had languished in an unfinished state since the late Middle Ages, became an icon of this project, galvanised by French occupation of the Rhineland, and when work was finally completed in 1880 Germany had indeed been unified under Bismarck.

In Britain, perhaps unsurprisingly given its cherished reputation as a bastion of liberty, architectural pluralism was the order of the day between 1789 and 1830, as it had been throughout the eighteenth century. Nevertheless, one particular contest of styles may be read as defining much of the architectural history of the period, just as a quite different contest had given the flavour to early Georgian Britain. In the first half of the eighteenth century, Palladianism, a form of classicism derived from the Venetian architect Andrea Palladio's (1508–80) strict interpretation of the only surviving architectural treatise from ancient Rome, vied with the reigning Baroque, iconically represented by Christopher Wren's St Paul's Cathedral. James Stevens Curl argues that Palladianism, which produced highly symmetrical, flat-fronted buildings (often with a portico) following one of the three Roman orders (systems of design, distinguished chiefly by the type of column and entablature), was the house style of the Whig oligarchy and Hanoverian faction, while the Baroque, expressed in much more richly ornamented and ostentatious buildings, was associated with the Tories, France, and popery[24] – demonstrating again the extent to which architecture can be governed by larger forces of cultural politics. Palladianism was superseded in the second half of the century by a purer brand of neoclassicism stimulated by a closer first-hand acquaintance with Roman remains and by the excavations at Pompeii and Herculaneum, which finally shed light on Roman domestic architecture. Then, towards the end of the century, attention shifted eastwards to an earlier antiquity, in the spirit of the Greek Revival described in Chapter 7.

Many of the differences between Roman and Greek classical architecture are difficult to discern for the untrained eye, but the most important feature of the Greek Revival was the rediscovery of the oldest Greek order, the Doric (characterised by baseless, fluted columns with very plain capitals), which was criticised as 'ugly, barbaric, primeval, sub-human'[25] by supporters of Rome, but prized by its acolytes for its very primitivism, strength, and simplicity. It was a familiar Romantic contest between nature and sophistication, with nature coming out on top by about 1800. Contemporaneous with the Greek Revival was the increasing vigour and visibility of the British Gothic Revival, which began in the 1750s with playful projects that could amount to little more than (in today's parlance) 'makeovers', but which gradually became more scholarly and, ultimately, a matter of passionate principle for its partisans. The style is identified with castle-style houses, often built to an asymmetrical 'picturesque' plan, and by pointed arches, elaborate tracery, pinnacles and spires in church design. Greek versus Gothic was therefore the major expression in the Romantic period of what J. Mordaunt Crook has called the 'dilemma of style'.[26] The contest is most dramatically encapsulated, in images that will come readily to mind for most readers (though the buildings themselves post-date the period), in the positioning at opposite ends of Whitehall in London of William Wilkins's National Gallery in Greek Revival style (1834–8) and Charles Barry's and Augustus Pugin's Gothic Houses of Parliament (1840–60);

another telling juxtaposition is in Edinburgh, where the unfinished Doric temple on Calton Hill that was to be the Scottish National Monument (1822–5) is a short walk from George Kemp's Gothic spire-like Scott Monument (1840–6). Both Revival modes could have ideological meanings attached to them – Curl says that the severe Greek style 'seemed ideal to express both the times and the aspirations of a growing, educated, mercantile, professional, and middle class' in post-war Britain, while Bergdoll points out that Gothic became linked with the campaign to regenerate the Anglican Church and counter the threat of the Nonconformist sects (whose chapels tended to be plain rectangular boxes)[27] – but these meanings were constantly shifting, and most architects freely switched from one style to another according to professional demands. Equally, there were some important architects, such as Sir John Soane (best known for his Bank of England, construction of which spanned the entire period, from 1788 to 1833), who developed a highly individual style that is difficult to pigeon-hole according to a crude dichotomy of Greek and Gothic.

Brief mention should also be made of several other important architectural developments and innovations of the period. The industrial revolution was a major factor in altering the built environment: factories, banks, and stock exchanges made a visual impact in many parts of the country, and factories in particular, where revolutionary use was made of structural iron in place of timber, were as important in design terms as the technology they housed. One visiting German architect's response to the Manchester cotton mills was 'awe and horror . . . mixed with a certain grudging admiration for sheer scale', indicating that sublimity was not the prerogative of the natural landscape.[28] Although most businesses were accommodated in buildings identical to private houses, the first purpose-built offices began to appear towards the end of the period, and Soane's magnificently domed and vaulted Bank of England aimed to inspire confidence in the market at a time of economic turmoil. It was in London that the clear division of a city into commercial and residential spaces (the City and the West End) first came about in this period, and here and in other cities, such as Bath and Edinburgh, pioneering exercises in town planning took place, creating unified squares, terraces, and crescents, shopping arcades, and detached 'villas' that were the germ of modern suburbia.

Painting

The late eighteenth and early nineteenth centuries were an exciting and transformative period for British and European painting, and familiarity with some of the major developments and figures, especially the two most important British painters, Constable and Turner, is a major advantage to the student of British Romantic literature. The difficulties of trying to offer a brief overview in a book format that does not permit illustrations are obvious, although they are alleviated by the easy availability now of images on the Internet, notably the online galleries of the National Gallery, London, and the Victoria and Albert Museum, and the magnificent Turner Online resource hosted by Tate Britain.

A general view of the state of painting in the period must take into account the declining importance of aristocratic patronage and the increasing role of institutions in displaying art, supporting artists, and conserving the nation's artistic heritage; the much-increased accessibility of paintings to a more socially diverse audience; and the difficulties faced by the art world in coming to terms with a more commercial and consumeristic society. The annual exhibitions of the Royal Academy of Arts, held since 1780 in the sumptuous surroundings of Somerset House on the Strand in London, were a barometer of many of these changes: founded by royal charter with a mission to promote British art, instruct young artists, and raise the standard of public taste in line with the ideals of high art espoused by Sir Joshua Reynolds, in reality the Academy's exhibitions featured a teeming variety of pictures in genres both high and low competing for the attention of potential buyers, and were attended by large, socially heterogeneous crowds containing many visitors who were there to see and be seen rather than to look at paintings. In David Solkin's words, the exhibitions, while 'designed as a showcase for the laudable achievements of the British School, and as an engine for the edification and improvement of society at large', were actually 'a doubly commercial enterprise, operating as both a highly profitable spectacle and a marketplace for expensive luxury goods'.[29] Solkin reflects the fact that paintings were now consumer items or investments for a moneyed clientele extending down to the 'respectable' middle classes, as well as entertainment for a still broader viewing public; this larger community of spectators and patrons, serviced by a growing number of art dealers and art critics, was inevitably perceived as a threat to the aristocracy's stranglehold on taste and to the cultural authority of the highly educated minority who identified with their values. This threat was magnified by the further opportunities for viewing and buying art afforded by complementary institutions that emerged in the period, such as the British Institution, founded in 1805 to showcase the work of contemporary British artists, and various commercial or promotional galleries, of which the best-known was John Boydell's Shakespeare Gallery, designed for new paintings that would then be engraved for an upmarket illustrated edition of Shakespeare's plays. Artists themselves differed in their response to this changing environment, some welcoming the improved opportunities for marketing their work, some uncomfortable at the thought of prostituting their talent to the changing tide of fashion. The emergence of institutional patronage was deplored by the essayist William Hazlitt, whose normally democratic instincts went into arrest on matters of art: he ridiculed the notion that new talent could be nurtured on the model of a fish farm, and argued that academies merely multiplied the number of people who presumed without sufficient knowledge or understanding to pronounce on artistic matters. For Hazlitt, genius cannot be bought and sold, and 'the public taste is ... necessarily vitiated, in proportion as it is made public'.[30]

The mixing of aristocratic connoisseurs with the 'vulgar crowd' in the Royal Academy galleries had a parallel in the *rapprochement* of high and low in the subject-matter of painting. History painting, the highest genre, was deflected from its tradition of the idealising and morally uplifting treatment of themes from national history, the classics, or the Bible to take on a wide range of contemporary and secular material. Benjamin West's *Death of General Wolfe* (1770) is often taken as pioneering this trend, representing the climax of the Anglo-French struggle for Canada and clothing the actors in modern dress rather than flowing classical robes. West did not follow up this success, but John Singleton Copley produced pictures commemorating the death of the Prime Minister, Pitt the Elder, the defence of Jersey against the French in 1780, and Britain's victory in the *Siege of Gibraltar* (1791). Henry Singleton is notable as the artist of the only known British heroic treatment of *The Destruction of the Bastile* (1792). In France itself, Jacques-Louis David put the grand manner to work in the service of the Revolution, and, subsequently, the Napoleonic Republic and Empire: *The Tennis-Court Oath* (1791) memorialises one of the defining moments in the early history of the Revolution; *Death of Marat* (1793) gives a Christ-like quality to the Jacobin martyr and turns 'a gruesome murder into timeless art';[31] while the iconic *Napoleon at St.-Bernard* (1800) is an unembarrassedly majestic portrayal of the First Consul and gives a powerful sense of destiny and progress. In Spain, Francisco Goya provided a very different but equally memorable interpretation of the Napoleonic era: although his most remarkable testimony to the horrors of the French occupation and guerrilla opposition is arguably the posthumously-published series of eighty etchings, the *Disasters of War*, Goya also produced two large contemporary history paintings of a popular insurrection on *The Second of May, 1808* and the French reprisals on *The Third of May, 1808*, the latter painting mixing documentary accuracy and Christian symbolism to become at the same time a bleak indictment of the inhumanity of war and 'a national icon of Spanish resistance'.[32]

Just as history painting descended to embrace 'lower' subjects (if only human rather than superhuman affairs), so the aspirations and status of the other established genres – portraiture, landscape, genre (scenes of ordinary life), and still life – rose. Probably the most important development for the student of Romantic literature was the elevation of landscape painting. Nature became a more important component of both history paintings and portraits, and landscape painting itself acquired a new confidence and ambition as it discovered new geographical territories, new themes and techniques, and new potential in a formerly subordinate medium, watercolour. This was a multi-national phenomenon – Caspar David Friedrich and Philipp Otto Runge in Germany, Georges Michel and Camille Corot in France, Thomas Cole in America, and Johan Dahl in Norway, are among the names that would feature in a more expansive account – but the 'British school' was remarkable for the serious pretensions it gave to landscape painting. One reason for this, Michael Rosenthal suggests, is that with Britain at war in the 1790s and early 1800s and travel rendered difficult, 'the native scene inevitably not only came under greater scrutiny but also represented what the British were fighting for'.[33] This insight certainly applies to the two most important British landscapists, John Constable and J.M.W. Turner, on whom these brief observations must dwell.

Constable famously devoted himself, in a letter of 1802, to the practice of a 'natural painture', which involved confronting nature direct (as opposed to imitating other artists) in order to achieve 'a pure and unaffected representation of the scenes that may employ me'.[34] He never left England, and travelled little within the country, but instead determined early on to establish himself as the painter of the Stour Valley in his native Suffolk. It is these 'scenes', therefore, that he learned to treat with a naturalism that was bold and unconventional in its time, but which can now appear trite through overfamiliarity. Constable was well-read in English nature poetry and conversant with modern aesthetic theory, and the earliest of his many studies of Dedham Vale are exercises in the picturesque: *Dedham from Langham* (1802), for instance, looks as though the artist has searched for a viewpoint from which the countryside can be composed into a Claudean landscape – it is an application of formal principles to an intimately known locality. At this stage, there is no significant moral content to Constable's landscapes. However, as his art developed he veered towards 'agricultural' landscapes giving an impression of a stable, industrious, and prosperous rural order – a perspective clearly congenial to the landowning class to which his family belonged. *The Hay Wain* (1821), his most reproduced painting, with its line of distant mowers indicating the destination of the cart crossing the river in the foreground, perfectly illustrates this aesthetic pattern, just as it also exemplifies his quasi-religious feeling for natural beauty. The vein of pastoral idyll that some commentators detect in the painting may be partly due to its retrospective quality – it was painted after Constable had left his home in Suffolk. The well-publicised explosion of rural riots and protests in the county the following year meant that this serenity became anachronistic. Thereafter, in Michael Rosenthal's view, Constable's art became more experimental, more self-referential, more self-sustaining: he explored a 'naturalism of sensation' rather than a 'naturalism of appearance', painted in a more expressionistic way (with increasingly tragic undertones), and incorporated elements of political and Christian allegory. Painting became therapy, as he created in his studio 'a kingdom of [his] own' in response to the loss of the rural world he had depended on emotionally and artistically.[35]

Turner was in many ways a complete contrast to Constable. He was, for a start, a compulsive traveller, both in Britain and on the Continent, finding material everywhere for his prolific art. He was much more versatile as an artist, able to work simultaneously in very different pictorial modes. And whereas politics seems almost to have taken Constable by surprise in 1822, Turner took a keen interest in contemporary affairs, although his personal politics are very uncertain (for example, his *Slavers Throwing Overboard the Dead and Dying* (1840) suggests liberal sympathies, but he also worked for slave-traders). However, it is as Britain's greatest and most original landscape artist that Turner is best known, and makes a fruitful comparison with

Constable. Like him, Turner was well acquainted with modern aesthetic doctrines and with the traditions of landscape painting, and had early experience of architectural drawing and professional topography; all this fed into the several substantial series of 'picturesque views' – watercolours prepared for engraving and reproduction – that he produced in the 1810s and 1820s as a pictorial record of his own country. But whereas Constable is associated most readily with a definitive interpretation of picturesque beauty, Turner's most memorable achievements in landscape are arguably his explorations of the sublime.

Snowstorm: Hannibal and his Army Crossing the Alps (1812), a much-discussed painting and one of the largest Turners on display at the Tate, makes the necessary points. The eponymous snowstorm, appearing as an awesome vortex that would become a signature in Turner's work, seems full of personalised menace as it hangs like a scorpion's tail over the puny humans below. As Hannibal's rearguard falls victim both to the elements and to the guerrilla tactics of native defenders, the overriding impression is of a raw natural energy challenging 'the very destiny of man and history'.[36] As John Gage points out, *Snowstorm* exemplifies Henry Fuseli's theory that painting excels when it manages to 'dart rays back to the past and forward to the future', for it offers a rebuke to the imperial ambitions of the modern Hannibal, Napoleon, who had also invaded Italy via the Alps.[37] In his later, increasingly 'abstract' work, Turner abandons the conventional vocabulary of sublimity (such as darkness and obscurity) and instead pursues Burke's observation that intense light can also be so overwhelming as to produce a sublime effect. The mysterious *Light and Colour (Goethe's Theory) – the Morning after the Deluge – Moses Writing the Book* (1843) has a verse caption that undermines the initial promise of the biblical theme and his use of the 'plus' colours (red, yellow, and green) in Goethe's colour theory, but in the sublime radiance that appears to come forward to envelop the spectator Turner suggests, as Sam Smiles says, that 'Beyond the (earthly) delusions of hope lie intimations of transcendence in nature'.[38]

Prints

Both Constable and Turner, the two British artists highlighted in the previous section, took a keen interest in the means by which their landscapes were reproduced and hence made available to a larger buying public. For three decades Turner's production of watercolours was dominated by work destined for the engraver – resulting in the several topographical series of 'picturesque views' of England and Wales – and he took a close personal interest in this professional 'translation' of his art. He also produced a series of landscape prints, his *Liber Studiorum* (1807–19), which doubled as an exposition of the different categories of landscape painting and an advertisement for his own achievements in the field; Turner contributed the etched outlines himself and mezzotint (scraping and burnishing a roughened copper plate, producing a better approximation of oil painting than line engraving) was added by a professional engraver. Constable also chose mezzotint – professionally executed – for the twenty prints that made up his *Various Subjects of Landscape Characteristic of English Scenery* (1830–3), a bid to obtain wider public recognition for his ideals of pictorial beauty. Like Turner, he superintended the manufacture of the plates with extreme care, sometimes uncomfortably so for the much-put-upon engraver. Both Constable's and Turner's attempts to escape the restrictions of the Royal Academy and private patronage and reach a more popular audience involved them in the highly diverse and stratified industry of printmaking, which reached its highest point of development in the period.

Prints – essentially, reproducible designs or images, with or without accompanying text – were used for a wide range of purposes, from the relatively high-cultural replication of paintings to the production of illustrated broadsides for sale by street hawkers. This diversity of functions was paralleled by a diversity of printing methods, with line engraving, a time-consuming technique that was brought to an astonishing level of sophistication in the eighteenth century, enjoying the highest reputation in a very status-conscious profession. Other high-ranking methods of illustration were the less laborious etching (whereby the design is incised on a plate coated with an acid-resistant 'ground', and then burned out to receive ink by the operation of acid), mezzotint, and aquatint (which uses several 'bitings' of acid on a rough sandy ground, producing an effect similar to a watercolour). These methods all required any text to be carefully inscribed on the same plate, but the illustrative methods associated with the bottom end of the market, woodcuts (a relief method in which the illustrator works with the grain of the wood) and wood engraving (in which the lines to be printed are cut into the end-grain), could be incorporated with a typeset page and printed in a single pull of the press. The huge success of wood engraving, perfected by the Newcastle-based Thomas Bewick, in making possible cheap illustrated material meant that the new chemical process of lithography was not widely adopted in the period. The interrelationships of the different print genres could be extremely complex: Brian Maidment has shown, in an analysis of the flood of images inspired by the burning of the Albion Flour Mill in Southwark, an icon of modern industrial architecture, in 1791, how ideological and aesthetic choices can to some extent be cross-matched with particular print media.[39]

An area of the industry of particular interest to students of literature is the production of satirical prints and political caricatures, which rose massively in output and popularity during the reign of George III, played a major role in mediating the propaganda war surrounding the French Revolution in the 1790s, and flourished again as the political temperature rose in the troubled years after Waterloo. Topical prints, which were the ancestor of modern political cartoons, were typically hand-coloured etchings, displayed to the public in printshop windows or in exhibition rooms, and sold as single sheets to be framed up, pasted on the wall or other suitable surface, or collected in portfolios or albums, as circumstances and propriety demanded. Production of caricatures, which dealt mainly with national and international politics and high society life, was centred on London, but well-established distribution networks carried the goods, along with their culture of wit and irreverence, to the provinces and abroad. Diana Donald writes of the remarkable invisibility of Georgian caricaturists, even artists like James Gillray and Thomas Rowlandson who are venerated today, in contemporary discourse: they were, for example, generally ignored by obituarists. The fact that most satirists were hard-nosed professionals, did not let their personal politics get in the way of a good commission, and 'habitually switched from one side to the other, sometimes within weeks and in relation to the same issue', did not help their artistic reputations by the standards of the day. In fact, everything about caricature, Donald shows – its ephemerality, its partisanship, its *ad hominem* mode of attack, its bondage to the shifting tides of public opinion, its focus on human imperfection and corruption – guaranteed critical disdain: 'low' subject matter had a low value and implied a 'low artist' who chose to represent only the worst types or facets of humanity.[40] Nevertheless, the sheer popularity of satirical prints, the undeniable technical brilliance of many of the artists, and the fact that wit and ridicule could be seen as important to a nation supposedly more at ease with itself than during the religious turmoil of the seventeenth century, all helped to complicate the status of the medium, and to further fray the boundaries between 'high' and 'low'.

The upsurge of caricature prints in the charged atmosphere of the 1790s coincides with what Donald describes as a transition already under way in the nature of political satire – an abandonment of an older emblematic tradition (using personifications of Fortune and Justice, devils and monsters, animal allegories, and so on) that evidently tapped into popular political consciousness, in favour of more sophisticated and ironic methods (employing much parody and burlesque, across a wide range of historical, biblical, and literary references) designed to appeal to an expanding polite audience. This would suggest that the new satire, hard-hitting as it could be, was 'not so much an affront to high culture as a playfully antithetical form which confirmed its hegemony'.[41] However, the confidence of this triumph was shaken in the 1790s as conservative propagandists found themselves obliged to communicate across the class divide, fighting crudeness with crudeness if necessary, to counter the radical message and inspire patriotic consensus. The course of the propaganda war, in which prints (and their reproduction in other media) played a central part, can be followed in David Bindman's exhibition catalogue, *The Shadow of the Guillotine*. As Bindman says, 'The extent and diversity of the types of image produced in England . . . suggest a widespread belief in the efficacy of images as a means of persuasion, especially of the uneducated.'[42] Most of the surviving print material is pro-government, not because of the complete success of official and voluntary censorship, but because of the greater ephemerality of demotic material like handbills and broadsides that carried more of the radical message, and because radicals favoured other visual media (such as coins, medals, mugs, even sweet wrappers) that were more likely to escape hostile attention. Among the recurrent themes of loyalist prints are the contrast between the freedom and prosperity enjoyed by Britons and the anarchy and poverty of revolutionary France; the unrestrained brutality of the Parisian sans-culottes and the perpetual terror of the guillotine; the perfidious behaviour of the Opposition leader, Fox; the nobility of the executed French king; and, later in the decade, the threat of a French invasion carried out in collusion with the Whigs. Radicals responded by reclaiming, in ironic assertive mode, Burke's contemptuous image of the people as a 'swinish multitude'. The visual front of the propaganda war was most hotly contested around the time of the Treason Trials and the Two Acts in 1794–5, succumbing to a repressive pro-government consensus by the end of the decade. Gillray's personal career is a microcosm of this trend: beginning with deeply ambivalent treatments of the main personalities and events, then alternating between character assassinations of Fox and equally unsparing caricatures of Pitt, then foursquare behind the government position once his services had been bought with a government pension.

The conflictive print culture of the revolutionary decade was re-created in the years after Waterloo as the parliamentary reform movement gathered steam, and with particular fervour in the aftermath of the Peterloo massacre. Prints sympathetic to the reformers depicted the events in documentary fashion, emphasising the orderly and disciplined behaviour of the demonstrators, or went for maximum emotional power in presenting the latter as victims, highlighting the participation of women and children; their opponents concentrated on precisely this aspect, since public opinion had difficulty coming to terms with the mass politicisation of women. However, the big success in visual culture of the post-war years was the remarriage of text and illustration in the work of William Hone (and his many imitators), whose shilling pamphlets enlivened with woodcuts, beginning with the seductive nursery-rhyme parody of *The Political House That Jack Built* (1819), found a uniquely popular way to disseminate the message that the entire system was corrupt. Pioneering as these were in publishing history terms, they cut the legs off Georgian political caricature: with the market for illustrated reading matter expanding ever down the social scale, the latter's 'personal vindictiveness' and 'black pessimism' increasingly looked 'trapped in a set of attitudes which repelled the idealists of the new age'[43] – an age that lies beyond the horizon of the present book.

Notes

1. *Reading in Detail: Aesthetics and the Feminine* (New York and London, 1987), pp. 11–22.

2. *Discourses on Art*, ed. Robert R. Wark (New Haven and London, 1975), pp. 44–5, 244.

3. *Essays on the Nature and Principles of Taste* (Edinburgh, 1790), pp. 10, 61–2.

4. *An Analytical Inquiry into the Principles of Taste*, 2nd edn (London, 1805), p. 145.

5. See Rosemary Ashton, *The German Idea: Four English Writers and the Reception of German Thought 1800–1860* (Cambridge, 1980).

6. *On the Naïve and Sentimental in Literature*, trans. Helen Watanabe-O'Kelly (Manchester, 1981), pp. 36, 51.

7. *On the Aesthetic Education of Man, in a Series of Letters*, ed. and trans. Elizabeth Wilkinson and L.A. Willoughby (Oxford, 1967), pp. 35, 139–41, 215, 41.

8. *Aesthetics: Lectures on Fine Art*, trans. T.M. Knox, 2 vols (Oxford, 1975), I, 55.

9. 'On Incomprehensibility', in *The Origins of Modern Critical Thought: German Aesthetic and Literary Criticism from Lessing to Hegel*, ed. David Simpson (Cambridge, 1988), pp. 184–5.

10. *A Philosophical Enquiry into the Origin of our Ideas of the Sublime and Beautiful*, ed. Adam Phillips (Oxford, 1990), p. 36.

11. *Critique of Judgement*, trans. J.C. Meredith (Oxford, 1952), Part I, p. 35.

12. *The Picturesque: Studies in a Point of View* (London and New York, 1927), p. 4.

13. *Claude Lorrain* (London, 1989), pp. 9, 64.

14. *Three Essays: On Picturesque Beauty; on Picturesque Travel; and on Sketching Landscape*, 3rd edn (London, 1808), p. 8.

15. *An Essay on the Picturesque*, revised edn (London, 1796), p. 105.

16. *The Landscape, a Didactic Poem*, 2nd edn (London, 1795), p. 18, Book I, ll. 263–6.

17. *Landscape and Ideology: The English Rustic Tradition, 1740–1860* (Berkeley and Los Angeles, 1986), pp. 68, 70.

18. John Dixon Hunt, *The Picturesque Garden in Europe* (London, 2003), p. 40. My brief observations on the landscape garden draw heavily on this excellent survey.

19. *The Art of Landscape Gardening*, ed. John Nolen (Boston and New York, 1907), p. 57.

20. Stephen Daniels and Charles Watkins, 'A Well-connected Landscape: Uvedale Price at Foxley', in *The Picturesque Landscape: Visions of Georgian Herefordshire*, ed. Daniels and Watkins (Nottingham, 1994), pp. 40–4 (p. 43).

21. Hunt, *Picturesque Garden*, pp. 75–6.

22. *Essay*, pp. 62–7.

23. *European Architecture, 1750–1890* (Oxford, 2000), p. 105.

24. *Georgian Architecture* (Newton Abbot, 2002), p. 23.

25. Nikolaus Pevsner and S. Lang, 'The Doric Revival', in *Studies in Art, Architecture and Design*, 2 vols (New York, 1968), I, 197–211 (p. 206).

26. See *The Dilemma of Style: Architectural Ideas from the Picturesque to the Post-Modern* (London, 1987), esp. ch. 1.

27. Curl, *Georgian Architecture*, p. 90; Bergdoll, *European Architecture*, pp. 156–8.

28. L. Ettlinger, 'A German Architect's Visit to England in 1826', *Architectural Review*, 97 (May 1945), 131–4 (p. 133).

29. '"This Great Mart of Genius": The Royal Academy Exhibitions at Somerset House, 1780–1836', in *Art on the Line: The Royal Academy Exhibitions at Somerset House 1780–1836*, ed. David H. Solkin (New Haven and London, 2001), pp. 1–8 (p. 8).

30. *Complete Works*, XVIII (1933), 46.

31. Robert Rosenblum and H.W. Janson, *Art of the Nineteenth Century: Painting and Sculpture* (London, 1984), p. 30.

32. Rose-Marie and Rainer Hagen, *Francisco Goya* (Cologne, 2003), p. 62.

33. 'Landscape as High Art', in *Glorious Nature: British Landscape Painting 1750–1850* (London, 1993), pp. 13–30 (p. 16).

34. Quoted in Michael Rosenthal, *Constable: The Painter and his Landscape* (New Haven and London, 1983), p. 27.

35. Rosenthal, *Constable*, pp. 192, 211.

36. Rosenblum and Janson, *Art of the Nineteenth Century*, p. 89.

37. *J.M.W. Turner: 'A Wonderful Range of Mind'* (New Haven and London, 1987), p. 193.

38. *J.M.W. Turner* (London, 2000), p. 66.

39. *Reading Popular Prints 1790–1870* (Manchester and New York, 1996), ch. 2.

40. *The Age of Caricature: Satirical Prints in the Reign of George III* (New Haven and London, 1996), pp. 26, 27–31.

41. Donald, *Age of Caricature*, p. 74.

42. *The Shadow of the Guillotine: Britain and the French Revolution* (London, 1989), p. 35.

43. Donald, *Age of Caricature*, p. 184.

Chronology

DATE	VERSE, DRAMA, FICTION	OTHER WORKS	HISTORICAL/ CULTURAL EVENTS
1789	Blake *Songs of Innocence*	Price *Discourse on the Love of Our Country*	French Revolution begins Mutiny on the *Bounty*
1790	Radcliffe *Sicilian Romance*	Bruce *Travels to Discover the Source of the Nile* Burke *Reflections on the Revolution in France* Kant *Critique of Judgement*	
1791		Paine *Rights of Man*, Part One Bartram *Travels*	Birmingham riots Louis XVI's flight to Varennes
1792	Bage *Man As He Is*	Gilpin *Three Essays* Paine *Rights of Man*, Part Two Wollstonecraft *Vindication of the Rights of Woman*	Abolition of monarchy in France; republic declared September Massacres in Paris London Corresponding Society formed Loyalist associations formed
1793	Blake *America* More *Village Politics*	Godwin *Political Justice*	Execution of Louis XVI Britain and France at war Reign of Terror begins Macartney embassy to China
1794	Blake *Songs of Experience* Godwin *Caleb Williams* Radcliffe *Mysteries of Udolpho*	Paine *Age of Reason* Paley *Evidences of Christianity* Price *Essay on the Picturesque* Knight *The Landscape*	Treason Trials Habeus Corpus suspended Execution of Robespierre
1795	Lewis *The Monk* More *Cheap Repository Tracts*	Hutton *Theory of the Earth* Hearne *Journey to the Northern Ocean*	'Two Acts' Food riots Methodist secession Britain takes Cape Colony from Dutch
1796	Coleridge *Poems on Various Subjects*		Napoleon's Italian campaign Turner exhibits first oil paintings

1797	Smith *Elegiac Sonnets*	Wilberforce *Practical Christianity*	Naval mutinies Invasion scare
1798	Wordsworth and Coleridge *Lyrical Ballads* Wollstonecraft *Wrongs of Woman*	Edgeworth *Practical Education* Malthus *Principles of Population*	France invades Switzerland Napoleon lands in Egypt; Battle of the Nile Irish Rebellion suppressed
1799	Wordsworth Two-Part *Prelude*	Park *Travels* More *Strictures on Modern System of Female Education*	Napoleon becomes First Consul Six Acts against radical activities
1800	Edgeworth *Castle Rackrent* *Lyrical Ballads*, second edition		Volta generates electricity Act of Union with Ireland
1801	Southey *Thalaba the Destroyer*		Pitt government falls First census of England and Wales
1802	Scott *Minstrelsy of the Scottish Border*	Paley *Natural Theology*	Peace of Amiens *Edinburgh Review* founded
1803	Darwin *Temple of Nature*	Lancaster *Improvements in Education*	Resumption of war with France France sells Louisiana Territory to United States
1804	Blake *Milton*	Davies *Celtic Researches*	Pitt returns as Prime Minister Napoleon crowned Emperor
1805	Scott *Lay of the Last Minstrel* Wordsworth *The Prelude* (completed in manuscript)	Knight *Principles of Taste*	Napoleon victorious at Ulm and Austerlitz Battle of Trafalgar; Nelson dies
1806			Deaths of Pitt and Fox Napoleon establishes trade blockade
1807	Wordsworth *Poems in Two Volumes*	Turner *History of the Anglo-Saxons*	Abolition of slave trade Davy isolates sodium and potassium
1808	Goethe *Faust*, Part One	Dalton *New System of Chemical Philosophy*	Peninsular War begins
1809			*Quarterly Review* founded
1810	Crabbe *The Borough* Scott *Lady of the Lake*		George III goes permanently insane
1811	Austen *Sense and Sensibility*		Prince of Wales becomes Regent Luddite riots

1812	Barbauld *Eighteen Hundred and Eleven* Byron *Childe Harold's Pilgrimage* I–II		Assassination of Spencer Perceval Napoleon invades Russia United States declares war on Britain
1813	Austen *Pride and Prejudice* Shelley *Queen Mab*	Owen *A New View of Society*	Napoleon loses Battle of Leipzig East India Company monopoly ended
1814	Austen *Mansfield Park* Byron *The Corsair* Scott *Waverley* Wordsworth *The Excursion*		Napoleon abdicates; restoration of monarchy Stephenson builds steam locomotive
1815	Peacock *Headlong Hall*		Napoleon escapes; Battle of Waterloo brings war to end Corn Law passed
1816	Byron *Childe Harold's Pilgrimage* III Shelley *Alastor*	Cobbett *Political Register*	Economic depression Spa Fields riot Elgin Marbles purchased for British Museum
1817	Byron *Manfred* Coleridge *Sibylline Leaves* Keats *Poems*	Ricardo *Principles of Political Economy* Mill *History of British India*	Pentridge uprising *Blackwood's Magazine* founded
1818	Byron *Childe Harold's Pilgrimage* IV Keats *Endymion* M. Shelley *Frankenstein* Austen *Northanger Abbey* and *Persuasion*		Church Building Act
1819	Byron *Don Juan* I–II Hone *Political House that Jack Built* Scott *Bride of Lammermoor*	Lawrence *Lectures on Physiology, Zoology, and the Natural History of Man*	Peterloo massacre 'Six Acts' restricting radical activity
1820	Clare *Poems Descriptive of Rural Life and Scenery* Maturin *Melmoth the Wanderer* Shelley *Prometheus Unbound*		Death of George III; accession of George IV Trial of Queen Caroline Cato Street Conspiracy Oersted discovers electromagnetism
1821		De Quincey *Confessions of an English Opium-Eater*	Greek War of Independence begins
1822	Shelley *Hellas*		Castlereagh commits suicide

1823		Hazlitt *Liber Amoris* Lamb *Essays of Elia*	
1824	Hogg *Confessions of a Justified Sinner*		Trade unions given right to exist National Gallery founded
1825		Hazlitt *The Spirit of the Age*	Stockton–Darlington railway opens
1826	M. Shelley *The Last Man*		London Zoological Society founded
1827			Reform of criminal law University of London founded Society for the Diffusion of Useful Knowledge founded
1828	Hemans *Records of Woman*		Repeal of Test and Corporation Acts
1829		Coleridge *On the Constitution of the Church and State*	Catholic emancipation Peel creates police force
1830	Tennyson *Poems, Chiefly Lyrical*	Cobbett *Rural Rides* Lyell *Principles of Geology* (vol. 1)	Death of George IV Whigs take power July Revolution in France Greek independence secured

General Bibliographies

Place of publication is London, unless otherwise stated.

General contextual studies

Butler, M. *Romantics, Rebels and Reactionaries: English Literature and its Background 1760–1830* (Oxford, 1981). (An important book in renewing interest in Romanticism's historical contexts.)

Gaull, M. *English Romanticism: The Human Context* (New York and London, 1988). (Enormously detailed.)

McCalman, I. (ed.) *An Oxford Companion to the Romantic Age: British Culture 1776–1832* (Oxford, 1999). (Indispensable reference work, despite some startling omissions; excellent topic essays.)

Politics and economics

Daunton, M.J. *Progress and Poverty: An Economic and Social History of Britain 1700–1850* (Oxford and New York, 1995). (Authoritative modern synthesis.)

Dickinson, H.T. (ed.) *Britain and the French Revolution, 1789–1815* (1979). (A balanced set of bicentenary essays.)

Doyle, W. *The French Revolution: A Very Short Introduction* (Oxford, 2001). (A godsend for undergraduates.)

Emsley, C. *British Society and the French Wars 1793–1815* (1979). (Expert treatment of a strangely neglected topic.)

Evans, E.J. *The Forging of the Nation: Early Industrial Britain 1783–1870* (London and New York, 1983). (Includes an excellent compendium of information.)

Goodwin. A. *The Friends of Liberty: The English Democratic Movement in the Age of the French Revolution* (1979). (Standard work.)

Hobsbawm, E.J. *The Age of Revolution: Europe 1789–1848* (1962). (Comprehensive account of politics and culture.)

Mellor, A.K. *Romanticism and Gender* (New York and London, 1993). (Chs 2–4 offer the best overview of the revolutionary ideology developed by women in the period.)

Mori, J. *Britain in the Age of the French Revolution* (2000). (Good on the interweaving of politics, economics, and religion.)

Rudé, G. *The French Revolution* (1988). (Very readable account, more detailed than Doyle.)

Thompson, E.P. *The Making of the English Working Class*, 2nd edn (Harmondsworth, 1968). (Inspirational 'history from below'.)

Travel and exploration

Bohls, E.A. *Women Travel Writers and the Language of Aesthetics, 1716–1818* (Cambridge, 1995). (For gender aspects of the topic.)

Chard, C. and H. Langdon (eds) *Transports: Travel, Pleasure, and Imaginative Geography, 1600–1830* (New Haven, 1996). (Elegant interdisciplinary collection.)

Dalrymple, W. *White Mughals* (2002). (Absorbing account of a colonial culture in transition.)

Fulford, T. and P. Kitson (eds) *Romanticism and Colonialism: Writing and Empire, 1780–1830* (Cambridge, 1998). (Includes two excellent survey essays.)

Hulme, P. and T. Youngs (eds) *The Cambridge Companion to Travel Writing* (Cambridge, 2002). (Contains much of relevance to the Romantic period.)

Jarvis, R. *Romantic Writing and Pedestrian Travel* (Basingstoke, 1997). (On the unique contribution of walking to the Romantic experience of the world.)

Leask, N. *Curiosity and the Aesthetics of Travel Writing 1770–1840* (Oxford, 2002). (Major theoretical study.)

Leed, E.J. *The Mind of the Traveller* (New York, 1991). (Brilliantly clarifies changes in attitudes and motives.)

Pratt, M.L. *Imperial Eyes: Travel Writing and Transculturation* (1992). (Set the standard for work in this field.)

Stafford, B.M. *Voyage into Substance: Art, Science, Nature, and the Illustrated Travel Account, 1760–1840* (Cambridge, Mass., 1984). (Richly thought-provoking.)

The literary marketplace

Altick, R.D. *The English Common Reader: A Social History of the Mass Reading Public 1800–1900* (Chicago, 1957). (Classic study.)

Erickson, L. *The Economy of Literary Form: English Literature and the Industrialization of Publishing* (Baltimore and London, 1996). (Some revealing case studies.)

Feather, J. *A History of British Publishing* (1988). (Useful survey.)

Klancher, J.P. *The Making of English Reading Audiences, 1790–1832* (Madison and London, 1987). (Focuses on periodical literature.)

McGann, J. *The Textual Condition* (Princeton, 1991). (Applies a socialised model of literary production to Romantic writing.)

Manguel, A. *A History of Reading* (1996). (Quirky and insightful.)

Martin, H.-J. *The History and Power of Writing* (Chicago and London, 1994). (Places the printing revolution within longer history.)

Newlyn, L. *Reading, Writing, and Romanticism: The Anxiety of Reception* (Oxford, 2000). (Relates major Romantics to the growth of the reading public and the rise of criticism.)

Sullivan, A. (ed.) *British Literary Magazines: The Romantic Age, 1789–1836* (Westport, 1983). (Alphabetical guide to periodicals.)

Twyman, M. *The British Library Guide to Printing: History and Techniques* (1998). (Succinct guide to changing technologies.)

Education and the family

Anderson, M. *Approaches to the History of the Western Family 1500–1914* (Basingstoke, 1980). (Compact yet detailed.)

Ariès, P. *Centuries of Childhood: A Social History of Family Life* (New York, 1962). (Classic study of the invention of childhood.)

Barnard, H.C. *A History of English Education from 1760* (1961). (Informative survey.)

Borer, M. *Willingly to School: A History of Women's Education* (1976). (Colourful account.)

Davidoff, L. and C. Hall *Family Fortunes: Men and Women of the English Middle Class 1780–1850*, revised edn (2002). (Influential feminist history.)

Flint, C. *Family Fictions: Narrative and Domestic Relations in Britain, 1688–1798* (Stanford, 1998). (Subtly connects family and literary history.)

Hofstetter, M. *The Romantic Idea of a University* (Basingstoke, 2001). (Compares German and British developments.)

Pollock, L. *Forgotten Children: Parent–Child Relations from 1500 to 1900* (Cambridge, 1983). (Uses diaries and autobiographies as source-material.)

Richardson, A. *Literature, Education, and Romanticism: Reading as Social Practice, 1780–1832* (Cambridge, 1994). (Well-researched, illuminating.)

Stone, L. *The Family, Sex and Marriage in England 1500–1800* (1979). (Richly documented, always interesting.)

Science

Aesch, A. Gode-Von *Natural Science in German Romanticism* (New York, 1941). (Standard work on relationship between science and literature.)

Burwick, F. *The Damnation of Newton: Goethe's Color Theory and Romantic Perception* (Berlin, 1986). (Enthralling study of a pivotal figure.)

Cunningham, A. and N. Jardine (eds) *Romanticism and the Sciences* (Cambridge, 1990). (A first-rate essay collection.)

Knight, D. *The Age of Science: The Scientific World-View of the Nineteenth Century* (Oxford, 1986). (One of many useful works by a great expositor and populariser.)

Levere, T. *Poetry Realized in Nature: Samuel Taylor Coleridge and Early Nineteenth-Century Science* (Cambridge, 1981). (The most detailed case study of a major poet's engagement with contemporary science.)

Rehbock, P. *The Philosophical Naturalists: Themes in Early Nineteenth-Century British Biology* (Madison, 1983). (Very helpful study of British science in European context.)

Uglow, J. *The Lunar Men: The Friends Who Made the Future, 1730–1810* (2002). (Brings to life a provincial centre of science and invention.)

Religion

Canuel, M. *Religion, Toleration and British Writing, 1790–1830* (Cambridge, 2002). (Interesting new slant.)

Clark, J.C.D. *English Society 1688–1832: Ideology, Social Structure and Political Practice during the Ancien Regime* (Cambridge, 1985). (Influential account of the religious politics of the period.)

Hempton, D. *Religion and Political Culture in Britain and Ireland: From the Glorious Revolution to the Decline of Empire* (Cambridge, 1996). (Clear and incisive.)

Hole, R. *Pulpits, Politics and Public Order in England, 1760–1832* (Cambridge, 1989). (Strong thesis about changing Church priorities.)

MacIntyre, A. *A Short History of Ethics*, 2nd edn (London, 1998). (The later chapters are relevant and very helpful.)

Prickett, S. *Origins of Narrative: The Romantic Appropriation of the Bible* (Cambridge, 1996). (How the Bible became 'a different book' in the Romantic period.)

Priestman, M. *Romantic Atheism: Poetry and Freethought, 1780–1830* (Cambridge, 1999). (Provides a detailed picture of 'infidel' activity.)

Ryan, R. *The Romantic Reformation: Religious Politics in English Literature, 1789–1824* (Cambridge, 1997). (Interprets the spirit of the age in religious terms.)

Ward, W.R. *Religion and Society in England 1790–1850* (London, 1972). (A good general survey.)

Watts, M.R. *The Dissenters*, 2 vols (Oxford, 1978, 1995). (Impressively researched, expansive argument; can be read selectively.)

The sense of the past

Bahn, P.G. *The Cambridge Illustrated History of Archaeology* (Cambridge, 1996). (Lively and informative.)

Carruthers, G. and A. Rawes (eds) *English Romanticism and the Celtic World* (Cambridge, 2003). (On the literary interactions between the 'centre' and its peripheries.)

Chandler, A. *A Dream of Order: The Medieval Ideal in Nineteenth-Century English Literature* (1971). (Contextualises the medieval revival.)

Chandler, J. *England in 1819: The Politics of Literary Culture and the Case of Romantic Historicism* (Chicago and London, 1998). (Essential reading.)

Collingwood, R.G. *The Idea of History* (Oxford, 1946). (Contains an illuminating section on the 'history of History'.)

Hobsbawm, E. and T. Ranger (eds) *The Invention of Tradition* (Cambridge, 1983). (For the essays by Morgan and Trevor-Roper.)

Smith, O. *The Politics of Language 1791–1819* (Oxford, 1984). (Explains what was at stake in competing theories of the origins of language.)

Tsigakou, F.-M. *The Rediscovery of Greece: Travellers and Painters of the Romantic Era* (New York, 1981). (Lively, well-illustrated.)

Webb, T. *English Romantic Hellenism 1700–1824* (Manchester, 1982). (Selection of primary sources with helpful commentary.)

Whitney, L. *Primitivism and the Idea of Progress in English Popular Literature of the Eighteenth Century* (Baltimore, 1934). (Good on the philosophical background.)

Aesthetics and the visual arts

Bergdoll, B. *European Architecture, 1750–1890* (Oxford, 2000). (Excellent on the cultural context of architectural developments.)

Bindman, D. *The Shadow of the Guillotine: Britain and the French Revolution* (1989). (Exhibition catalogue that brings the Revolution debate to life.)

Copley, S. and P. Garside (eds) *The Politics of the Picturesque: Literature, Landscape and Aesthetics since 1770* (Cambridge, 1994). (Essays reflecting modern critical interest in the picturesque.)

Donald, D. *The Age of Caricature: Satirical Prints in the Reign of George III* (New Haven and London, 1996). (Sophisticated yet entertaining account of print culture.)

Franklin, A. and M. Philp *Napoleon and the Invasion of Britain* (Oxford, 2003). (Stunning exhibition catalogue on Britain at war.)

Hipple, W.J. *The Beautiful, the Sublime and the Picturesque in Eighteenth-Century British Aesthetic Theory* (Carbondale, 1957). (Major study.)

Hunt, J. Dixon *The Picturesque Garden in Europe* (2003). (Very scholarly, and a visual feast.)

Hussey, C. *The Picturesque: Studies in a Point of View* (London and New York, 1927). (Still the best general survey.)

Rosenblum, R. and H.W. Janson *Art of the Nineteenth Century: Painting and Sculpture* (1984). (Illuminating discussions of individual works.)

Vaughan, W. *Romanticism and Art* (1994). (A good general introduction.)

Individual Authors
Notes on biography, major works, and suggested further reading

This section contains brief notes on a number of significant British writers featured in this book whose lives, or whose major writings, fall within the Romantic period. Place of publication is London, unless otherwise stated.

BENTHAM, Jeremy (1748–1832), philosopher, jurist, and social reformer, was an infant prodigy who entered Oxford University at the age of twelve. He was admitted to the bar, but decided to work at reforming the law (along with other institutions), rather than practising it. His *Introduction to the Principles of Morals and Legislation* (1789) advanced the theory of utilitarianism, which became the creed of a group of 'philosophical radicals' who used the *Westminster Review* to press for change. His other works include a *Defence of Usury* (1787), *A Plan of Parliamentary Reform* (1817), and the *Rationale of Judicial Evidence* (1827). Bentham's works were widely translated and he achieved a global reputation.

Burns, J.H., general ed., *The Collected Works of Jeremy Bentham* (1968–).

See: Dinwiddy, J., *Bentham* (Oxford, 1989).

BURKE, Edmund (1729–97), statesman and political philosopher, was born in Dublin, and was educated at a Quaker school in Co. Kildare and at Trinity College, Dublin, before leaving for London to read, inconclusively, for the bar. Burke belongs chronologically to the eighteenth century but looms over the entire Romantic period. He was an MP from 1766 until his death, aligning himself first with the Rockingham Whigs and then with Charles James Fox, and advocating conciliation with the American colonies, reform of the colonial administration in India, and Catholic emancipation. His passionate opposition to the French Revolution finally caused a break with Fox, and Burke spent his final years as something of a parliamentary outcast. His early *Philosophical Enquiry into the Origin of our Ideas of the Sublime and Beautiful* (1757) had a lasting influence, while the celebrated *Reflections on the Revolution in France* (1790) became the fulcrum of political debate in the 1790s. He maintained his assault on the Revolution and defence of 'old Whig' principles in *An Appeal from the Old to the New Whigs* (1791) and *Letters on a Regicide Peace* (1795–6).

Langford, P., general ed., *The Writings and Speeches of Edmund Burke* (Oxford, 1981–).

See: Kramnick, I., *The Rage of Edmund Burke: Portrait of an Ambivalent Conservative* (New York, 1977).
Macpherson, C.B., *Burke* (Oxford, 1980).

COBBETT, William (1762–1835), radical journalist and politician, was born in Surrey, worked as an agricultural labourer, and later enlisted in the army. A disastrous attempt to reveal corruption in the army led to him fleeing to America, where he established himself as a journalist in the pro-British camp. In 1800 he returned to England, and two years later founded the weekly *Political Register*, which reflected his shift from conservative to radical and built a sustained critique of 'Old Corruption'. In the renewed agitation that followed the end of the Napoleonic wars, Cobbett reached out to a labouring-class audience by selling his editorials as broadsheets for two pence. During a second American exile, he wrote *A Year's Residence in the United States of America* (1818–19) and his *Grammar of the English Language* (1818). In the 1820s, back in England, he toured the rural nation, chronicling its destruction and distress in *Rural Rides* (1830). Having campaigned for parliamentary reform, Cobbett became an MP in 1832 in the first election conducted under the new system.

Nattrass, L., ed., *William Cobbett: Selected Writings*, 6 vols (1998).

See: Sambrook, J., *William Cobbett* (1973).

DARWIN, Erasmus (1731–1802), doctor, poet, and scientist, was educated at St John's College, Cambridge and the University of Edinburgh, and practised medicine at Nottingham, Lichfield, and Derby. He was a member of the 'Lunar Society' of scientists, industrialists, and other Midlands luminaries. His main achievement was in versifying contemporary scientific developments, as in *The Loves of the Plants* (1789) and *The Economy of Vegetation* (1791). The prose medical treatise, *Zoonomia* (1794–6), and the posthumous *Temple of Nature* (1803) presented unique interpretations of biological research and advanced towards a theory of evolution. Darwin also produced a liberal *Plan for the Conduct of Female Education* (1797).

See: King-Hele, D., *Erasmus Darwin* (1986).

DAVY, Sir Humphry (1778–1829), chemist, was born and educated in Cornwall, and was apprenticed to a surgeon before turning to a life of science. He conducted research on the medicinal properties of gases at Thomas Beddoes's Pneumatic Institution in Bristol between 1798 and 1801, when he took up a post at the newly founded Royal Institution in London. Here, with lavish funding, he made a series of important discoveries in electrochemistry and became a celebrated public lecturer. His work in the field of applied science included the miner's safety lamp that bore his name. He was knighted in 1812 and became president of the Royal Society in 1820. Among his important works were *Researches, Chemical and Philosophical* (1799) and *Elements of Chemical Philosophy* (1812).

Davy, J., ed., *The Collected Works of Sir Humphry Davy*, 9 vols (1839–40).

See: Knight, D., *Humphry Davy: Science and Power* (Cambridge, 1992).

EDGEWORTH, Maria (1767/8–1849), novelist, children's author, and educationalist, was born in Oxfordshire and educated partly at home and partly at schools in Derby and London. In 1773 she accompanied her father to Ireland, where she assisted him in running the family estate and educating her younger siblings. Her most substantial non-literary work, co-authored with her father, was *Practical Education* (1798), a manual of rational, progressive teaching methods. *Letters for Literary Ladies* (1795) was a cleverly constructed intervention in the debate on female education. She again collaborated with her father on *Essays on Professional Education* in 1809, although from 1800 onwards her energies were directed mainly to her novels and children's literature.

See: Butler, M., *Maria Edgeworth: A Literary Biography* (Oxford, 1972).

GILPIN, William (1724–1800), clergyman and theorist of the picturesque, was born near Carlisle, educated at Queen's College, Oxford, and ordained in 1746. He worked as a schoolmaster in Surrey for thirty years, before becoming vicar of Boldre, in the New

Forest, in 1777. He produced a series of tour narratives describing the travels he had undertaken in various parts of the country over many years, beginning with *Observations on the River Wye* (1782). These stimulated domestic tourism and established the cult of picturesque beauty, an interest further fuelled by the more theoretical *Remarks on Forest Scenery* (1790) and *Three Essays: On Picturesque Beauty; on Picturesque Travel; and on Sketching Landscape* (1792).

See: Barbier, C.P., *William Gilpin: His Drawings, Teaching, and Theory of the Picturesque* (Oxford, 1963).

GODWIN, William (1756–1836), political philosopher and novelist, served as a Dissenting minister before turning atheist in the 1780s and subsequently earning his living by writing. His *Enquiry Concerning Political Justice* (1793) elaborated his creed of rational anarchism and inspired a generation of young radicals. Godwin married Mary Wollstonecraft in 1797 and published dangerously frank *Memoirs* (1798) of her following her death soon after giving birth to their daughter. He also produced works of political biography, history, and educational theory, in addition to six novels, of which the best-known is *Caleb Williams* (1794).

Philp, M., general ed., *The Political and Philosophical Writings of William Godwin*, 7 vols (1993).

See: Locke, D., *A Fantasy of Reason: The Life and Thought of William Godwin* (1980).

HAZLITT, William (1778–1830), essayist and critic, was the son of a Unitarian minister and was educated for the ministry himself, but deserted the vocation to pursue his interests in painting and philosophy. Based in London from 1812, he made his living as a prolific journalist, writing for many of the leading journals of the day. Better known for his contributions on literature, theatre, and politics, Hazlitt was also an important writer on aesthetics and the fine arts, though *Sketches of the Principal Picture Galleries in England* (1824) was his only collection of essays on such topics to appear in his lifetime. His son produced an edition of his *Criticisms on Art* in 1843–4.

Howe, P.P., ed., *The Complete Works of William Hazlitt*, 21 vols (1930–4).

See: Bromwich, D., *Hazlitt: The Mind of a Critic* (New York and Oxford, 1983).

HUTTON, James (1726–97), geologist, was educated at the University of Edinburgh, and turned his hand to law, medicine, and farming before devoting himself to his scientific interests. He first set out his uniformitarian principle of geology, accounting for landforms by the regular operation of observable natural processes over vast periods of time, in two papers published in *Transactions of the Royal Society of Edinburgh* in 1788, later expanding his argument in *Theory of the Earth* (1795).

See: Dean, D., *James Hutton and the History of Geology* (Ithaca and London, 1992).

KNIGHT, Richard Payne (1750–1824), Whig MP, antiquarian, collector, and aesthetician, was heir to estates at Downton, Herefordshire, built on wealth from ironworks. As an authority on ancient art and mythology he was largely self-educated. His controversial, privately published *Discourse on the Worship of Priapus* (1786) was reissued in modified form as *An Inquiry into the Symbolic Language of Ancient Art and Mythology* (1818). His other major works were *The Landscape* (1794), a long verse contribution to the picturesque debate, and *An Analytical Inquiry into the Principles of Taste* (1805).

See: Ballantyne, A., *Architecture, Landscape and Liberty: Richard Payne Knight and the Picturesque* (Cambridge, 1997).

MALTHUS, Thomas (1766–1834), economist, demographer, and clergyman, was educated at Jesus College, Cambridge, and subsequently ordained. He had a long career in the Church, though from 1805 he also worked as a professor of economics and history at the East India College in Hertfordshire. His most important publication was his first, the *Essay on the Principle of Population* (1798), which brought him fame and controversy and influenced the debate on poor law reform. His other works include *An Inquiry into the Nature and Progress of Rent* (1815) and *Principles of Political Economy* (1820).

See: Winch, D., *Malthus* (Oxford, 1987).

MORE, Hannah (1745–1833), poet, playwright, essayist, and conservative propagandist, taught at a family-run girls' school in Bristol, and later established a network of Sunday schools in rural Somerset. She was a prominent member of the Clapham sect of evangelical reformers and a passionate anti-slavery campaigner. The success of her 1792 anti-Paineite pamphlet, *Village Politics*, led to a series of mass-produced *Cheap Repository Tracts* (1795–8) aimed at a working-class audience. Other important works were her *Strictures on the Modern System of Female Education* (1799) and the didactic novel, *Coelebs in Search of a Wife* (1809).

Hole, R., ed., *Selected Writings of Hannah More* (1996).

See: Kowalewski-Wallace, E., *Their Fathers' Daughters: Hannah More, Maria Edgeworth, and Patriarchal Complicity* (Oxford, 1991).

PAINE, Thomas (1737–1809), radical philosopher and political activist, was born in Norfolk, and worked as a corset-maker and excise officer before emigrating to America in 1774, where he achieved fame with his pamphlet *Common Sense* (1776), advocating independence from Britain. In 1787 he returned to Britain, where he led the response to Burke's *Reflections* with his *Rights of Man* (1791–2), defending the French Revolution and pressing a radical programme of political and economic reform. Indicted for treason, Paine fled to France, where he was elected to the National Convention, though he was imprisoned and narrowly escaped execution after falling out of favour during Robespierre's ascendancy. His anti-Christian *Age of Reason* (1794–5) alienated many friends and supporters, and after returning to America in 1803 he spent his final years as an outcast.

Foner, P.S., ed., *The Complete Writings of Thomas Paine*, 2 vols (New York, 1945).

See: Philp, M., *Paine* (Oxford, 1989).

PALEY, William (1743–1805), Anglican cleric, university teacher, and Christian apologist, was born in Peterborough and educated at Giggleswick Grammar School and Christ's College, Cambridge. He became a fellow of his college in 1766, and was ordained a year later. He subsequently obtained various Church appointments, the most notable being the archdeaconry of Carlisle (1782). His major works were *The Principles of Moral and Political Philosophy* (1785), which married Christianity and utilitarianism, *A View of the Evidences of Christianity* (1794), a defence of revealed religion that became a standard textbook at Cambridge, and *Natural Theology* (1802), uniquely embodying the argument from design.

See: LeMahieu, D.L., *The Mind of William Paley: A Philosopher and His Age* (Lincoln, Nebr., 1976).

PRICE, Sir Uvedale (1747–1829), Whig MP and aesthetician, was educated at Eton and Christ Church, Oxford, and did the Grand Tour with Charles James Fox in 1767.

His major publication, the *Essay on the Picturesque* (1794), was highly influential on landscape gardening and architecture, and Price put his aesthetic principles into practice on his own estate at Foxley, Herefordshire.

See: Daniels, S. and C. Watkins, 'Picturesque Landscaping and Estate Management: Uvedale Price and Nathaniel Kent at Foxley', in *The Politics of the Picturesque*, ed. S. Copley and P. Garside (Cambridge, 1994), pp. 13–41.

RITSON, Joseph (1752–1803), antiquarian, anthologist, and critic, was born in Stockton-on-Tees and educated at a local school before training for the law. In 1775 he moved to London, and in 1780 set up as a conveyancer on his own account; nine years later he was called to the bar. His long-standing interest in folk culture and national antiquities bore fruit in a series of collections of popular songs and ballads, including his *Select Collection of English Songs* (1783), *Pieces of Ancient Popular Poetry* (1791), *Ancient Songs* (1792), and *Robin Hood* (1795). The commentaries accompanying these works involved him in a bitter war with fellow antiquarian, Thomas Percy, on a mixture of editorial and ideological grounds. Ritson was also a militant vegetarian, and published *An Essay on Abstinence from Animal Food as a Moral Duty* (1802) shortly before succumbing to insanity.

See: Bronwich, B.H., *Joseph Ritson: Scholar at Arms* (Chicago, 1938).

SPENCE, Thomas (1750–1814), agrarian reformer and radical activist, a shoemaker's son, was born in Newcastle, where he worked for a time as a schoolmaster. In 1775 he read a paper advocating the parochial ownership of land to the Newcastle Philosophical Society, which promptly expelled him. He subsequently published the paper in a number of forms, including *The Meridian Sun of Liberty* (1795). In 1788 he moved to London, where he became an enthusiastic member of the London Corresponding Society, set up as a bookseller, and propagandised in various media, including a radical weekly called *Pig's Meat*. He was arrested many times and had two significant spells in prison, the latter following a conviction for seditious libel. His works include *The End of Oppression* (1795) and *The Rights of Infants* (1797).

See: McCalman, I., *Radical Underworld: Prophets, Revolutionaries, and Pornographers in London, 1795–1840* (Cambridge, 1988).

WILBERFORCE, William (1759–1833), Tory MP, philanthropist, evangelical crusader and social reformer, was born into the wealthy Yorkshire commercial class and was educated at St John's College, Cambridge. He entered Parliament in 1780 and, after a religious conversion several years later, rapidly became the leading anti-slavery campaigner at Westminster. As a key figure in the so-called Clapham sect of evangelicals he had a passionate interest in moral reform, a cause he pressed in his *Practical View of the Prevailing Religious System of Professed Christians, in the Higher and Middle Classes of this Country, Contrasted with Real Christianity* (1797). He also published an *Appeal to the Religion, Justice, and Humanity of the Inhabitants of the British Empire, in behalf of the Negro Slaves in the West Indies* (1823).

See: Pollock, J., *Wilberforce* (1977).

WOLLSTONECRAFT, Mary (1759–97), miscellaneous writer and pioneer feminist, left home at the age of nineteen and earned her living as a teacher and governess before establishing herself as a writer. In the 1790s she became part of the radical circle centred on the London publisher, Joseph Johnson. Johnson published her *Vindication of the Rights of Men* (1790), an immediate response to Burke, and the feminist treatise, *Vindication of the Rights of Woman* (1792), her most important work. Among her other non-fictional works were *Thoughts on the Education of Daughters* (1787), *An Historical and Moral View of the Origin and Progress of the French Revolution* (1794), and an innovative piece of travel writing, *A Short Residence in Sweden, Norway and Denmark* (1796).

Todd, J. and M. Butler, eds, *The Works of Mary Wollstonecraft*, 7 vols (1989).

See: Kelly, G., *Revolutionary Feminism: The Mind and Career of Mary Wollstonecraft* (Basingstoke, 1992).

Index

Longman Literature in English Series

General Editors:
David Carroll, formerly University of Lancaster
Chris Walsh, University College Chester
Michael Wheeler, Director of the Gladstone Project

Pre-Renaissance English Literature
English Literature before Chaucer *Michael Swanton*
English Literature in the Age of Chaucer *Dieter Mehl*
English Medieval Romance *W. R. J. Barron*

English Poetry
English Poetry of the Sixteenth Century *Gary Waller (Second Edition)*
English Poetry of the Seventeenth Century *George Parfitt (Second Edition)*
English Poetry of the Eighteenth Century, 1700–1789 *David Fairer*
English Poetry of the Romantic Period, 1789–1830 *J. R. Watson (Second Edition)*
English Poetry of the Victorian Period, 1830–1890 *Bernard Richards (Second Edition)*
English Poetry since 1940 *Neil Corcoran*

English Drama
English Drama before Shakespeare *Peter Happé*
English Drama: Shakespeare to the Restoration, 1590–1660 *Alexander Leggatt*
English Drama: Restoration and Eighteenth Century, 1660–1789 *Richard W. Bevis*
English Drama of the Early Modern Period, 1890–1940 *Jean Chothia*
English Drama since 1940 *David Rabey*

English Fiction
English Fiction of the Eighteenth Century, 1700–1789 *Clive T. Probyn*
English Fiction of the Romantic Period, 1789–1830 *Gary Kelly*
English Fiction of the Victorian Period, 1830–1890 *Michael Wheeler (Second Edition)*
English Fiction of the Early Modern Period, 1890–1940 *Douglas Hewitt*

English Prose
English Prose of the Seventeenth Century, 1590–1700 *Roger Pooley*
English Prose of the Nineteenth Century *Hilary Fraser with Daniel Brown*

Criticism and Literary Theory
Criticism and Literary Theory, 1890 to the Present *Chris Baldick*

The Intellectual and Cultural Context
The Seventeenth Century, 1603–1700 *Graham Parry*
The Eighteenth Century, 1700–1789 *James Sambrook (Second Edition)*
The Victorian Period, 1830–1890 *Robin Gilmour*
The Romantic Period, 1789–1830 *Robin Jarvis*

American Literature
American Literature before 1880 *Robert Lawson-Peebles*
American Poetry of the Twentieth Century *Richard Gray*
American Drama of the Twentieth Century *Gerald M. Berkowitz*
American Fiction, 1865–1940 *Brian Lee*
American Fiction since 1940 *Tony Hilfer*
Twentieth-Century America *Douglas Tallack*

Other Literatures
Irish Literature since 1800 *Norman Vance*
Scottish Literature since 1707 *Marshall Walker*
Indian Literature in English *William Walsh*
African Literatures in English: East and West *Gareth Griffiths*
Southern African Literatures *Michael Chapman*
Caribbean Literature in English *Louis James*
Canadian Literature in English *W. J. Keith*